*Fast and Feast*

premierement sist laurench
de Reims Apres seoit
lempereur Apres seoit
le Roy dangleterre en mylieu
du front de la sale Apres
le Roy de france seoit le roy

des romains Et auoit auταle de distance
du Roy au Roy des romains come du
Roy a lempereur Et auoient lempereur
le Roy et le Roy des romains chascun se
parement ung ciel de drap dor broke de velu
au aus armes de france et par dessus ceul

# Fast and Feast

## Food in Medieval Society

Bridget Ann Henisch

The Pennsylvania State University Press
University Park, Pennsylvania

Library of Congress Cataloging in Publication Data

Henisch, Bridget Ann.
   Fast and feast.

   Bibliography: p. 271
   Includes index.
   1. Food habits—Europe. 2. Gastronomy—History.
3. Medieval civilization. 4. Food—History. I. Title.
GT2853.E8H46      394.1'094      76-15677
ISBN 0-271-01230-7
ISBN 0-271-00424-X (pbk.)

Printed in the United States of America


Seventh printing, 1999

*Frontispiece:* Entertainment at a Feast.
*Les Chroniques de France,* French, ca. 1379 (Paris, Bibliothèque Nationale,
MS. fr. 2813, fol. 473v). Photo. Bibl. nat. Paris.

*To Heinz*

# *Acknowledgments*

This study is based mainly on English sources of the thirteenth, fourteenth, and fifteenth centuries. Supplementary material has been drawn from other countries and other periods.

My greatest debt is to the shadowy host of editors, commentators, and translators whose labors over the centuries have made the book a possibility. I am grateful to the staff of the Pattee Library of The Pennsylvania State University for their helpful response to innumerable requests.

Special thanks are due to Miss Lorna Walker, of St. Andrew's University, Scotland, for her help and advice, to Mrs. Sandra McBride, for the matchless skill which turned illegible notes into ordered typescript, and to my husband, heroic trencherman at every feast and fast, for his unfailing support throughout this long endeavor.

B.A.H.

# Contents

# 1

# Introduction

While his poem *Childe Harold* was at the height of its success, Byron noted ruefully in his journal: "The . . . Edinburgh bookseller once sent an order for books, poesy, and cookery, with this agreeable postscript: 'The *Harold* and *Cookery* are much wanted.' Such is fame."[1] A touch of cross surprise may be detected in the observation, surprise that a mere cookbook could sell as well as a Romantic's masterpiece. The irritation is understandable, for Byron was that unfortunate creature, a fashionable poet with a weight problem, yet even he should have realized that the compliment was all to the poem. The public's response to poetry is notoriously erratic, but cookery books are always in demand. Mundane yet magical, their sober instructions fire man's dreams, whet but never sate his appetite.

A taste for such productions shows itself here and there throughout the medieval period. The two earliest copies that still survive of the Roman recipe book attributed to Apicius were made in the ninth century at the monasteries of Tours and Fulda.[2] During the first, fifteenth-century days of printing, a cookbook, *Küchenmeisterei* (Nürnberg, 1482), was reprinted at least eight times, while in the next century a lady in Paris left only three books in her will: a Book of Hours, a romance, and *L'Art de faire confitures*.[3]

Amid all that may be bewildering about the Middle Ages to the modern reader, there is something reassuringly familiar about medieval attitudes to food. Then as now, children sealed friendship with an apple or a pear, and baked mud pies in makeshift ovens.[4] Then as now, on cold winter days sensible men preferred creature comforts to army maneuvers: "When I am beside the brasier and I hear the wind blowing and see the full spit turning before the fire and the good wine brought up from the cellar, then I want to eat and drink and rest beside a coal fire. If I have a fat capon, I feel no itch to attack a tower."[5] Then as now, unfamiliar meals intensified the miseries of the homesick. Even the austere Carthusians in 1422 allowed an Italian brother to leave a monastery in London for his native Lombardy, "in case he should not be able to adapt himself to the English food."[6] Then as now, home cooking was properly appreciated. According to a late thirteenth-century life of Christ, when anxious angels asked Jesus what he would like to eat after his long fast in the desert, they received the prompt reply: "Go to my beloved mother . . . I eat no food as gladly as hers." [7]

Such glimpses reveal a recognizable world; yet occasionally, in this chorus of relaxed enjoyment, dark and disconcerting notes are sounded. When a fifteenth-century priest is advised not only to eat slowly, laying down his knife between mouthfuls, but to meditate on death while he does so, because "the man who thinks of death does not eagerly desire any elegance, any delicacy, any exquisite food," we become conscious of strange currents flowing beneath the placid surface.[8]

Man must have food. So much is simple, but in every age his attitude toward this basic fact of life is complicated by the ideas which shape his own society. Medieval man looked to the Church for guidance, but the Church's feelings about the subject were mixed and its teachings in consequence confused. On the one hand, eating and feasting were sanctified by biblical example; on the other, Christianity was shot through with desire to detach the soul from the world, to help it grow impervious to life's enchantments. Only a saint could hope to reconcile the two ways of thinking in his life. Ordinary man had to be content with uneasy compromise and endless tug-of-war.

The Bible brims over with references to food, from that meal prepared by Abraham and Sarah for three angels on the plain of Mamre to the picnic by the sea of Tiberias for Jesus and his disciples after the Resurrection. Jesus himself graced the board of a remarkable number of dinner parties, perhaps thereby fulfilling to the letter Isaiah's enigmatic prophecy about the Messiah: "Butter and honey shall he eat, that he may know to refuse the evil, and choose the good" (Isaiah 7:15). Of such occasions, a handful became inextricably woven into the teaching of the Church. The Marriage at Cana, the miracle of the loaves and fishes, and the Supper at Emmaus were of immense significance in Christian doctrine, analyzed in commentaries, discussed in sermons, and commemorated in services. The Last Supper itself was recalled and relived in every mass. In all these, the offering of food and drink was seen as an expression of love, the act of eating together as a symbol of communion and fellowship.

In Psalm 23, God comforts the poet with a feast: "Thou preparest a table before me in the presence of mine enemies: thou anointest my head with oil; my cup runneth over." In the parable of the prodigal son, the reconciliation between wayward boy and loving father is sealed with a kiss and a banquet. Just before his arrest, Jesus promises his disciples a future reward for their steadfast loyalty: "Ye may eat and drink at my table in my kingdom" (Luke 22:30).

Such familiar texts and much-loved stories had their effect on men's attitudes toward God and His world. John Myrc, an early fifteenth-century English priest, encouraged his readers to share their food with the hungry poor, "and then God wyll fede you of his borde [from his table] yn Heven."[9] Berthold von Regensburg, a thirteenth-century Franciscan, developed the idea with zest. His paradise is a sumptuous restaurant, packed with gourmet souls happily sampling an endless stream of bewitching creations and subtle sauces from the hands of God, the master chef.[10] In another sermon Myrc said that every Easter, while Christians rejoice on earth, God gives a feast in heaven to celebrate His son's victory.[11]

God was pictured as a genial and thoughtful host on earth as well as in heaven. The image lived on long after the Middle Ages had slipped into the shadows. In the seventeenth century, George Herbert used it to express his vision of the beauty and order of a world whose master knew exactly what each of His creatures needed to sustain itself, and took care to supply it from a never-empty cupboard. No detail was neglected, not an insect overlooked. Even flies had "their table spread, ere they appear."[12]

This divine example set the standard of good behavior in human society. Hospitality was honored and meanness condemned. The cheerful host flourished under the protection of his patron, Saint Julian, while Charity itself was sometimes personified as a woman holding out a loaf in one hand and a cup in the other.[13] To feed the hungry was one of the seven works of mercy, proposed by Jesus as a simple way to express love for himself. When a bewildered questioner asked, "Lord, when saw we thee an hungred, and fed thee? or thirsty, and gave thee drink?" the answer came, clear and firm: "Inasmuch as ye have done it unto one of the least of these my brethren, ye have done it unto me" (Matt. 25:31–40). The reward for such generosity was the hope of a place in heaven.

On the other hand, in the teaching of the Church one of the all too many branches of gluttony was represented by the churlish diner steadily munching his way through a meal and refusing to share it with any companion, however desperate.[14] Of this deplorable type the most notorious example was Dives, the rich man tortured with thirst in hell because he had ignored Lazarus, the beggar starving at his gate (Luke 16:19–31). The story was very well known and endlessly illustrated. In the thirteenth century, Henry III used it as a somewhat inhibiting motif for the decoration of three of his great dining halls, to catch the eye of every guest whenever he chanced to glance up from his plate.[15]

The message was plain, and most people paid a little more than lip service to the ideal of charity, yet alms were not always given with good grace. St. Bernardino of Siena told of the time he went begging for food through the streets and so irritated a housewife that she hurled a very hard old loaf straight at his head. "It hurt me very much," he said, and added demurely, "perhaps she did not give it with a glad heart."[16] Nevertheless, however reluctantly, she did let him have something, for the hope of heaven was a great spur to generosity. Charity needs an object, and beggars were well aware of their value to their betters. "Paradise knocks on your doors," the destitute of Constantinople would murmur insinuatingly as they held out their hands, and they were seldom disappointed.[17]

The words of the Bible and their elaboration in the teaching of the Church shed a nobility and spiritual significance over the role of food and drink in everyday life. This is exemplified well in the design of one of the stained glass windows at Chartres. It was dedicated to St. Lubin, a local saint who had once been the cellarer of the abbey, and it was paid for by the tavern-keepers of the town. Round the edge of the window are clustered tiny scenes of the wine trade, of men with glasses in their hands, and carriers driving carts loaded with barrels to their destinations. In the center is the supreme moment of the Mass, the presentation of the cup of wine, "This is my blood of the new testament, which is shed for many" (Mark 14:24).[18]

The Bible, however, has proved to be a bottomless well, from which any number of contradictory lessons may be drawn. It is so rich and varied that it can offer something for every frame of mind, and the kind of treasure found in its pages has depended to some extent on the kind of man who happened to be conducting the search. Scriptural interpretation is a dangerously slippery tool in all but the hands of a master, as this story of Pope Julius and his peacock suggests. Julius III ("a porkish pope," the dourly Protestant chronicler Holinshed notes in an aside) was partial to cold peacock, and one evening he exploded in a tantrum of rage when his favorite dish failed to appear on the supper table. A cardinal attempted a gentle reproof: "Let not your holinesse, I praie you, be so moved with a matter of so small weight." At this, the pope burst out with triumphant, unanswerable logic: "If God was so angrye for one apple, that he cast our first parents out of Paradise for the same, whie may not I, being his vicar, be angrye then for a peacocke, sithens [since] a peacocke is a greater matter than an apple?"[19]

The sheer complexity of the Bible has made it just as happy a hunting-ground for those who stressed the ascetic side of Christianity as for those who rejoiced in its celebration of food as a symbol of life and love. To set against a happy occasion like the Marriage at Cana there is Jesus' forty-day fast in the wilderness; every encouragement to feast can be matched by another to self-denial and austerity. A roll call of such texts contains some of the best known words in the New Testament, phrases which by constant repetition have become familiar throughout the Western world. "He that loveth his life shall lose it; and he that hateth his life in this world shall keep it unto life eternal. If any man serve me, let him follow me . . . " (John 12:25–26); "Blessed are ye that hunger now, for ye shall be filled" (Luke 6:21); "Take no thought for your life, what ye shall eat" (Luke 12:22); "Man shall not live by bread alone" (Luke 4:4); "If any man will come after me, let him deny himself, and take up his cross, and follow me. For whosoever will save his life shall lose it, and whosoever will lose his life for my sake shall find it" (Matt. 16:24–25); "He that taketh not his cross, and followeth after me, is not worthy of me" (Matt. 10:30); "Strait is the gate, and narrow is the way, which leadeth unto life, and few there be that find it" (Matt. 7:14).

Verses like these were signposts to the path of discipline and mortification for the true Christian. To him, Jesus was the supreme example of self-sacrifice because he gave up his life willingly for love of mankind. In return, believers were not asked to follow him literally to a death on the cross, but to respond to that love by denying themselves the small pleasures of life. Such sacrifices had no intrinsic value; they were important only as means to an end, the proper ordering of the soul's priorities. The discipline was necessary to achieve a certain attitude of detachment toward the preoccupations of daily life. Once this had been gained it was possible to concentrate on the main task of the Christian, the loving renovation of his inner self in imitation of Jesus.

These ideals of conduct were developed during the early days of the new religion. While Christians formed a tiny, persecuted community within the Roman empire, their attitude was one of contempt for the world, its rulers, glories, pleasures, moral standards, and beliefs. Every effort was made to mark a sharp distinction between the behavior of church members and that of the pagans who menaced them. Austerity, self-denial, and rigorous self-discipline shaped the lives of the converted. Life on earth was regarded as a period of trial, and only those who persisted steadfastly in their faith could hope for a reward at the second coming of the Messiah. The Christian Church was a society of the spiritual élite. Indeed, none but the élite, the absolutely committed, could hope to reach such standards and stand firm against such outside hostility.

Once Christianity had been declared the official religion of the empire, attitudes inevitably changed. Its leaders held positions of worldly power and influence, and became inextricably involved in worldly diplomacy and worldly business. The Church was no longer an embattled handful of enthusiasts fighting for survival, but a state institution zealously intent on bringing everyone within its fold. Standards slipped a little. When thousands are converted at the whim of a prince or the point of a sword the highest flights of religious enthusiasm are not to be expected.

Over the centuries, church and society learned to live together in fair comfort, but there was a price to be paid for the alliance. Each was deeply penetrated by the other's influence. The Church was flawed and tarnished by the relationship, while society found itself caught in a network of rules and regulations spun around it by the Church. An early Christian might have been horrified by a certain laxness in the average medieval congregation, not to mention the average churchman. Nevertheless he would have noticed that for every member of society, not just the zealous few, the year had become marked by fasts and penances as well as feasts, ordained by the Church and maintained by innumerable pressures, which ensured general obedience no matter how weak the flesh or reluctant the spirit.

Officially, the Church took great pains to emphasize that fasting was merely a useful self-discipline. It was taught that everything in the world had been created by God, and every part of it was good. A fast was ordered not because food in itself was evil but because it was so necessary and so attractive to man that some form of abstention from it at certain times was considered to be very good for the soul.

Throughout the medieval period, however, this doctrine was in constant danger of distortion by rival theories. For a long line of heretics, of whom the best known are the Manichees of the third century and the Cathars of the twelfth, matter itself was evil. Satan was co-eternal with God, and the world was under his domination. It was an unclean prison, from which the soul must struggle to withdraw and so escape. The orthodox declared that the goodness of life on earth had been affirmed and enhanced by the Incarnation, when Jesus became man as well as God. Heretic theorists disagreed, maintaining instead that Jesus had remained God alone, wrapped in a cloak of humanity. Just as a cloak is quite separate from the man who wears it, so the physical body Jesus assumed was no part of his true nature.

Such heretics as the Cathars ate only the bare minimum required to keep themselves alive. Indeed, some of them carried their belief to its logical conclusion and deliberately committed suicide by slow starvation, with the solemn approval of their fellows.[20] They won much awed praise from the general public for the austerity and holiness of their lives, but they were ruthlessly hunted down and exterminated by the Church. The savage persecution was considered necessary because the heresy was so deceptively attractive. The outward result was a way of life which seemed to exemplify the ideal of Christian self-denial, but it grew from a diseased root of false doctrine. So sensitive were church authorities to any hint of the heresy that the Carthusians, most austere of all the monastic orders, found it wise to protect themselves from unwarranted suspicions. Their rules forbade the eating of meat at all times, even for invalid monks, and they were accused sometimes of avoiding meat because they considered it evil. In an early fourteenth-century treatise the order carefully explained its position: "The Carthusians, unlike certain heretics, hold like other Christians that all God's creatures are good and lawful to be eaten, where there is no vow to the contrary."[21]

The heretics were killed but their theories lingered on, to sharpen and strengthen a hostility toward the good things of life which always lurked just beneath the surface of society. A certain serenity and sense of balance are needed if a man is to practice austerities while asserting that the food he denies himself is perfectly good. Righteous rejection of the world's delights is much more invigorating and much easier to maintain, at least for short periods. Violent extremes of mortification had a special fascination for medieval man, and the life of a community or an individual might be punctuated from time to time by explosions of enthusiastic austerity.

As a fanatic young hermit, St. Bernardino of Siena disdained all normal foods known to man and decided to try thistles. In this he was typical of a hundred zealous converts; what sets the saint apart is the modesty and humor with which he described the experiment many years later: "I picked a thistle . . . I placed it in my mouth and began to chew. I chewed and chewed—it would not go down. 'Let us try,' said I, 'a sip of water.' In vain! The water went down, the thistle stayed in my mouth." When one of his listeners criticized him for the failure, and pointed out that St. Francis of Assisi had done far better by fasting forty days without touching a crumb, not even a thistle, St. Bernardino had a disarming reply: "He could do it—and I could not."[22]

The same determination to find virtue in making life as disagreeable as possible sometimes ruffled the calm waters of scriptural commentary. According to the Bible, St. John the Baptist was sustained in the desert by a diet of locusts and wild honey (Matt. 3:4), and to the general reader this seemed meager enough to satisfy the most demanding purist. To the gimlet eyes of certain early commentators, however, "locusts" held alarming suggestions of meat, and "wild honey" evoked nightmare visions of some delicious, spiritually debilitating dessert. Determined efforts were made to clean the record, by interpreting "locust" as a kind of unpalatable plant or tree-pod and emphasizing that honey from "wild" bees was specially bitter. Once these changes had been made to everyone's satisfaction, St. John the Baptist could be safely praised again for his extraordinary mortification.[23]

Hospitality and austerity were given equal honors by the Church but proved to be uneasy bedfellows. Their reconciliation posed a problem so knotty that most men gave up the unequal struggle and allowed temperament to sway them one way or the other. For those who faced the question, however, an exquisitely simple and satisfactory solution, an ideal of behavior, could be found in the lives of the first Christian hermits.

From the end of the third century to the fifth a stream of men and women turned their backs on society and escaped to the deserts of Egypt and Palestine, to live in poverty and solitude and meditate on God. Stories of their lives and collections of their sayings were copied and circulated throughout the Christian world from the fifth century to the end of the Middle Ages. They were read and cherished in every century, had a marked influence on monastic thought, and found their way into the teachings of the Church. Their popularity is confirmed by the flurry of vernacular translations, intended for laymen, which were turned out by the new printing presses in the late fifteenth century in Venice, Augsburg, Strassburg, and Paris. Caxton just managed to complete an English translation before he died in 1491, and his assistant, Wynkyn de Worde, had it ready for sale in London in 1495.[24]

The best of these hermits achieved a beautiful balance between the stern demands they made on themselves and the kindness they offered to their fellows. Their lives were proof that austerity could be sweetened and hospitality refined when the two were practiced together and nourished by love. Fasting was a personal, private discipline, to be followed rigorously but set aside without a moment's hesitation if the occasion demanded it. The admired ideal was austerity tempered by thoughtfulness. The truly good man was severe with himself but sensitively considerate as host, guest, and master.

When a party of visitors from Palestine called on a hermit in Egypt he left his prayers and prepared a meal for them. Having emptied their bowls they rudely proceeded to criticize him for laxness and compare him unfavorably with the hermits they had left at home. Their host offered this gentle explanation and re-proof: "Fasting is ever with me, but I cannot keep you ever here; and though fasting be indeed useful and necessary, it is a matter of our own choosing, but love in its fulness the law of God requires at our hands. So, receiving Christ in you, I must show you whatever things be of love, with all carefulness: but when I have sent you away, then may I take up again the rule of fasting."[25]

Many such stories were told of censorious purists cut down to size by older, wiser men. One who prided himself on his abstinence came to see a hermit and found him already surrounded by a small group of other visitors. The hermit courteously prepared some vegetable soup, and everyone settled down to eat. Ostentatiously, the righteous pilgrim waved away the soup, produced from his wallet one small, exceedingly dry pea, and proceeded to chew it in forbidding silence. Conscious guilt showed in every other face, appetites faded, and gloom settled over the party. After the ruined meal, the hermit drew aside the culprit, and said what every host would like to say to every dieting guest: "Brother, if thou comest to any one, do not show off to him thy way of life: if thou dost wish to keep to thine own way, abide in thy cell and go nowhere from it."[26]

Bad hosts did not escape criticism. When a young man boasted that he was too busy with his prayers to cook anything, and so "the grass is growing up my chimney," he was deflated by the tart comment: "And you have driven away hospitality."[27]

Personal austerity was not to be imposed on others. When an experienced old hermit and his young disciple visited a monastery they accepted an invitation to dine with the monks. Once on the road and on their own again they passed a well, and the disciple wanted to drink there, but he was stopped by his master with the reminder, "today is a fast." Understandably, the other protested: "But, Father, did we not eat today?" The old man acknowledged this, but explained why they had broken their fast in the company of others: "That was love's bread, my son: but for us, let us keep our own fast."[28]

St. Cyriac had a little vegetable garden around his desert cell, guarded by a faithful lion. However strict his own fast, the saint never forgot to give the lion an ample dinner of bread. It may be that he had an imperfect grasp of his companion's true preferences, for it has to be admitted that two visitors one day spotted the lion in a secluded corner, munching a wild goat. Nevertheless, the story was told as a record of Cyriac's kindness and an example to all good masters.[29]

Stories like these, glimmering down the centuries, offered society an ideal of courtesy to emulate. In 1187, when Abbot Samson of Bury St. Edmunds heard of the Saracens' capture of Jerusalem, he swore to eat no more meat: "None the less he desired that meat should be placed before him when he sat at table, that so our alms might be increased."[30] The food left untouched by the abbot was distributed to the poor after the meal, and so by this order Samson made sure that no one but himself would suffer for his personal penance.

This religious ideal, of private austerity coupled with public generosity, dovetailed very smoothly into the social assumptions of the whole medieval period. In the cut-throat realities of everyday life, to nourish was not so much an act of love as a demonstration of power. Anyone who hoped to retain authority and influence in this world had to show himself the source of all good things for his dependents, and to equal, or preferably surpass, the magnificence of his allies and enemies. Lavish generosity was the hallmark of the important man. To err on the side of reckless extravagance might bring financial embarrassment; to err on the side of frugality could achieve nothing but contempt. In a fifteenth-century survey of past kings of England it is the generous ones who are fondly recalled: Henry I, "an excellent mete gever," and Hardicanute, famed for the splendor of his feasts and the number of his cooks. This king packed a lot of good living into a bare two-year reign, and his death is recorded with terse regret: "He deyid drinking at Lambethe."[31]

Against a background of such assumptions, no one foolish enough to inflict his own privations on his guests was going to stand very high in public opinion. Thomas Becket, Archbishop of Canterbury in the mid-twelfth century, won high praise from his contemporaries because he curbed his own appetite but kept a superb table for his visitors. At dinner he himself, as a mortification, drank "water used for the cooking of hay," but he never forgot his duties as a host: "He was always, however, the first to taste the wine before giving it to those who sat at table with him."[32] In dismal contrast to this princely style, the prosperous citizen of the end of the fifteenth century was beginning to cut a very shabby figure. A Venetian visitor to London around 1496–97 noted disapprovingly that Englishmen were "very sparing of wine when they drink it at their own expense. And this, it is said, they do in order to induce their other English guests to drink in moderation also."[33]

Pettiness of this kind in an ordinary man might provoke no more than laughter and gossip among his friends. Detected in the great it could have the most serious consequences, for retrenchment was a sure indication of waning power, a signal to sharp-eyed observers that liberties could be taken, loyalties realigned. Henry III was so impressed with this hard fact of life that he had a motto inscribed round the edge of his chessboard as a helpful reminder: "He who does not give what he has, will not get what he wants."[34] Einhard, Charlemagne's ninth-century biographer, reports that some of the emperor's officials were worried by the number of foreign guests entertained at court, but Charlemagne was confident of his own political good sense: "He considered that his reputation for hospitality and the advantage of the good name which he acquired more than compensated for the great nuisance of their being there."[35]

Charlemagne's advisers were probably perturbed by the thought of all the extra mouths to feed, because they knew much better than their master the high cost of unstinting generosity and endless entertainment. Banquets could be alarmingly expensive. The hero of the late fourteenth-century romance *Sir Cleges* brings himself to the brink of ruin by spending all his fortune on Christmas feasts for rich and poor and on lavish presents for the minstrels who provided the entertainment.[36] Such habits were endearing, and only proper for a hero, but they did make life very difficult. Once matters had got so far out of hand there was no easy answer to the question of how to set a man's affairs in order again. To get into debt was bad, but any attempt to cut down expenses by cutting out dinner parties was far worse, an open invitation to the brutal mockery of one's peers and the knowing titters of subordinates.

Poor Henry III, despite that motto round his chessboard, was always in financial hot water, and his halfhearted efforts to struggle out of debt were felt by contemporaries to do him very little credit. Matthew Paris noted with disapproval in his chronicle for the year 1250: "The king, shamefully deviating from the track of his ancestors, ordered the expenses of his court and the amusements of his usual hospitality to be lessened; an inexcusable act, and bringing on him even the charge of avarice."[37]

Any tightening of the belt had to be done more discreetly than this if it were to be both effective and socially undamaging. The art lay in knowing which corners could be cut without undue offense to those who mattered. A beginning might be made on days when no one of any consequence had been invited. Grand dinners were made possible by private economies. An old French proverb and its seventeenth-century translation put the matter in a nutshell: "Après la feste et le jeu, les pois au feu"; "when costlie Feasts and Games are ended, fond wast [foolish waste] by thrift let be amended."[38]

Firm distinctions were drawn between the quality and amount of the food served at high table to the master and his honored guests and that served to the rest of the company. These helped to balance budgets and send stewards contentedly to bed. The same Venetian who commented unfavorably on English drinking habits was pained by the national meanness to servants: "The

English, being great epicures, and very avaricious by nature, indulge in the most delicate fare themselves and give their household the coarsest bread, and beer, and cold meat baked on Sunday for the week."[39] This bland reversal of the admired ideal of denial to self and generosity to others was not, of course, confined to England. Dante spent long years of exile from Florence in various Italian courts and knew only too well the bitter humiliations of the unwanted, unimportant guest, dependent for his dinner on some grudging host:

> How salt the bread of strangers is, how hard
> The up and down of someone else's stair.[40]

The most drastic remedy for straitened circumstances and empty purses was to give up entertaining altogether. This was a desperate move, for it was an unmistakable signal to society of waning powers and slackening influence. Henry III brought shame on himself in 1250 with the miserable inadequacy of his feasts; by the following Christmas he had sunk beyond reproach. Far from binding his subjects to himself with displays of regal hospitality, he had been reduced to hobbling from one household to another, hoping for a free dinner: "He now, without shame, sought his lodgings and his meals with abbots, priors, clerks, and men of low degree."[41]

Some eccentrics, of course, took a perverse delight in flouting the cherished beliefs of their contemporaries. In 1166 the Sicilian chronicler Hugo Falcandus drew a malicious portrait of the Archbishop of Reggio: "He would willingly endure hunger and thirst beyond the limits of human tolerance in order to save money. Never happy at his own table, he was never sad at those of others, and would frequently spend whole days without food, waiting to be invited to dinner."[42]

Such behavior provoked not merely the sneers of society but the disapproval of the moralists. The man unwilling to fulfill his obligations, too mean to entertain worthily but ready enough to feed at someone else's expense, stood condemned for adding one sin to another, avarice to gluttony. A fourteenth-century treatise describes the tug-of-war between this man's belly and his purse, each clamoring, "I wole be ful." Their distracted master hits on the perfect solution, filling the one at his friend's table and the other at his own, but the writer leaves no doubt that the Devil's wheelbarrow is drawn up in the wings, ready to trundle him off to Hell.[43]

Those who tried to avoid this fate by plunging dutifully into a whirl of entertaining might still find that wheelbarrow waiting for them at the end. When hospitality is regarded as a status symbol it degenerates all too easily into ostentation. Commentators were not slow to offer their analysis of the unseemly passions seething behind the smiling masks of host and guest.

Splendid dinner parties earned the moralists' displeasure because far too much money was lavished on them. Rare delicacies might cost more "than XL. men myghte lyve by."[44] Moreover, too much time was frittered away on the preparations. The anxious and ambitious host worried over the details of the menu, fretting himself into a fever over what dishes to choose and what sauces should accompany them, "al for to savoure wel in the palet of the mouth."[45] Still more time was wasted afterward, in minute discussion by host and guest of the whole sumptuous occasion: how many dishes had been served, how much they had probably cost, how they had been presented, whether the sauces had been sharp enough.[46] In short, had the host triumphed, or had he failed the test?

Regrettably, guests seldom received the feast in a spirit of becoming gratitude. Failure provoked mockery and success sharpened envy. When Richard Whittington was Lord Mayor of London in 1422 he had a running battle with the Worshipful Company of Brewers, and he was constantly hauling them over the coals for minor infringements of the law. In their record book, the brewers noted this petty persecution and attributed it entirely to the mayor's jealous displeasure at seeing particularly fine, fat swans on the table at their company feast on St. Martin's Day. By 1424, the brewers had learned tact. They smoothed the feathers of the next Lord Mayor at his inauguration by gracefully presenting him with a magnificent ox and a boar, to form the basis of his own banquet. They had their reward, as they demurely recorded in their book: "He did no harm to the Brewers."[47]

Moralists particularly deplored the fact that all this time and money, effort and ingenuity, went to please the eye and palate, not to fill an empty stomach. More and more dishes were expected by the demanding guest, and yet when he sat down to the banquet he could not touch half the food spread out before him: "Hit happeth ofte tymes in grete festes and dyners that we be fylde wyth the sight of the noble and lichorous [delicious] metis, and whan we wolde ete we ben saciat [sated] and fild."[48]

With such warnings and exhortations ringing in their ears, men stumbled uncertainly through a maze of contradictory assumptions about food and its role in life. They were lured hither and thither by conflicting ideals and conflicting advice, tugged to and fro by the insistent demands of their Church, their society, and their purse. The ways in which these ideas and pressures affected the preparation and presentation of meals will be explored in the rest of this book.

# 2

# Mealtimes

Adam lay I-bowndyn, bowndyn in a bond,
fowre thowsand wynter thowt he not to long;
And al was for an appil, an appil that he tok . . .
Ne hadde the appil take ben, the appil taken ben,
ne hadde never our lady a ben hevene qwen;
Blyssid be the tyme that appil take was,
Ther-fore we mown syngyn, "deo gracias."[1]

Moralists, while dourly acknowledging the correctness of this happy conclusion, never allowed it to deflect them from a highly critical examination of the act which made it possible. Man's first, disastrous lapse in Paradise hinted only too broadly at more of the same to come. In consequence, gluttony was listed among the seven deadly sins and labeled as the one which revealed man's true place on the scale of life to be distinctly closer to the animals than the angels. As John Myrc, an early fifteenth-century sermon writer, remarked, the devil knew he could scarcely fail with an apple, for "yche best of kynde ys sonnest taken wyth mete [every creature by nature is most readily caught with food]."[2]

Medieval discussion of any one of the major sins took the form of meticulous analysis: each of the possible forms it might assume was pinpointed, each of its many disguises rudely stripped away and the horrid realities beneath laid bare. Rigorous diets when endured merely for the sake of health received as little sympathy from sharp-eyed commentators on gluttony as ostentatious dinner parties. Dieting for fashion had not yet been invented, but we may be sure that moralists would have risen with relish to the challenge.

The object of this exercise, the minute examination of a sin as it showed itself in a host of humdrum incidents and attitudes every day, was to jolt a complacent audience into self-recognition. Certainly these words on gluttony must have caused a few uneasy twinges: "The first braunche of this synne is to ete er tyme be [before the proper time] . . . as a man synneth to ete bifor tyme, right so synneth a man to ete over late."[3]

The medieval code word for eating "over late" was *reresoper.* The last respectable meal of the day was supper, preferably eaten together by the whole household after work had finished. Thomas Tusser in the sixteenth century recommends that the housewife should be making her preparations for it as the hens settle down on their roost. A comfortable time afterward, the well-ordered establishment would retire to bed, ready to get up briskly at daybreak for the morning's tasks. The reresoper was an extra, an extravagance and an indulgence, much disapproved of by churchmen and economical heads of families except, of course, when discreetly enjoying one themselves. It might be a sizable meal for a party, or just some tempting tidbit, eaten late in the evening with one or two cronies, washed down with a considerable amount of drink and accompanied by much regrettable frivolity.

Simple or elaborate, it was condemned on two counts. First, it was unnecessary. Dinner and supper satisfied hunger; reresopers placated greed. Second, it was anti-social. Although there was a slow, steady growth of desire for privacy throughout the period, it was always stoutly maintained that a decent meal was shared by the entire company. Ideally, master and man sat down together in the hall. It was considered furtive, even faintly disreputable, to wish to slip away and huddle in a corner with a friend. Bishop Robert Grosseteste, in the thirteenth century, advised the Countess of Lincoln to "forbid dinners and suppers out of the hall, in secret and in private rooms, for from this arises waste, and no honour to the lord or lady."[4] To this was added the rider that she must keep an eye on the leftovers intended for the poor after the company had eaten, in case they were spirited away to the servants' quarters for midnight feasts.

Not only were reresopers a form of annoyingly unofficial consumption of good food and candles; moralists unraveled a spider's web of association between them, loud laughter, low jokes, acrimonious games of chess, and gross flirtation. In the Prologue to the fifteenth-century *Tale of Beryn,* the Pardoner hopes to seduce the barmaid of his inn after a reresoper of roast goose and a caudle, a nourishing nightcap with a mulled wine base.[5]

Always frowned on, these meals were particularly disapproved of when planned for a Thursday, or any other evening before a fast day. On such nights the black sheep of the flock might be found sitting up late, fortifying themselves for the rigors ahead:

> And overlong ete flesshe and drunke
> Aftyr that mydnyght ys runge.[6]

Those who will not learn to "be waar [beware] of nodding hee-dis and of candil light"[7] find themselves the next morning with a distinct disinclination to leave their beds. Thomas Hoccleve, in fifteenth-century London, presents himself as a melancholy ex-ample. While a young man, working in the Privy Seal, he could sit up drinking later than all his fellow clerks but, as always, there was a penalty to pay:

> On the morn was wight of no degree
> So looth as I to twynne fro my cowche.[8]

Poor Hoccleve would have got cold comfort for his aching head from the sermon writers who, with the malice of the strictly sober, liked to describe such a crumpled survivor from the night before as "the develes bolster," because "the feend restyth in him as in his softe fedyrbed."[9]

This reluctance to get up, this tendency to loll in bed until "IX of the clok or X,"[10] would seem on the face of it to lead to the vice of eating too late in the morning, not too early. As the moralists persist, however, in coupling the sin of eating "over late" at night with that of eating "er tyme be" in the day, the question may be asked: When was the proper time to eat the first meal? The short answer is: after the first devotions. By saying his prayers or, ide-ally, by attending mass, a man paid his respects to God before attending to his stomach. The day should be prefaced by worship, just as a meal was prefaced by grace. Both practices showed a man's love for God and protected him against temptations and sudden hazards. If tragedy struck during the day, morning devo-tions could help someone to salvation, even though no priest was with him when he died:

> . . . hyt may the save
> Yyf housel ne shryfte thou mayst have
> [if you cannot receive communion or absolution].[11]

The danger of failing to say grace or at least cross oneself before eating is alarmingly illustrated by a story about a young woman who omitted to do either before nibbling a lettuce leaf. Invisible to her, a devil happened to be sitting on the leaf at the time. Once swallowed, he refused to come out again, and the priest who arrived to exorcise him heard through the girl's lips an aggrieved little voice complaining: "Allas! whatt hafe I done? I satt opon the letes [lettuce], and sho come and tuke me up and bate [bit] me."[12]

The rule that devotions should come before the first meal applied of course particularly to Sundays and other holy days, but all in a position to do so were encouraged to obey it every day. In the fourteenth-century romance *Sir Gawain and the Green Knight,* it is noted carefully by the poet that Bercilak, up before daybreak for a hunt, "ete a sop hastyly" only "when he hade herde masse."[13] Andrew Boorde, in the early sixteenth century, outlines an ambitious program of spiritual and physical exercises for his reader, to be carried out between waking and eating:

> Walke in your gardayne or parke a thousande pace or two; and than great and noble men doth use to here masse, and other men that cannot do so, but must applye theyr busynes, doth serve God with some prayers . . . before you go to your refection, moderatly exercyse your body . . . playing at the tennys . . . or paysyng wayghtes or plomettes of ledde in your handes [lifting weights] . . . to open your poores [pores].[14]

*Mens sana in corpore sano* indeed. For the Hoccleves of this world, their heads throbbing after the reresopers of the night before, such aggressive, all-round virtue was far out of reach. Pale on his pillow, the reveler would murmur instead: "I may noght faste, ne do penauns, ne go to cherch, ne bydde my bedys, for I have a badde heued . . . I schal noght ben wel at ese tyl I have drunkyn agen."[15] Straightaway, an affable devil settled himself on the bed, coaxing the sufferer to eat a morsel, just to keep his strength up to serve God all the more vigorously later in the day: "thou most kepe the in hele of body for any holynesse."[16] As this always seemed by far the best, indeed the only course of action, it prompted a virtuous rummage in the bedside cupboard for some small sustaining snack. Tusser tartly observed:

> Some slovens from sleeping no sooner get up,
> But hand is in aumbrie, and nose in the cup.[17]

No wonder commentators never failed to link eating "over late" with eating "er tyme be" in the first branch of Gluttony.

Such decadence was frowned upon, and practiced sinners found it politic to observe the letter of the law. Erasmus, in his

*Praise of Folly* (1511), shows how this could be done with the least discomfort. Courtiers who felt the need to recruit their strength after a hard night slept brazenly until midday, but made sure to have "a wretched little hired priest waiting at their bedside [who] runs quickly through the mass before they're hardly out of bed. Then they go to breakfast, which is scarcely over before there's a summons to lunch."[18]

Although grudgingly conceded to be better than nothing, this lightning combination of instant mass with instant nourishment was not exactly what the Church had in mind for her wily, wandering flock. Ideally, it was considered that the first and principal meal of the day was to be eaten at *none,* after many hours of hard and conscientious work. In this, as in so many other aspects of life, it was the Church which gave the medieval day its characteristic shape and punctuation points. By ecclesiastical law it had been decreed that devotions should be said or sung at certain times throughout the twenty-four hours. The main burden of this cycle of worship was borne by the monasteries, but its influence was felt everywhere. Although clocks became quite well-known and used in the later Middle Ages, the bells that rang to mark each service remained convenient, familiar timekeepers for the whole community. The many surviving Books of Hours made for laymen are clues to the widespread popularity of the devotions.

These times of prayer, though called the canonical hours, did not correspond to the sixty-minute unit. Instead, each covered a flexible period, roughly three hours in length. The hour of *none,* from which the word "noon" is derived, was the ninth hour after daybreak, and so fell in the early afternoon. As it also had to keep a certain distance from vespers, the sunset service, if precision had been demanded, constant adjustments would have been necessary to fit *none* and all the other hours into short winter days and long summer ones. In practice, *none* was deemed to stretch from midday to three P.M., and its appropriate service might be performed early or late within that span, depending on season and circumstance.

In monasteries, the main meal of the day was always eaten after *none* had been celebrated, and so the time for sitting down to dinner moved with the time of the service. Being calculated from sunrise, the devotions fell later in the day in winter than in summer, and dinner followed suit. The winter season began on 14 September and the summer one at Easter. Lent was treated as a separate period with its own rule: dinner was to be eaten penitentially late in the afternoon.

Amidst these shifting sands, one rock stood firm: the proper time of day for dinner was *none,* whenever that happened to be. Society at large paid faithful lip service to this rule, and *noonmeat* became a synonym for meal. As obedient sons of the Church, however, laymen learned to imitate her flexibility. *None* took on the present meaning of noon, and the dinner hour drew much closer to twelve than to three in the afternoon. Frequently, indeed, the main meal of the day was eaten even earlier. In a large household, for example, if the important diners were to sit down at noon, those whose job was to attend on them had to eat some time before or afterward. At Edward IV's court twenty-four squires waited on the king and queen, and in 1478 it was decided that twelve of these should eat before and twelve after the official meal. The "first meate" for such attendants was to be on the table by "nyne of the clock at the furthest."[19]

Perhaps because of such a shift system, Froissart was eating his dinner in the middle of the morning on 6 January 1367, during his stay at the royal court: "I was in Bordeaux, sitting at table, when King Richard [II] was born. He came into the world on a Wednesday, on the stroke of ten. At that hour Sir Richard de Pontchardon, who was Marshal of Aquitaine at the time, entered and said to me 'Froissart, write down and place on record that her Highness the Princess has been delivered of a fine boy.' "[20]

The determination of employers to see that the food they provided was well-earned combined with the Church's teaching to push the time of the main meal to a point several hours after everyone had got up. As work usually began at sunrise, however, it was possible to put in several hours of work and still sit down virtuously to dinner while the day was young. One fine summer morning, Thomas Betson, a fifteenth-century wool merchant, wrote a long letter from Calais to the little girl in England he was to marry, and ended with these words: " [written] at great Calais, on this side of the sea, the first day of June, when every man was gone to his dinner, and the clock smote nine, and all your household cried after me and bade me 'come down, come down to dinner at once.' "[21]

In his sixteenth-century treatise, *The Haven of Health,* Thomas Cogan calculates that "when foure houres be past after breakfast, a man may safely taste his dinner, and the most convenient time for dinner is about eleven of the clocke before noone."[22] He qualifies the statement with a story that applies as well to the medieval period as to any other: "Diogenes the philosopher, when he was asked the question what time was best for a man to dine, he answered, for a rich man when he will, but for a poore man when he maye."[23] While noon was the accepted time for dinner in the Middle Ages, the meal was tugged to and fro through the morning hours. Hunger pangs and dawn rising encouraged early sessions, preachers urged later ones. Masters favored, and frequently enforced, the break that fit best into the working day.

The ideal number of meals was considered to be two, dinner and supper. An everyday supper was a much lighter affair than dinner, and eaten by sunset. In his sixth-century *Rule* for monks, St. Benedict stressed the point: "At all times, they must so manage the hour of the meal . . . that it is in daylight."[24] Economical householders found no reason to quarrel with this as a guideline; the saving on light and heat was recommendation enough.

A festive supper for guests was a rather different matter. The thirteenth-century Franciscan Bartholomaeus Anglicus certainly conceded that the ideal supper must be "not to erly nor to late," but he found "plente of lyghte of candels" an important part of the pleasure, and considered it essential that the meal should proceed at a leisurely pace: "For men use, after full ende of werke and of traveyle to sytte longe at the supper . . . at the soupper men schulde eate by leyser [leisure] and not to hastely."[25]

Great men, of course, made their own rules. Froissart tells us that Gaston de Foix liked to get up at noon, sleep in the afternoon, and have his supper at midnight. Any critical comments on these habits ventured by the clergy attached to the household remain unrecorded.[26]

It is hard to decide how widely accepted breakfast became in the period. In theory it had no existence: grown men held out until the proper time. In practice it was not unknown: grown men were human. As a result, breakfast leads a slightly furtive existence in the records. To compound confusion, until the meal had been established, the word could be applied with perfect propriety to dinner. In the fifteenth-century, Lydgate's travelers "break fast" in this sense:

> Every Pilgryme . . . toke anon his hors . . .
> Whan the sonne roos in the est ful clyere,
> Fully in purpoos to come to dynere
> Unto Osspryng and breke ther our faste.[27]

A little later Caxton, in his *English and French Dialogues*, begins a specimen menu with the ominous words "We shall breke our fast with trippes [tripe]," goes on to list as the other features of the meal an ox foot, a pig's foot, and a head of garlic, and ends with evident satisfaction, "So shall we breke our faste."[28] It is dangerous to be unduly influenced by the soothing simplicities of toast and cornflakes, but Caxton's bill of fare seems dauntingly substantial for anyone to face fresh from his bed, and we may assume that here too the "break fast" intended is dinner.

In the same century, however, breakfast is listed as a meal coming before dinner and supper for Edward IV and his household.[29] Consisting as it did of bread, meat, and ale, the royal breakfast seems to have been designed to lay a sound foundation for the day ahead, but often the impression left by other references is that the meal, when eaten at all, was a snatched and hurried affair. As noted before, Bercilak ate only a "sop" after mass before heading for the hunt, a sop being a sliver of bread dipped in wine or some other liquid. Jorrocks would scarcely have approved.

Breakfast may perhaps be described, by the later Middle Ages, as an optional extra. Those who did hard, heavy work could expect to have a bite to eat before the midday meal, though Tusser briskly reminds employers that this is to be regarded as a privilege, not a right:

> No breakefast of custome provide for to save,
> but onely for such as deserveth to have.[30]

Regulations for the masons and carpenters building York Minster ca. 1352 laid down that they were to begin the working day at sunrise and eat their dinner at noon. In summertime, when dawn came early, they were allowed a break for breakfast "for the space of [time that it takes to walk] half a league"; in winter, with a much shorter morning, they were expected to have eaten before they arrived on the site.[31]

Other groups of people sometimes indulged with breakfast were the old, the sick, and the very young. Even in monasteries the invalids and the young novices were allowed to eat something before *none*. In society at large the privilege was probably taken for granted. A fifteenth-century schoolboy looked back nostalgically to the days when he was very small and very spoiled: "My brekefaste was brought to my beddys side as ofte as me liste to calle therfor, and so many tymes I was first fedde or I were cledde [fed before I was dressed]."[32] The memory made a painful contrast to the present state of his affairs: "Now at fyve of the clocke by the monelyght I most go to my booke and lete slepe and slouthe alon . . . brekfastes that were sumtyme brought at my biddynge is dryven oute of contrey and never shall cum agayne."[33]

Perhaps because of these associations with childhood and infirmity, there lingered on for a long time a certain feeling of apology and embarrassment when a grown man admitted to eating breakfast. It was often regarded as a weakness, to be disguised if possible as something quite different: "This is no brekefast: but a morsell to drynke with."[34] A businessman in fourteenth-century Prato carefully explained that the only reason he ate some roasted chestnuts every morning before going out was to please his wife: "she pampers me, as I do her."[35]

It seems likely that the habit took possession of society, inch by inch, its eventual victory assured by a fatal weakness in the defenders. Too many, then as now, found themselves not at their best on an empty stomach, and welcomed the invader with open arms. The Host in the Prologue to *The Tale of Beryn,* trying to decide who among his group of pilgrims is to tell the first story of the day, prefers not to rely on the drawing of lots for this privilege. An entertainer is required and, as he points out, the lot might fall to someone quite unsuitable: "som men fasting beth no thing iocounde."[36] For such cases Andrew Boorde, ever helpful, recommends a little green ginger first thing in the morning.[37]

Not only did workmen usually eat breakfast; they were also fortified in the course of the day with "nuncheons." These little snacks had become accepted fringe benefits by the fifteenth century, and they were noted down on wage sheets as a matter of course. In 1423, the Company of Brewers in London listed two kinds of payment, in money and in food, for the casual laborers it employed: "Robert, dawber, for his dawbyng" received four pence "with his noonnchyns"; two carpenters making a gutter got eightpence each "with here Nonsenches."[38]

A softening of attitude toward breaks in routine and eating on the job may be traced in pictures made throughout the period. In early Labors of the Months cycles, men are hard at work; in illustrated manuals on the virtues and vices, a peasant sitting idle in a field is Sloth personified.[39] Slowly, artists learned to relax, and revealed from time to time the incidental pleasures of the working day. The shipbuilders on a fifteenth-century misericord in St. David's Cathedral in Wales are drinking while their unfinished boat stands on its stocks behind them; many a harvester in late medieval calendar pictures for August enjoys his picnic in the shadow of the half-cut corn.[40]

Nuncheons, like breakfasts, helped workmen through the long laborious day. The lack of such a pretext, sad to say, deterred few of their betters from effortlessly acquiring the habit. Hoccleve, indeed, spent so much time and energy treating girls to sweet wine and "wafres thikke" that he sometimes found it impossible to drag himself back to the office for the rest of the afternoon, and went off boating on the Thames instead.[41] Though the Church thundered against those who "renneth to the mete or tyme be [before time], as doth a dombe best [dumb beast],"[42] many were delighted to follow the example of the mouse in Lydgate's story, who lay back on the sacks in the mill he made his home, fastidiously brushed the crumbs from his whiskers, and murmured:

> Thys is a mery lyfe . . .
> As I have appetyte, I dyne late or sone.[43]

Two meals a day might be deemed sufficient by moralists well into the sixteenth century; the true state of affairs is hinted at in pictures and poems, where people eat and drink in the garden, the bed, the bath (fig. 1), and any combination of these. The calendar scene for May in the early sixteenth-century Da Costa Hours shows four lovers serenading the spring in a boat. Prominent in the foreground is a large flagon of wine hung over the side to cool in the water. In a fifteenth-century poem, *The Flower and the Leaf*, some friends, scorched by the sun and drenched by a thunderstorm, are helped by strangers who have prudently sheltered beneath a tree. When the skies clear, these kindly bustle about to make the victims comfortable:

> . . . gadring
> Plesaunt salades, which they made hem ete,
> For to refresh their greet unkindly hete.[44]

That life kept pace with art may be deduced from a letter, written on 13 May 1482, by a wool merchant, Richard Cely, to his brother George. On the lookout for a wife, Richard had contrived an introduction to a lady at Northleach in the Cotswolds, a town regularly visited on his buying trips. Carefully noting that he declined an invitation to dinner, he lets slip the information that he, the lady, and two companions consumed between them one roast heron, a gallon of unspecified wine, and a "pottell of whyte romney," containing another half gallon. After all this, to no one's surprise, Richard found the lady "very well favoured and witty."[45]

The wine doubtless floated the party over awkward patches at

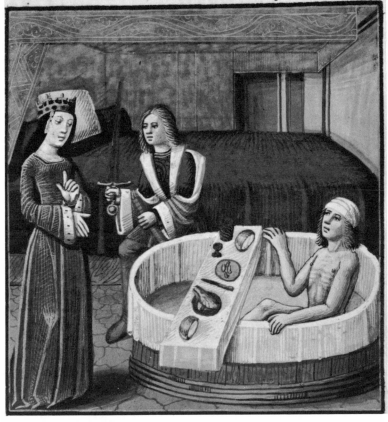

1. Bath and Board.
*Tristan,* Paris, 1494–95 (Paris, Bibliothèque Nationale, MS. Vélin 623, fol. 37). Photo. Bibl. nat. Paris.

this first meeting. Like cups of tea and coffee today, it helped to pass the time. As the Wife of Bath says with engaging frankness to the Prioress, in *The Tale of Beryn,* after dinner and a quick turn round the garden of their inn at Canterbury:

> I woll gyve yewe the wyne, and yee schull me also;
> ffor tyll wee go to soper wee have naught ellis to do.[46]

What could the Church do in face of this incurable human

tendency to nibble and sip, to stay up late for reresopers, only to wake with the first prayer of the day already on the lips: "A, lord God, what schule we ete today?"[47] Her only course was to make plain the consequences of self-indulgence, objectively and without concession to ingrained national tastes. Among the many cautionary tales, the Case of the Fatal Welsh Rarebit stands out:

> I fynde wryten amonge olde gestys, how God made Saynte Peter porter of heven and that God of his goodnes, soone after his passyon, suffred many men to come to the kyngdome of heven with small deservyng, at whiche tyme there was in heven a grete company of Welchemen whiche, with theyre krakynge and babelynge, trobelyd all the other. Wherfore God sayd to Saynt Peter that he was wery of them, and that he wolde fayne have them out of heven. To whom Saynt Peter sayde, "Good Lorde, I warrant you that shalbe shortly done." Wherfore Saynt Peter went out of heven gatys, and cryed with a loude voice, "Cause bobe," that is as moche to say as "rostyd chese," whiche thynge the Welchmen heryng ran out of hevyn a great pace. And when Saynt Peter sawe them al out, he sodenly went in to heven and lokkyd the dore, and so sparryd all the Welchmen out.
>
> By this ye may se that it is no wysdome for a man to love or to set his mynde to moche upon ony delycate or worldly pleasure wherby he shall lose the celestyall and eternall Ioye.[48]

# 3

# Fast and Feast

The medieval year resembled a chessboard of black and white squares. It was patterned with periods of fast and feast, each distinct and limited in time, yet each dependent on the other for its significance and worth. To give true spiritual refreshment, feast and fast had to follow each other like the seasons. A Church feast was ushered in by a period of fasting; a fast was rewarded with not only a feast in this life but the hope of a celestial banquet in the next. To be of value, each had to be a deliberate, conscious offering by the individual or by society. Endless, thoughtless wining and dining by the prosperous was nothing but gross indulgence; the nagging, perpetual undernourishment of the poor, "in suche bare places where every day is Lent,"[1] was nothing but misery.

Fasting, the dark square on the board, was undertaken for several different reasons. It was a form of self-discipline, a private mortification for one's personal sins and a public mortification for those of society. It might be an individual's act of propitiation, a spring cleaning to freshen the soul and make it ready to receive God's grace, or an imitation of Jesus' fast in the wilderness, a thorough preparation by the whole community for the great feasts of the Church's year: Christmas and Easter. In every case, a fast was to be endured for its spiritual benefit: dazzling displays of willpower and austerity were frowned on.

Anyone might choose to practice a private regime of abstinence on any ordinary day of the year. In the *Swinfield Accounts* for 1289/90, it is made plain that a few members of the bishop's household decided to fast one extra day a week in November and December. They are referred to as "the fasters," and as they had decided to eat no meat on their special day, fish had to be ordered for them.[2]

In this case, the steward and cook might well have felt privately irritated by the extra trouble involved, but everyone else went on contentedly munching his way through an ordinary, hearty meal. It was always heavily emphasized that a private fast must be combined with consideration for others. A fast was not to be regarded by a frugal housekeeper as a heaven-sent excuse for belt-tightening and cheese-paring. No money was to be saved on meals; the usual amounts had to be prepared and then given away to the needy.[3]

There can be problems when a guest on a private diet comes to dinner. The sight of a righteous diner waving away a delicacy has left many a host regrettably unedified, many a fellow guest resentful. In the fifth century, St. Augustine solved the problem with great tact. For many years he had denied himself meat, but when invited to a splendid dinner party in Carthage, he found a roast peacock brought to the table in his honor. On the spur of the moment, he decided to create a diversion by conducting a scientific experiment. The Church had adopted the peacock as a symbol of everlasting life because its flesh was believed to be imperishable. The question was vexed, debate was hot. Here was a perfect opportunity to put the matter to the test: "I took a fair slice of the breast and had it put to one side. After as many days as it takes for any other cooked meat to become high, I had it brought out before me. There was no offensive odour whatever. I then had the same piece of meat kept for more than a month. I still found no change in it. Then, after a whole year, the only difference was that it was somewhat dried and shrivelled."[4]

In several passages, Augustine drops a hint that he himself found undereating rather hard. Wine presented no problem, but good food was a real temptation, all the more vexing because it was one to be struggled with every single day. He buoyed himself with the faint comfort that moderation was good for his physical health.[5] Such a consolation was rudely brushed aside by a more robust, and less sophisticated, sermon writer in the fifteenth century. A diet attempted for any reason other than spiritual improvement, and in particular for such irrelevancies as health and beauty, was nothing but a mockery: "Yet schalt thou dye for all that phisyk."[6]

Any personal, private diet betokened commendable zeal, because it was an addition to those official fast days with which the Church attempted to cleanse and discipline society. In each week there were three fast days, of which the most strictly observed was

Friday, in memory of the crucifixion. To this were added Wednesday and Saturday: Wednesday because it was the day when Judas accepted money for his promise to betray Jesus; Saturday because it was the day consecrated to Mary and the celebration of her virginity. Society was encouraged to observe these days, although, as with all fasts, the very old, the very young, the very sick, and the very poor were held excused. There were of course exceptions. St. Nicholas showed his holiness early in life by refusing to take his mother's milk more than once on Wednesdays and Fridays:

> Seint Nicholas . . .
> . . . so yong to Crist did reverençe.[7]

Four times a year these ordinary weekday fasts on Wednesday, Friday, and Saturday were observed with special seriousness: early in Lent, just after Pentecost, in September, and in December during Advent. At these punctuation points in the year, the days were called Ember Days. The Church took over and adapted the Roman practice of holding ceremonies to ask the gods for help with the farm year. In June the Romans prayed for a good harvest; in September for a good vintage, and in December for a good seedtime. By the fifth century A.D. the Church had added a fourth occasion, in February or March. The days always retained their links with the farm cycle, and in the services designed for them the lessons are shot through with the imagery of sowing, reaping, and harvesting.

The Church, however, was only partially concerned with the fruits of the earth. Its principal interest was in the fruits of the soul, and so the idea of harvest in the field became overlaid with that of spiritual harvest. An early fifteenth-century sermon by John Myrc, commenting on the significance of the Ember Days, draws the necessary parallels between the seasons of the earth and the soul. In March, cutting winds dry up the sodden soil and make it workable; the fast will cleanse and ready the soul. In summer, as the plants shoot up, men fast to make their virtues grow. In September, men hope to gather in a harvest of good works; in December, as the shriveling cold kills off the earth's weeds, the fast kills off the weeds of vice.[8]

The origin of the name, Ember, is obscure. It is now thought to be a corruption of the Latin *quatuor tempora*, the four times, but Myrc has a much more intriguing explanation. According to him, on these days little cakes used to be baked among the fire embers.

It was always a matter of luck whether the cakes would be rescued at just the right time, or reduced to cinders in the heat. Frequent disasters forcibly reminded the cooks that man too would turn to ashes, a gloomy thought which put them in the proper frame of mind for fasting on blackened buns.[9]

The two longest and most important fasts were Advent and Lent, which ushered in the greatest feasts of the year, Christmas and Easter. The season of Advent covers a span of about four weeks and always contains four Sundays. It begins on the first of these, Advent Sunday, and this day marks the start of the ecclesiastical year. It is a period of preparation for Christmas, a time when man tries to turn over a new leaf and start again. One fifteenth-century sermon writer points the parallel between the Church and the individual: just as the Church makes a fresh beginning on Advent Sunday, "so owe ye to begynne and renewe youre lyff."[10]

Lent, however, is the season immediately thought of when the subject of fasting comes to mind. Its length, six weeks, was chosen in imitation of Jesus' fast of forty days in the wilderness. In spirit, it is a long drawn-out prayer for forgiveness of sin, a call for help, a begging for God's grace to save man from himself. Its last week is darkened by an intensive meditation on man's betrayal of Jesus at the crucifixion. Whereas the services for Advent are shot through with the excitement and joy of the birthday just about to dawn, the tone of Lent is sober, only occasionally lightened by the promise of salvation and of Jesus' victory over death. It was a long and dreary stretch of time, to be endured as a penance; a quite considerable sacrifice to be offered up to God in gratitude for His mercies, and sorrow for man's inadequacies. In the farm year, a tenth of a man's harvest, a tithe, had to be handed over to his lord or his parish priest. Of the year's three hundred and sixty-five days, Lent's forty made up a generous tenth, and were sometimes called "the tithe days of the year."[11]

The form of a fast varied very much from occasion to occasion. Indeed, the term fast scarcely applies to an ordinary Friday, for an ordinary layman. The amount eaten could be just as ample as usual, and the only change expected was, for reasons to be discussed later, a change in the main ingredient of the menu, from meat to fish.

Lent was a rather different matter, the major fast of the year. The first hardship to be endured in this season was a limitation in the number of meals to be eaten each day. Instead of the usual two, and sometimes three if the household indulged in breakfast, only one was officially allowed. Matters were not improved in the early centuries of the Church's history by the rule that this solitary meal was not to be eaten until the early evening, after the hour of vespers which marked the end of the ecclesiastical day. According to popular belief, this rule was made to strengthen Lent's character as an imitation of Jesus' fast in the wilderness. While Jesus had managed to survive his forty days without eating a morsel, this was impossible for ordinary men, and so dinner time in Lent was set in limbo, as it were, between the official end of one day and the official beginning of the next.[12]

By a series of equally ingenious intellectual maneuvers the time for dinner was gradually, over the centuries, pushed back to noon, but it remained the one proper meal of the day. Moreover, the fact that it was the only one was not considered a legitimate excuse to increase its size. The one concession to human weakness was the collation, a very light snack, no more than a drink and a morsel of bread, to be eaten just before bedtime. This was first officially sanctioned in a decree of 817, which permitted monks to have a drink while they listened to the regular evening reading of a passage from Cassian's *Collationes*.[13] Thus, a word which today denotes a delicate, elegant little meal, comes, by way of a grudging admission of man's frailty in the ninth century, from a fifth-century anthology of wise thoughts culled from the early hermits in the Egyptian desert.

This sharp cut in the number of meals eaten each day was trying enough, but the change in diet was much harder to bear. For six weeks, no meat of any kind could be eaten. The formal reason for this had its roots in the significance of the season. Lent was a period of reflection on man's sin, which could be traced back to Adam's fall. When God discovered what Adam had done, He said: "Cursed is the ground for thy sake."[14] The earth and earth's creatures were flawed by man's failure, and therefore at the time of the year when attention was most focused on that failure, in memory of it no animal that was born and bred on land was to be eaten. Exceptions, as always, were made for the very poor, young, old, and sick, but the rule was otherwise strictly enforced and seriously obeyed. Nevertheless, it posed certain delicate problems for thoughtful commentators. In the Church's teaching, the whole of God's creation was good; it was a heresy to state that any being was by its nature evil and untouchable. As St. Paul says: "For every creature of God is good, and nothing to be refused, if it be received with thanksgiving."[15] It had to be constantly and carefully emphasized, therefore, that meat was good, and given up in Lent only as a daily reminder of man's fall and God's anger. Meat was also, incidentally, enormously enjoyed, so the long deprivation was a very real punishment.

The prohibition was often stretched to cover other animal products: butter, cheese, milk, and eggs. The rules about these were interpreted a little less strictly than that about meat; nevertheless, it was the custom for eggs at least to vanish after Shrove Tuesday, and reappear, in all their hardboiled glory, on Easter Sunday.

In theory, the diner's attitude of mind was more important than what he found on his plate; as St. Augustine remarked: "It is the uncleanness of gluttony that I fear, not unclean meat. For I know ... that John the Baptist ... was not polluted by the flesh of living creatures, the locusts which were granted him as food. On the other hand I know that Esau was defrauded by his greed for a dish of lentils."[16] While thoughts are invisible, food is not, and in practice the Church did all in its power to make sure that menus, if nothing else, met its exacting requirements.

Its most stalwart members would have been happy to impose a stern regime of bread and water on society, but more moderate counsels prevailed. If meat, butter, cheese, eggs, and milk were all forbidden, what could keep body and soul together for six long weeks? The answer was fish. Fish, providentially, had escaped God's curse on the earth by living in the water. Water itself was an element of special sanctity, washing away the sins of the world in Noah's Flood, and the sins of the individual in baptism. Its creatures might be said to share something of its virtues. Once the choice had been justified, the rest was easy. Fish was plentiful, fish was cheap, and in the season of Lent, fish was king.

Any fish that finned its way obligingly within man's reach was welcome on fast days, but in England and northern Europe, at least, the one that leaped irresistibly to mind when the subject of Lent cropped up was the herring. Passing northern coasts in enormous shoals each autumn, he was easy to catch, easy to salt, dry, and store, and easy to buy. He was nourishing, plentiful, and very cheap. He was King Herring, who mounted his throne on Ash Wednesday, and stayed there, however much his subjects grumbled, until Easter Sunday. As Thomas Nashe in the sixteenth century puts it: "he weares a coronet on his head, in token that hee is as he is."[17]

Whatever a man's luck, whether he could enjoy the luxury of variety, or had to munch his way resignedly through six long weeks of dried herring, his eating habits were turned upside down by Lent's imperious demands. These affected society in many ways. Even children's games changed with the seasons. Alexander Barclay describes a year's round of amusements, and for autumn, when pigs were killed for the winter, shows children playing in the streets with a football made from a pig's bladder. Froissart, looking back to his own childhood, remembers a game he used to play in Lent with a pile of sea shells.[18] More important, Lent had a considerable effect on household and business arrangements. Careful planning went into the making of a Lent that was no less comfortable than it absolutely had to be.

Those fortunate enough to possess large and varied estates were inclined to take the easy way out, and move their household to the one with the most fish within its boundaries. Roger II of Sicily liked to migrate to his pleasure garden at Favara for the season because among its charms were several well-stocked fish ponds.[19] Lesser men had to show more ingenuity. The English army, campaigning in France in 1359, traveled everywhere with a number of little leather boats packed into their wagons. Whenever a stretch of water was reached, these were unloaded and launched for fishing expeditions. Froissart comments drily: "This was a great standby for them at all seasons, including Lent, at least for the lords and the royal household, but the common soldiers had to manage with what they found."[20]

The owner of a fish stew, or pond, was lucky because he could brighten his diet of preserved saltwater fish with some newly caught, freshwater ones. However, privilege had to be paid for with precautions. The sixteenth-century Thomas Tusser recommended September as the month in which to stock the stew-pond for Lent:

> Thy ponds renew,
> Put eeles in stew,
> To leeve til Lent,
> and then be spent.[21]

During Lent itself, the precious pond had to be guarded from the greedy:

> knaves seld repent
> to steale in Lent.[22]

The prudent householder bought as much fish as he could afford and store in the autumn. To wait for the panic days just before a major fast was to ask for trouble. Prices shot up as shoppers grew desperate, while during the fast, inevitably "the fysshe mongers wynneth this lente."[23] Indeed, it was not always possible for the improvident to find a fish at all if he left the search too late. The *Swinfield Accounts* for 1289/90 reveal that in one October week the usual Wednesday fast had to be switched to a Thursday because there was no fish to be had on the right day.[24]

In the fifteenth century there was a flourishing trade between England and Iceland. English ships left for Iceland between February and April and returned, loaded with cod, between July and September. The cod was salted down at sea, or dried in the air to a boardlike consistency. Thus treated, it became the most plentiful and least loved of Lenten delicacies, the stockfish.[25] Herring fleets also brought in their catch in the autumn, and offered both white and red for sale. White herrings had been preserved in salt, while the red ones were both salted and smoked, in double protection. Tusser advised his farmer-reader that the best time to buy the main stock of dried fish for the year was in the weeks after harvest, when there was a slack period on the farm, and prices were low.[26] He might have added that weather in the early autumn could be relied on to be reasonable enough to make transportation by road or water less of a headache than in February.

It was most convenient to buy fish already prepared for storage, but most economical to preserve it at home, whenever practicable. Margery Cressy, in her will (ca. 1180), made arrangements for five cartloads of alder wood to be delivered to the nuns of Godstow each year in the first two weeks of October and used "to drye their heryng."[27]

Slowly but surely, fast flowed into feast. The prudent housekeeper had to make the same long-term plans for Easter as for Lent, if she had no wish to pay a fortune for a morsel of meat on Easter Saturday. Tusser set Martinmas, 11 November, as the critical date.[28] This was the season for the main slaughter of cattle, so meat was plentiful and prices low. A piece of beef hung up then to smoke in the chimney through the long winter months would make a most economical centerpiece for the Easter dinner.

The necessities of a long fast encouraged, indeed, a battle of wits between the wily citizen and the wilier businessman. The latter, of course, wore innumerable disguises, many of them ecclesiastical. However carefully a household planned, it was always necessary to buy some fish in Lent itself. Abingdon Abbey, well aware of this, plumped out its money bags by imposing a toll on every barge laden with herring that sailed past the abbey walls on its way up the Thames during Lent.[29] Bury St. Edmunds, noting that it straddled the main route from Yarmouth to London, hit on the idea of levying a toll on all London-bound carts from Yarmouth laden with pickled herrings. London merchants had to take a firm line and threaten to pull down some new stone houses just built that year by the Abbot of Bury before the matter could be smoothed over.[30]

Fast days made fish very big business. As Thomas Nashe exuberantly claimed: "To trowle in the cash throughout all nations of Christendome, there is no fellowe to the red herring."[31] The demand for fish created jobs. Ropemakers, sailmakers, net weavers, coopers, cleaners, packers, carriers, workers in the salt houses—prosperity for all of them depended on society's need for fish. As salt fish make men thirsty, even brewers benefited. Money poured into a town like Yarmouth because the herring "draweth more barkes to Yarmouth bay, than Helen's beautie did to Troy."[32]

The economic effects of strict and steady fasting may be judged by the gloom which descended on English government officials in Elizabeth I's reign, when the Reformation had loosened the Catholic Church's grip on society. Although for a long time after the Reformation some fast days continued to be observed, particularly Fridays and the season of Lent, many, like Wednesdays, were no longer official fish days, and even in Lent the use of fish was not so automatic as it had been. As a result, the number of English ships at sea had dramatically declined, and in February 1563, a government document was drawn up entitled "Arguments in Favour of Establishing Wednesday as an Additional Fish Day," with this explanation of its contents: "Arguments to prove that it is necessary for the restoring of the Navye of England to have more fishe eaten and therefor one daye more in the weeke ordeyned to be a fissh daye, and that to be Wednesdaye, rather than any other."[33] The essay is studded with regretful calculations of the number of fish days observed by the whole country in the bad old times before the coming of the light, and shot through with desire to have the best of both worlds by pouring scorn on the superstition while preserving all its profits.

Long after the Reformation, fasting was encouraged for a variety of secular reasons. Farmers believed that fish days helped to prevent too great a drain on a country's meat supplies:

> The land doth will, the sea doth wish,
> Spare sometime flesh, and feede of fish.[34]

In the seventeenth century, that fervent fisherman, Izaak Walton, believed that the weakening of the rules about fasting lay at the root of England's medical problems: "It is observed by the most learned physicians, that the casting off of Lent, and other fish days . . . hath doubtless been the chief cause of those many putrid, shaking, intermitting agues, unto which this nation of ours is now more subject, than those wiser countries that feed on herbs, salads, and plenty of fish."[35]

These ripples of memory, spreading out through the centuries, are an indication of fasting's profound effect on society. Testimony to the seriousness with which its rules were regarded in the Middle Ages is easily found in a hundred stories. In 1381, the citizens of Ghent endured a long siege. Stocks of food dwindled away, and there was great suffering. Half-starved, the people still had strength enough to be shocked by a new and unavoidable crisis: "And whan the tyme of Lent came, than were they in great dystresse, for they had no Lenton stuffe."[36] Joinville, captured by Saracens while on the Seventh Crusade, in 1250, lost track of days and seasons. On one occasion while he was eating his dinner, a visitor was brought to see him, a fellow countryman, from Paris: "When the man arrived he said to me: 'My lord, what are you doing?' 'Why, what can I be doing?' said I. 'In God's name,' he replied, 'you're eating meat on a Friday.' As soon as I heard this I put my bowl behind me. . . ." Poor Joinville was so ashamed of his lapse that he imposed an extra punishment on himself: "I did not cease to fast on bread and water every Friday in Lent from that time onwards."[37]

Inevitably, the season of Lent, which stretched over such a long period and brought with it such a change in atmosphere and eating habits, was entered with some sinking of the heart. Tension was heightened by the very fact that Lent did not creep gradually into place, could not be put off for a day or two until a man felt ready to face its rigors. Only in fantasy could Lent be either shortened or delayed. A fifteenth-century Italian story tells of a country priest whose arithmetic became hopelessly muddled when he tried to calculate the dates of Easter and Ash Wednesday. One year, happily enjoying a day's holiday in a neighboring town, he was disconcerted to find the citizens celebrating Palm Sunday, while his own Lent had not even got started. Rushing back to his parish, he explained that Lent had just come puffing over the mountains, and felt so worn-out by his climb that this year he had strength for only one week of fasting before the Easter celebrations.[38]

Less fortunate parishioners found that Lent stalked in remorselessly on Ash Wednesday, and the old, unregenerate, meat-eating life ended with a bang the day before. On Shrove Tuesday, every morsel of fresh meat had to be eaten up, and the last, precious hours were spent in one long frenzy of self-indulgence: "Always before Lent there comes waddling a fat gross bursten-gutted groom, called Shrove Tuesday . . . He devours more flesh in fourteen hours, than this whole kingdom doth . . . in six weeks after. Such boiling and broiling, such roasting and toasting, such stewing and brewing, such baking, frying, mincing, cutting, carving, devouring, and gorbellied gormondizing, that a man would think people did . . . ballast their bellies with meat for a voyage to Constantinople. . . ."[39]

Eggs had to be gobbled up with the same mad abandon. Ambrosial extravaganzas were created over the centuries to ensure that a thousand eggs slipped effortlessly down a hundred ravening throats. The wafer-thin pancake, sugared, spiced, and fried to perfection, was one invention; "pain perdu" another. In this, a humble slice of bread is magically metamorphosed into a royal delicacy once it has been soaked in wine and rosewater, rolled in beaten eggs, sugared, fried, and sugared again. Cotgrave, in 1611, lists in his dictionary under *"pain"* the phrase *"Le Jour de pain perdu,"* and offers the English translation: "Shrovetewsday." Shrove Tuesday derives its name from the verb *shrive*, to hear or make confession, and this riot of self-indulgence did not begin officially until after confessions had been heard in the morning. The sound of bells ringing out to summon men to church was inextricably associated with the feast to follow. Long after the Reformation, when their original significance had been forgotten, the bells still rang on Shrove Tuesday morning. Confessions had vanished, but no self-respecting cook would begin to heat his frying-pan until the "Pancake Bell" was heard.

The violent contrast between Shrove Tuesday and Ash Wednesday created an atmosphere of tension and nervous excitement. The conflict between the two is personified by Peter Brueghel the Elder in *The Fight Between Carnival and Lent* (1559). The figure of Carnival is enormous, seated on a wine barrel, and wearing a large pie cocked over one eye. He tilts at Lent with a long spit crowded with sausages and chickens. Behind him a woman surrounded by eggs is cooking pancakes, while everyone else is enjoying himself. On the ground is a rather nasty litter of egg shells, bones, and playing cards. Lent is thin and gloomy, and his lance is a paddle with two fish on it. Mussel shells are strewn on the ground beside him, and large baskets of shells and bread stand nearby. Behind, fishmongers do a roaring trade, and beggars are lined up for alms from the charitable.

Personifications reveal something of the popular attitude to Lent, the dislike of its monotony which lurked just beneath respectful obedience to its rules. Rabelais' King Lent is "a huge greedy guts, a glutton for peas, a crook-fingered splitter of herring-barrels, a mackerel snatcher . . . that cockroach bastard of a Lent."[40] John Gladman of Norwich, in 1448, arranged a procession of the months and seasons, each wearing a suitable costume. Lent marched along, "cladde in white with redde herrings skinnes and his hors trapped with oyster shelles after him in token that sadnesse and abstinence of merth shulde followe and an holy tyme."[41]

Carnival—that is, Shrove Tuesday and the days preceding it—was much preferred to Lent, but too much feasting can fray the best of tempers, and the season was notorious for its quarrels and sudden spurts of violence. The University of Paris was banished for a while from the city in 1228 because of a Carnival riot in which some students beat up an innkeeper and poured his stock of wine into the street.[42]

On the other hand, Lent itself hardly sweetened tempers. The second lesson of the mass on Ash Wednesday urges men to face the coming weeks with cheerfulness: "When you fast, do not show it by gloomy looks, as the hypocrites do."[43] Despite this suggestion, belt-tightening and salt herrings wreaked havoc on the human spirit. The English friar Robert Holcot had to preach a sermon to the University of Oxford one Lent in the early fourteenth century, in which he deplored "rows at night and riots, blows, slaughter, homicide and wicked conspiracy by day."[44] In 1543, the Earl of Surrey was clapped into the Fleet jail in London for breaking windows in Lent. While cooling his heels there he made the blood pressure of his neighbors rise still higher by the pious claim that he had smashed their windows only to startle them into thinking about their own shortcomings.[45]

Lent was, decidedly, a strain, and the muffled cries of protest can be heard from one end of the Middle Ages to the other. Early in the ninth century, Charlemagne is explaining to sympathetic ears that "he could not go long without food, and . . . fasting made him feel ill."[46]

In the fifteenth century, a schoolboy grumbles in his private notebook: "Thou wyll not beleve how wery I am off fysshe, and how moch I desir that flesch wer cum in ageyn. For I have ete none other but salt fysh this Lent, and it hathe engendyrde so moch flewme [phlegm] within me that it stoppith my pypys that I can unneth [scarcely] speke nother brethe."[47]

Dogs, of course, detested the season, that "hard siege by Lent and fish bones,"[48] and did everything they could to circumvent it:

> Watch therefore in Lent, to thy sheepe go and looke,
> for dogs will have vittles, by hooke or by crooke.[49]

For all but the most devout, indeed, Lent was much too long, and it began to feel too long at some time on Ash Wednesday morning. Dunbar (ca. 1460–1513) makes fun of the faint-hearted when he pictures two Scottish matrons consoling themselves on Ash Wednesday with a pot of wine, and sighing as they sip: "This lange Lentrune hes maid me lene [This long Lent has made me lean]."[50]

Of all Lent's ingredients, perhaps the most loathed was the red herring. Very cheap and very plentiful, it haunted every menu, turned up on every plate. Devising "goodbyes," not "au revoirs," to the red herring became one of the small, sweet consolations of the season. At St. Rémy in France, clerks walked in procession to church on Maundy Thursday, just before Easter, each pulling a red herring on a string, each trying to tread on the herring in front, while guarding his own from the man behind.[51] As late as the nineteenth century, Queen's College in Oxford preserved a memory of its own farewell. On Easter Sunday, the first dish sent up to high table was a red herring, riding away on horseback: "That is to say, a herring placed by the cook, something after the likeness of a man on horseback, set on a corn sallad."[52]

After six long weeks of austerity, Easter was welcomed as the radiantly happy commemoration of the Resurrection, the day of days on which, in celebration, all the good things to eat came trooping back. To emphasize that Lent was a season of mourning and penitence, the Church forbade the singing of the joyful "alleluia" in services throughout the whole period. At Easter, the "alleluia" rang out once more and, with a sigh of contentment, the world returned to normal:

Soone at Easter cometh alleluya,
With butter, chese and a tansay
[egg mixture flavored with the herb tansy].[53]

It is the nature of man to build the most complicated cage of
rules and regulations in which to trap himself, and then, with
equal ingenuity and zest, to bend his brain to the problem of
wriggling triumphantly out again. Lent was a challenge; the game
was to ferret out the loopholes. Its dreary length might be neither
ignored nor shortened, but its sorrows could be drowned in
drink. From an early period it had been accepted that drinking
did not break the fast; determined rummagers through the Bible
could back up the Church's decision on the matter with such texts
as this, from an impeccable authority, St. Paul: "Drink no longer
water, but use a little wine for thy stomach's sake."[54]

Perhaps the consumption of so many fish in Lent made minds
turn to thoughts of liquor. Certainly, consideration for the fish
formed the classic drinker's excuse, as this fifteenth-century sermon reveals: "In this time of Lent, when by the law and custom of
the Church men fast, very few people abstain from excessive
drinking: on the contrary, they go to the taverns, and some im-
bibe and get drunk more than they do out of Lent, thinking and
saying: 'Fishes *must* swim.' "[55]

The phrase had been tripping effortlessly from the reveler's
tongue for many centuries. At the splendid Roman dinner party
in the *Satyricon,* Trimalchio coaxes his guests to drink after a fish
course with the same tempting logic: "Gentlemen, I want you to
savour this good wine. Fish must swim, and that's a fact."[56]

Salted fish, of course, made Lent's diet thirsty work for the most
conscientious diner. In polite society, care was taken to cut off the
salt-impregnated skin of a fish before it was offered to a guest, but
even so a need was felt to disguise the flesh itself.[57] By the second
half of Lent, desperate measures were demanded to blot out the
taste of hated herring. A large dollop of mustard was the favored
disguise, and for centuries the two went hand in hand in the
popular imagination: "The red Herring and Ling never came to
the boord without mustard, their waiting maid."[58] This formidable partnership of hot mustard with salt herring must have
been the answer to a brewer's prayer, a confirmation that peniten-
tial seasons did indeed do good.

Perhaps on the principle that alcohol can be disastrous to an
empty stomach, authority turned a blind eye on the practice of

ballasting each drink with a little snack. At least two of the year's variety of breads and buns were specially associated with Lent: the *wig*, a small, wedge-shaped cake, and the *crakenel*, a hard, twice-baked rusk. Each may have been quite uninteresting in itself, but each was blessedly solid, and each designed expressly for dipping in the cup and sopping up the drink.

These might be described as the poor man's comforters. More exciting additions to a meager diet were also allowed. None of Lent's rules and regulations forbade the use of sweetmeats and spices. Provided that it was too tiny to be deemed a meal, the most luxurious tidbit could be sucked and nibbled.[59] A pungent spice berry might be rolled round the mouth for hours, a scrap of crystallized ginger, or a morsel of almond butter, made from ground almonds pounded and bound together with sugar and rosewater, could sweeten tempers soured by the long breakfast-less, supperless hours. The only disadvantage of these delicious consolations was their expense. The idea of frittering away a small fortune on a dish or two of candied violets did not appeal to every solid citizen. Francesco, a very prosperous merchant in four-teenth-century Prato, was scolded by one friend for his superhu-man self-control: "To save 12 *soldi*, you will pass this Lent without comfits. You are one of those who would keep money in their purse, and hunger in their belly."[60]

To soften Lent's rigors, and brighten its menus, there was a constant, hopeful search for interesting and permissible ingredi-ents. Already by the fourth century, St. Jerome was fighting a rearguard action against his weaker, but determined, brethren: "What advantage do you hope to receive by refraining from the use of oil, whilst at the same time you seek out rare and exquisite fruits—Carian dried figs, pepper, dates of the palm tree, bread made of fine flour, pistachio-nuts? The garden is ransacked to furnish palatable dainties which turn us aside from the narrow way to heaven. Plain ordinary bread ought to content him who fasts."[61]

For northern Europe in particular, this search proved an ex-pensive business. Lent comes round each year at a peculiarly bleak and barren time for the gardens there. As no native fruits and nuts are in season then, the best solution was to import dried fruits and nuts from the East and the Mediterranean basin. Figs, dates, raisins, currants, and almonds found an easy, eager market throughout the winter and especially in Lent. Figs, indeed, were so associated with the season that Cotgrave in his dictionary lists under the word *"Caresme"* (Lent) the phrase *"Figue de caresme,"* with the translation: "A drie figge . . . Lenten figge." The cost of transportation, however, was a distinct drawback, and a merchant had to time his shipments with care. Prices that were paid with pleasure in Lent were thought outrageous once Easter had arrived. Nicholas Palmer, a Bristol merchant in the fifteenth century, sailed to southern Spain and took on board a load of dried fruit, but because of bad weather his ship missed the Lent market by a week or two and limped home to England after Easter. It was impossible then to sell the fruit at a profit and the whole venture was a financial disaster.[62]

The luckiest people lived beside the sea. They had no need to chew their way through six weeks of red herrings, varied with an occasional eel, pike, or other river fish. Instead they could hope for good weather to bring a glorious variety of fresh saltwater fish to their tables. A fifteenth-century schoolboy sighed over the unfairness of the arrangement: "Wolde to god I wer on of the dwellers by the see syde, for ther see fysh be plentuse and I love them better than I do this fresh water fysh, but now I must ete freshe water fyshe whether I wyll or noo."[63]

Agreeable and luxurious ingredients might divert attention from the absence of meat, but what Lent, indeed any fast day, cried out for was a master cook, whose skills and inspired imagination could transform by magic irksome penance into rare delight. The Eastern Church took the heroic position that a lack of talent in the kitchen sharpened the mortification of a fast and so increased its spiritual value. The only consolation allowed to Byzantine monks after a melancholy meal was the sight of the cooks kneeling to beg forgiveness for their incompetence.[64] Most Western churchmen set their sights considerably lower, and put their faith in velvet diplomacy. In 1082, the first Norman appointed to be prior of Winchester arrived to find the whole monastery disobeying rules by eating meat. He coaxed the brethren back into the fold with exquisitely prepared fish recipes.[65]

Where the Church was prepared to lead, the laity were sure to follow. In the fourteenth-century romance *Sir Gawain and the Green Knight*, the hero arrives at a castle on Christmas Eve, the last day of the Advent fast. Officially, therefore, the dinner must be meatless: nevertheless, the cooks have contrived a dazzling prelude to the Christmas festivities, working their inspired variations on the theme of fish: fish baked, fish grilled, fish simmered, fish attended by a hundred subtle sauces. The host's apologies for "this penaunce" are mere polite pretense, the modesty becoming a winner. Fast has been triumphantly metamorphosed into feast.[66]

An occasional official effort was made to give another turn to the screw, and make even Lent's permitted ingredients less appetizing than usual. In 1417, for example, it was ordained in London that no fine breads could be baked that Lent; only coarse loaves were to be put on sale.[67] Such busybody zeal ran counter to the prevailing belief that obedience to the letter of Lent's law was hard enough for ordinary mortals, who needed the encouragement of a little self-indulgence and pampering along the way. Cooks who could make the six weeks palatable were the Church's secret weapon: "I am as willing to fast with him [Jack a Lent] as to feast with Shrove-tide; for he hath an army of various dishes, an host of divers fishes, with salads, sauces, sweetmeats, wines, ale, beer, fruit, roots, raisins, almonds, spices, with which I have often . . . made . . . good . . . shift to fast. . . ."[68]

Medieval recipe books make it clear that the cook's main concern in Lent was to find satisfactory substitutions for forbidden ingredients in familiar dishes. Because no butter, eggs, or meat products could be used, major changes had to be made in cooking techniques. Pastry could not be bound together with egg yolks; food must be fried in oil, not animal fat; alternatives to meat stock had to be found for a stew or a sauce. The cook who could afford to do so relied heavily on the almond. The nut added nourishment and bulk to a meatless diet; blanched, ground, and steeped in water it yielded a liquid, "milk of almonds," more interesting than plain water, with a distinctive flavor of its own. *Latte di mandorla* is still a favorite drink in southern Italy. This "milk" was used as a basis for stews and soups, and as a binding ingredient for pastry. A fifteenth-century recipe book offers two recipes side by side for little pastry turnovers, charmingly called "hats" because they are to be shaped "in the maner of an hatte." A hat made on a meat day had its pastry kneaded together with egg yolks; on a fish day, milk of almonds takes their place.[69]

Economically, almonds could be steeped two or three times and so yield several batches of milk. A liquid thickened with ground almonds became something more substantial, a moist purée, and was known as "cream of almonds." Whereas egg yolks or beef marrow might be used on a meat day to thicken a sauce, on a fish day this cream could take their place. Thus, at the end of a recipe for "Custard lumbarde" comes the sentence: "And if hit be in lenton, take creme of Almondes, And leve [leave out] the egges And the Mary [marrow]."[70]

The cook on a tighter budget had to look for less expensive alternatives. A yeast dough might be used instead of pastry for a crust, and bread crumbs take the place of ground almonds. Thus, for "Lent fritters" a dough of flour, salt, saffron, and yeast is suggested, and a soup for Lent is made from a mixture of water and wine simmered together with honey, heavily spiced, and thickened with crumbs.[71]

Fish was the obvious substitute for meat, and so in the two recipes for "hats" just discussed, the turnovers are simply filled with fish instead of meat in Lent.[72] Fruit fillings also took the place of meat on a fast day: "Lent fritters" are explicitly modeled on "fritters of fflesh," but contain apples.[73]

Despite this ingenuity and loving care, cravings for banished pleasures would sidle into mind from time to time. When these moments came, the good cook rose to the crisis and comforted his wistful flock with some inspired simulation of the longed-for delicacy. Judging from the cookery-books, the specialty most in demand was the Mock Egg. The simplest of many recipes will serve as an example of the trouble lavished on the project. Blanched, ground almonds were simmered in boiling water, then the liquid was drained away and the soft purée sweetened with sugar and divided into two parts. One was left white, the other colored yellow with saffron, ginger, and cinnamon. After this, the contents of a real egg were blown out, and the shell washed in warm water. It was then stuffed with the white and yellow almond mixture, roasted in the ashes, and served up in triumph as a hardboiled egg.[74]

Given his head, a master cook came to regard the rules of a fast as obstacles round which to race in a grand slalom display of dazzling virtuosity. In a wealthy and self-indulgent monastic community, whose vow of year-round abstinence from meat allowed ample time for reflection on the problem of eating well while breaking not a single rule, the art of turning fast into feast could reach its apogee. Giraldus Cambrensis was impressed, despite his disapproval, by the meatless dinner to which he was invited by the monks of Canterbury, in Kent, in 1179: "You might see so many kinds of fish, roast and boiled, stuffed and fried, so many dishes contrived with eggs and pepper by dexterous cooks, so many flavourings and condiments, compounded with like dexterity to tickle gluttony and awaken appetite ... wine, metheglin, claret, must, mead, mulberry juice . . . beverages so choice that beer, such as is made at its best in England and above all in Kent, found no place among them."[75]

Monks on a perpetually austere regime developed the special skill of splitting hairs, of nosing out each loophole in a list of prohibitions. The thirteenth-century French preacher Jacques de Vitry illustrated this tendency with a story of some monks who were not allowed to eat any meat except game that had been hunted. The rule was deftly turned to their advantage when one bright spirit smuggled in some hounds, to chase round the cloister pigs raised on the monastery farm, and so, at a stroke, transform them into game.[76] Food for thought might be found even in the sixth-century *Rule of St. Benedict,* the code which gave Western monasticism its shape and tone. St. Benedict, with a beginner's innocence, stipulated that monks must not eat the meat of "quadrupeds." Eagle eyes were quick to spot the word, sharp wits to point out that not even the most rigorous interpretation could stretch the term to cover birds.[77]

The rule about meat-eating was expertly whittled away over the centuries in all but the most austere monasteries. Because the rule was relaxed in any case for a sick monk, it had become the custom by the thirteenth century for a rota of all monks to dine each day in the infirmary, where meat was served to strengthen invalids. Meals for the community as a whole were taken in the refectory, and there evolved a theory that only in this room did the rule apply. Inevitably, every effort was made to avoid eating there. At Rochester in the same century, the cellarer sat at his own table in a room beneath the refectory, while at many monasteries a special room, called, appropriately, the misericord, was set aside for extracurricular dining, and a number of monks enjoyed a holiday there every day. Caution and quotas were flung to the winds at Blyth in 1287. In that year Archbishop Romeyn visited the monastery and, tactlessly arriving at dinnertime, found the refectory deserted and the entire community eating in the misericord. Such blatant flouting of the rules could bring only trouble to a monastery. More prudent communities regulated their own excesses with discretion. At Malmesbury Abbey a plan was drawn up in 1293 to insure that about a quarter of the members ate in the refectory every day, and so each monk had to endure its rigors on seven or eight days in every month.[78] No wonder Dante contrasted the lean and hungry look of the first apostles with the comfortably rounded girth of their thirteenth-century heirs:

Pastors today require to be propped up
On either side, one man their horse to lead
(so great their weight!) . . . [79]

The Church not only learned to view its own austerities with indulgence, but came to realize the financial rewards to be found in releasing the laity from theirs. The rules about meat were never relaxed in Lent or Advent, but it was quite possible in the later Middle Ages to pay cash for permission to eat butter and other dairy foods. One of the splendid fifteenth-century towers of Rouen Cathedral is known as the Butter Tower because its costs were covered by money paid for butter dispensations in Lent. Pleased as posterity must be by this enlightened use of the contributions, the Church was to regret bitterly its bland and businesslike sale of such indulgences. In one of his three treatises of 1520 which helped to spark the Reformation, Luther encouraged the princes and magistrates of Germany to reform the Church which had refused to reform itself, and seized on the butter question as an example of the abuses that shocked and angered educated Europe: "The fasts should be matters of liberty, and all sorts of food made free, as the Gospel makes them. For at Rome they themselves laugh at the fasts, making us foreigners eat the oil with which they would not grease their shoes, and afterwards selling us liberty to eat butter and all sorts of other things."[80]

The rule forbidding meat on a fast day was the one most strictly enforced and conscientiously obeyed, but some desperate ingenuity was applied to the definition of meat and fish. Reluctantly it had to be conceded that the beaver was a mammal, even though he spent so much of his life in the water, but his tail, being covered with scales, looked distinctly fishy. It was permissible, therefore, to brighten a fish menu with a dish of beaver tail. In the fifteenth-century, John Russell lists it for consideration in his chapter "Of the Kervying of Fische."[81]

Birds, even water birds, were classed as animals on fast days, but it was possible to enjoy one with a quiet conscience by claiming it was that very special bird, the barnacle goose. The rumors about this seem to have originated in the Celtic lands of Ireland and Brittany, and the earliest written account discovered so far is by Giraldus Cambrensis, describing Ireland in 1187. He asserted that these birds started life in shells that clung to driftwood in the sea. After forcing open its shell, each tiny, embryonic bird hung on by its beak to the floating timber until its feathers had grown and its wings were strong. Then it dropped off into the water and flew away. In later versions, the shells hung from trees growing at the water's edge.[82] The story may have been developed as a theory to explain why the migrating geese which appeared each year over the waters of Europe were never seen to breed there. Certainly those who said they could be eaten rested their argument on the assertion that they were no ordinary birds because they were not born in the ordinary way. By no means everybody could bring himself to swallow the story. In the mid-thirteenth century, the Emperor Frederick II took the trouble to examine some barnacles, and tartly noted: "these bore no resemblance to any avian body. We therefore doubt the truth of this legend in the absence of corroborating evidence. In our opinion this superstition arose from the fact that barnacle geese breed in such remote latitudes that men, in ignorance of their real nesting places, invented this story."[83]

Few people, however, were of Frederick's inquiring turn of mind in these matters, and the story had a long and flourishing life. In 1597, Gerard devoted chapter 188 of his *Herball* to the Barnacle Tree, and not only told his readers that the current price for a "tree goose" in Lancashire was threepence, but described the log of wood smothered in shells which he himself pulled out of the sea "between Dover and Rumney." He took some of the shells home with him to London, and settled down to examine them: "After I had opened . . . I found living things that were very naked, in shape like a Bird; in others, the Birds covered with soft downe, the shell halfe open, and the Bird ready to fall out . . . I dare not absolutely avouch every circumstance of the first part of this history, concerning the tree . . . howbeit, that which I have seene with mine eies, and handled with mine hands, I dare confidently avouch, and boldly put downe for verity."[84]

Whatever Shakespeare may have thought, Bohemia has no coast-line, and perhaps because of this its citizens seem to have been unfamiliar with the barnacle goose. One of them, Leo of Rozmital, came on a mission to England in 1465/67, and his secretary set down a bemused account of the fast-day dinner to which they were invited in Salisbury by the Duke of Clarence:

> Among other dishes they gave us to eat what should have been a fish, but it was roasted and looked like a duck. It has its wings, feathers, neck and feet. It lays eggs and tastes like a wild duck. We had to eat it as fish, but in my mouth it turned to meat, although they say it is indeed a fish because it grows at first out

of a worm in the sea, and when it is grown, it assumes the form of a duck and lays eggs, but its eggs do not hatch out or produce anything. It seeks its nourishment in the sea and not on land. Therefore it is said to be a fish.[85]

Clearly, the Duke was brother under the skin to the fox in one of Henryson's fables. As a penance for his life of crime, the fox is ordered to eat no meat in Lent. Meekly accepting the sentence, he trots round the corner, catches a kid and carries it off to the river's edge. Brisk baptism follows, as he dips the body in the water with the genial cry: "Ga doun Schir Kid, cum up Schir Salmond agane! [Go down Sir Kid, come up Sir Salmon]."[86] After this bow to the proprieties, the sinner settles down to dinner with a smile.

Beguiled by the spectacle of man's heroic ingenuity in the circumvention of disagreeable rules, the modern reader may smile at the lapses and forget the high standards which made such falls from grace inevitable. A story told by the early hermits of the fourth and fifth centuries turns the tables and makes fun of those whose standards are high because they have never attempted to put them into practice. A party of monks from Egypt traveled into the desert to study the daily life of some hermits there. They came prepared to admire, but were shocked to find the holy old men wolfing down their food at dinnertime. Unknown to the visitors, the hermits had been on a strict fast for a week, and were understandably ravenous. One of them decided to teach the critical Egyptians a lesson, and persuaded them to stay and share the fast for two days. The result was interesting:

On Saturday the Egyptians sat down to eat with the old men. And they reached voraciously for their food. And one of the old men checked their hands, and said: "Eat like monks, in a disciplined way." One of the Egyptians threw off his restraining hand, and said: "Leave go. I am dying, I have not eaten cooked food all the week." And the old man said to him: "If you are so weak at a meal after a fast of only two days, why were you scandalized at monks who always kept their abstinence for a week at a time?"[87]

The term *fast* was an elastic one, and could be stretched to cover not only abstinence but many kinds of consumption, from the stern rigors of a bread and water diet to the elegant austerity of a splendid banquet, prepared with love and skill and vast expense.

Such diverse dinners were linked only by their official purpose, penance. Each fast day had been instituted as an occasion for the recollection of sin, and for remorse; each privation prompted man to spring-clean his soul.

*Feast* was another word which covered many occasions with a common keynote. A feast might be one of the great days of the Church's year, Christmas, Easter, Whitsun, or mark one of the highlights of the agricultural round, harvest or sheepshearing. It might be on a saint's day, or held to celebrate some entirely secular affair. It might be a very grand and public event or just a happy gathering of friends. Whatever its form and occasion, the feast's purpose was always celebration, the joyful commemoration of some event or person. A fast, however gilded, was marked by the absence of some cherished ingredient; a feast brought with it extra delicacies.

It was, however, the spirit much more than the substance which made one meal a feast and another merely dinner. Even a fast day could become a feast without the addition of a single forbidden ingredient to the menu. Thus, the fourth Sunday in Lent, known as Mid-Lent Sunday because it marks the halfway point of the season, was deliberately treated as a feast by the Church, in order to cheer up flagging spirits and spur them on to Easter.[88] The note of happiness was struck in the mass for the day by its gospel reading, which told the story of the Miracle of the Loaves and Fishes, and by the stirring words of its introit: "Be glad, Jerusalem . . . rejoice and be glad, you that were in sadness" (Isaiah 66:10, 11). The mood of the day was relaxed, and its meals were brightened by some little extra luxury. In the same way, Palm Sunday had an air of cheerful excitement about it, fostered by the Church as a release of tension and a preparation for the somber week still to be endured. It celebrated the triumphant entry of Jesus into Jerusalem, and its service looked forward to his victory on the cross. Once again there was a festive atmosphere to the day, and cooks put their best foot forward. Bishop Swinfield's staff, in 1289/90, unlocked their spice cupboards for the occasion and transformed the obligatory fish dinner with almonds, sugar, ginger, and mustard.[89] In the accounts of the Church of St. Mary Hill in 1510 appears this entry: "For palme flowrys and cake on Palme Sonday, 10d."[90]

Feasting was a favorite form of entertainment, and the medieval year was dotted with opportunities for agreeable self-indulgence. Societies held their annual dinners, sportsmen celebrated victory with a feast. On 17 August 1478, the married men among the English merchants living in Calais challenged the bachelors to a shooting match of twelve a side at a range of two hundred and sixty yards. Before the contest began, it was solemnly agreed in writing that the losers were to pay for a feast worthy of the day, costing not less than twelve pence a head.[91]

The satisfactory completion of a job obviously begged for a feast to mark the occasion. In the summer of 1497, the four newly appointed wardens of the Goldsmiths' Company in London gave a dinner to honor their predecessors on the day these officials formally retired and handed over their account books.[92] A more ingenious excuse for celebration was concocted in the Hôtel Dieu, in Paris. In this hospital, the counterpane of each bed was made of fur, and in the interests of hygiene thirty furriers were called in every July to clean them, remove any louse or flea, and mend the holes. The heroic task of beating, pounding, and inch-by-inch inspection took a whole month to complete and everyone joined in, including the patients. When at last the clouds of dust had vanished and peace came stealing back, professionals and volunteers sat down together to a grand feast provided by the management.[93]

The medieval calendar was so crammed with saints' days that it was quite impossible for each one to be honored everywhere. Only a few of the most important saints, like John the Baptist, could expect widespread celebrations. It is to be hoped that in heaven life's mysteries are made plain to the elect. Otherwise John, a prophet noted for his austerity, must have remained baffled for centuries by the feasting and drinking which took place every year on the day of his Nativity, 24 June, as an affectionate but singularly inappropriate tribute to his memory. Lesser saints were remembered by communities to which they were linked with special intimacy. When they were commemorated, the day's festivities were sweetened with a particularly good dinner and some traditional delicacy. The mayors of Bristol attended an annual ceremony held in the Weavers' Hall on the eve of St. Katherine's Day, when there were "drynkyngs with Spysid Cake brede."[94]

Of all the saints in the calendar, St. Nicholas was one of the most universally popular and venerated. His reputation for saving shipwrecked sailors and children, and his generosity to fathers with marriageable daughters but no money for their dowries, made him a very sympathetic figure, much loved and honored everywhere. Froissart mentions that Gaston de Foix's celebrations on the saint's day were as magnificent as those he ordained for Easter.[95] Among his many responsibilities, Nicholas was the patron saint of students, and his day marked one of the high points of the university year in both France and England, with a lavish dinner as the special attraction. In 1214, the town of Oxford even agreed to forget its feud with the university for the day and provide a free dinner for one hundred poor students.[96]

St. Nicholas was so universally popular that, according to one Russian folk story, a mutiny broke out in heaven among his envious peers, who heard rumors of the parties given for him on earth and felt distinctly sulky. St. John Cassian led the grumblers, and at last plucked up courage to complain to God about this blatant favoritism. The result was something less than satisfactory. God summoned St. Nicholas to speak for himself, but he was nowhere to be found. Two angels were dispatched to earth to find him, and when they brought him back he appeared with a half-drowned man in his arms: "God asked St. Nicholas what he was doing. St. Nicholas said that he was on the sea and had been working to save the sailors from a shipwreck. Then God turned sternly to St. Cassian and said, 'What have *you* done for the people, so as to win their honor and their gifts? To punish your impudence I order that your day be 29th February and so you will only have a feast once in four years.' "[97]

The monastic calendar was filled with small festivities to brighten the monotony of the official diet. By the beginning of the twelfth century it had become the custom for a man to leave a sum of money to a monastery, with the request that the monks should say a mass for his soul each year on the anniversary of his death, and celebrate his memory at dinner that day with some extra dish paid for out of the funds provided. The donation was known as a pittance, and the name soon came to be given to the dish as well. Today, the word suggests something meager, or disappointingly small, but in its heyday it stood for something delicate and fine, a luxurious tidbit. At Evesham, for example, a dish of salmon and an allowance of the best wine was added to the menu on the anniversary of a former prior, William de Walcote.[98]

A well-known monastery received many pittances, and an official was appointed to handle the funds and make sure that the right dishes appeared on the right day. Much of the charm of the pittance lay in the fact that it always remained an extra, not a staple of the diet. A community in need of money sometimes voted to give up its pleasures and use the pittance revenues for some necessity. Around 1200, the church tower at Evesham was built in this way.[99]

Not every monastery could rise to such heroic heights. On 23 June 1198 a fire broke out in the shrine of St. Edmund at the abbey of Bury St. Edmund. Abbot Samson blamed the disaster on his monks' preoccupation with food and drink, and suggested that the pittance money ought to be used for the repair of the box in which the saint's remains were kept. It was an awkward moment, but quick wits saved the day and the delightful dinners: "We all agreed that our pittancery should be assigned for this purpose; but this design was abandoned, since the Sacrist said that St. Edmund could easily restore his own feretory without any such assistance."[100]

While the saints to be honored, the benefactors to be remembered, varied from district to district and country to country, there were certain great festivals which marked the high points of the farm and church year all over Europe. The completion of each major task on the land was celebrated with a feast for all the workers. The year was punctuated with festivities which followed each other in a slow and steady progress through the months. Sheep-shearing, grain harvest, grape harvest, and seed-time had their appointed seasons and time-honored dishes.

For the Church, the seasons of greatest rejoicing were of course Easter and Christmas. Both were times of great joy, so much so, indeed, that they came to epitomize joy itself. In the early thirteenth-century poem *Tristan* by Gottfried von Strassburg, when Rivalin thinks about the radiant charm of Blancheflor he remembers "the joyous Easter Day that lurked smiling in her eyes."[101] The doctrinal significance and spiritual happiness of both occasions were expressed not only in elaborately beautiful services but in sumptuous feasting. The long periods of fasting that preceded them added a special gusto to the occasions. Trevisa goes to the heart of the matter with a simple definition: "Ester daie is a tyme . . . of ioiful refeccion and fedinge."[102]

The accounts of Bishop Swinfield's household expenses in 1289/90 show the dramatic swing from the somber austerity of Good Friday to the unbuttoned ease of Easter Sunday. Only bread, wine, and fish appear in the steward's notes for Good Friday, and of these some of the fish went untouched; on Easter Sunday, a party of eighty munched its way through the following: 1 ½ carcases of salt beef, 1 bacon, 1 ¾ carcases of fresh beef, 2 boars, 5 pigs, 4 ½ calves, 22 kids, 3 fat deer, 12 capons, 88 pigeons, 1400 eggs, bread, cheese, unlimited beer, and 66 gallons of wine.[103]

The sharp contrast between the two days is used by the Town Mouse in Henryson's fable to impress her country cousin with the splendor of a city larder when she grandly claims: "My Gude Friday is better nor your Pace [My Good Friday is better than your Easter]."[104]

There is no clue in the Swinfield accounts to the way the fourteen hundred eggs were served, but there are scattered hints in medieval records that the Easter egg was not unknown. It was the custom to bring the hardboiled egg of Lent to be blessed at church on Easter Sunday, and at Wycombe, in 1221, the vicar was given the right to a tenth of the eggs and cheese presented.[105] During the reign of Edward I of England, orders were given for four hundred eggs to be boiled and distributed to the royal household on Easter Sunday. Most of the eggs were colored with vegetable dyes but some, for special favorites, were covered with gold leaf.[106] This is the reference which most strongly suggests some custom comparable to the modern one. The idea of decorating the egg was a very old one: two goose eggs painted with stripes and dots were found in the grave of a Roman-Germanic child (ca. A.D. 320) at Worms in Germany.[107] The crusader Joinville discovered that Arabs too took pleasure in painted eggs. When he and his fellow prisoners were released in 1250, their Saracen captors prepared a cheerful send-off for them: "The food they gave us consisted of cheese fritters baked in the sun to keep them free from maggots, and hard-boiled eggs cooked three or four days before, the shells of which, in our honor, had been painted in various colors."[108]

Christmas was the very epitome of exuberant self-indulgence. Its various names were synonyms of the good life. Henryson's two mice, reveling in the larder, toast their luck with the shout: "Haill, Yule! Haill!" (*Yule* used here with the meaning "time of merrymaking").[109]

As with Easter, there was a sense of well-being, of wonderful release after fast. Christmas Day and the week that followed were given over to enjoyment; as one fifteenth-century sermon writer simply summed up the matter: " . . . in Cristenmasse wyke . . . then is no tyme to faste."[110] In Ben Jonson's *Masque of Christmas* (1616), one character says to Christmas: "Here's one o' Friday Street would come in," and Christmas replies: "By no means, nor out of neither of the Fish Streets admit not a man; they are not Christmas creatures; fish and fasting days, foh!"[111]

The good food and drink associated so agreeably with ecclesiastical feast days were intended to be merely incidental pleasures. A feast day ordained by the Church was a holy day, dedicated to reverent celebrations. Holy day became holiday when, to encourage attendance at services, the ordinary workday was shortened, but the holiness of the day grew somewhat obscured as human nature found a thousand regrettable uses for its leisure. As a fifteenth-century sermon points out acidly, Christmas week was designed to be a time of solemn joy and humble gratitude, but had become something quite different: "Now this is turned ynto pryde by dyverse gyses of clothyng . . . into envy, for on ys arayde bettyr then another; in gloteny by surfet of dyverse metys and drynkes; into lechery that seweth [follows] alway gloteny; into slouthe of Goddys servyce liyng yn the morow-tyde long yn bedde for owtrage wakyng over nyght [outrageously late nights]."[112]

In theory, a man who worked on a feast day was classed with the lowest riff-raff of society: "Comoun strumpettys [prostitutes], hasardourys [gamblers] and such othere, and halyday-werkerys."[113] In practice, rules were bent to suit convenience, because both employers and workmen found the number of feast days in the year as much a problem as a pleasure. Employers were irritated by interrupted work weeks and made brisk, arbitrary decisions on what in their view constituted a feast day worthy of the name. A feudal lord ruled his own peasants with a firm hand, and the number of their holidays depended on his whim. In the thirteenth century, Walter of Henley wrote a treatise on farm management and helpfully showed his readers how to pare holidays for peasants to the bone: "You know that there are in the year 52 weeks. Now take away 8 weeks for holy days and other hindrances, then are there 44 working weeks left."[114] Eight weeks seems a generous sum, until it is realized that it makes allowance only for fifty-two Sundays and four other days in the year.

Skilled craftsmen were better placed than peasants to protect their rights, yet while they could fight for their feast days they had very mixed feelings about them. Such breaks in the year's routine were pleasant in principle, but in fact brought with them an alarming loss in income, as no work meant no wages. Slowly, certain compromises were made, to satisfy both workers and employers. In a contract drawn up for masons and carpenters in Calais, in 1474, feast days were graded according to their importance; the time at which work finished depended on the dignity of the day. Thus, a minor feast, like New Year's Day, was not recognized as a holiday and work ended at the usual time, that is, five in the afternoon. On a more important feast, like St. Thomas of Canterbury's, work stopped at three in the afternoon, while on the greatest of all, like Christmas Day itself, tools were downed at eleven in the morning. Although this particular group of men was expected to work for a few hours even on Christmas Day, it was the general custom to take a holiday lasting several days in the Christmas and Easter weeks. At York in 1327, all work stopped from 24 December until the twenty-eighth, and at Westminster in 1331, the vacation lasted from 23 December to the thirtieth.

Workmen were paid for the number of hours they worked on a feast day, and sometimes employers would add their own spice of pleasure to the day by paying either for a round of drinks or for a whole, festive dinner. In 1421, the London bridgewardens paid 3s. 4d. "to all the masons and carpenters for their Shrovetide Feast, as is customary." Another compromise arrangement was made with men working on royal buildings in England in the mid-thirteenth century, whereby they were given full wages for one out of every two feast days on which nothing was done.[115]

Whatever the economic worries a feast day brought in its train, there is no doubt of the importance of the feast itself in medieval society. In theory, a feast was the epitome of love and fellowship, and while reality often failed to mirror this ideal, a ceremonial dinner was a visible demonstration of the ties of power, dependence, and mutual obligation which bound the host and guests. It was politic for the host to appear generous, because the lavishness of his table gave the clue to his resources; it was wise to be both hospitable to dependents and discriminating in the choice of guests of honor, because the number and caliber of diners in the hall revealed his importance and his power. As Thomas Nashe remarks:

> It is the honor of Nobility
> To keepe high dayes and solemne festivals:
> Then, to set their magnificence to view,
> To frolick open with their favorites,
> And use their neighbours with all curtesie.[116]

Feasts, quite simply, oiled the wheels of society. The host showered favors on his guests in the hope of favors in return. The last line of Tusser's verse on the virtues of hospitality puts the matter in a nutshell:

Of all the other dooings housekeeping is cheefe,
For daily it helpeth the poore with releefe;
the neighbour, the stranger, and all that have neede,
Which causeth thy dooings the better to speede.[117]

Even in the custom of leaving money in a will for a funeral feast may be detected a man's desire to keep his name alive and honored, and give evidence of his resources: "I pray yow that ye wald Brewe X buschellys of malt forto gef pore men of my paryche; and also that ye wolde bake VI buschellys of whete of smale Halpene [halfpenny] Loves, and gefe evere man and woman a Love and a galon of ale, als fer als it will go."[118]

Just as the host needed his guests, so they needed his invitation. They wished to show themselves to be a part of his family, and safely under the umbrella of his protection. To be dropped from a guest list could be very alarming, a fact of life that Abbot Samson of Bury St. Edmunds made use of in the late twelfth century to bring his townsmen to heel. Once, finding the burgesses of Bury fighting with his servants on 26 December, he was so angry he announced that he would not follow his usual custom of inviting the former to dine at his table on the first five days of Christmas. This awful threat so crushed the offenders that they begged his forgiveness and gained their reward: "All having been brought back to the blessing of peace, the burgesses feasted with their lord during the days that followed with much rejoicing."[119]

The interplay between host and guests, the favors given and the favors received, is suggested by the names of two of Christmas' attendants in Jonson's *Masque of Christmas:* New Year's Gift and Offering. New Year's gifts might be either presents exchanged between friends and equals or gifts from masters to servants, from the powerful to the dependent. An offering was a present offered in tribute to a superior, bluntly defined in a fifteenth-century dictionary: "*Offerynge,* a presaunt to a lorde at Crystemasse, or other tymys."[120] At a time of fast, the prosperous were expected to be specially generous to the less fortunate with no thought of any but spiritual gain, but at a feast there was mutual exchange, symbolizing interwoven needs.

Gratifying as it was to be present at a memorable feast, the sweetest satisfaction was the host's for devising such a pleasure. In the Church of St. Margaret in King's Lynn is the brass of Robert

Braunche, twice mayor of the town in the mid-fourteenth century. One feast he gave was so impressive that he had a picture representing it engraved beneath his feet along the bottom of the brass. It is not known whether the great occasion was a feast for St. Margaret, a dinner Braunche gave when he was mayor, or one to honor Edward III when he visited King's Lynn in 1344. The only certainty is that Braunche remembered the occasion with such pride that he wanted it to form part of his memorial.[121]

# 4

# Cook and Kitchen

As one peers down the tunnel of time, trying to catch glimpses of the medieval cook at work, there is at first disappointingly little to be seen. Neither he nor his equipment were considered worthy of a center-stage position, and so they must be hunted down patiently in the nooks and crannies of art and literature. Kitchen scenes are hard to find, but many a cauldron bubbles in exotic settings: devils tend their pots over the fires of hell in a Last Judgment, cooks stir their dinner on the back of a whale at the bottom of a page (fig. 2). A stewpot perched on the head of a rakish monster in a manuscript border, a stumpy little man carved on a bench end, clutching a ladle as long as himself, these are the scraps which make up the patchwork quilt of first impressions.

Such random clues suggest that cooks were exceedingly cross and their kitchens in perpetual uproar. Dogs were everywhere, looking for dinner. According to a proverb recorded in the sixteenth century, "The cook is not so sone gone as the doges hed is in the porigpot." Medieval dogs never deigned to wait for a back to be turned. A misericord in St. George's Chapel, Windsor, shows four enormous hounds piling into a cauldron, indifferent to the cook just poised to hurl his ladle. On another, at St. Mary Virgin Church in Fairford, Gloucestershire, a very fat dog is headfirst in the pot, while on a bench end at Sherborne Abbey, a woman has given up the unequal struggle and meekly holds out the bowl for her dog to lick.[1]

When dogs are not the problem, a fox is running off with a hen, the distracted housewife is in hot pursuit, and the family pig left behind to a leisurely exploration of the pots and pans.[2] In a fifteenth-century edition of Aesop's fables, two plump rats investigate the resources of a larder.[3]

Animals may have been incidental irritations in the kitchen, but the cook's principal distractions were his fellow humans. The scene which appears most frequently in art shows the cook repelling boarders, beating off the tasters and nibblers who hover hopefully round his precious stewpot. A polished flirt knew exactly how to make defenses crumble. In a border of the fourteenth-century *Smithfield Decretals,* he has one arm round the cook, while deftly fishing a joint out of her cauldron with the other (fig. 3).

Only lovers can get away with such shameless depredations; husbands are clouted as soon as they creep within range. On a misericord in Bristol Cathedral, the husband has actually managed to get as far as lifting the lid of the stewpan, but his wife has

2. Makeshift Kitchen.
*Queen Mary's Psalter,* English, first quarter of the fourteenth century (London, British Museum, MS. Royal 2B. VII, fol. 111). Courtesy of the British Library Board.

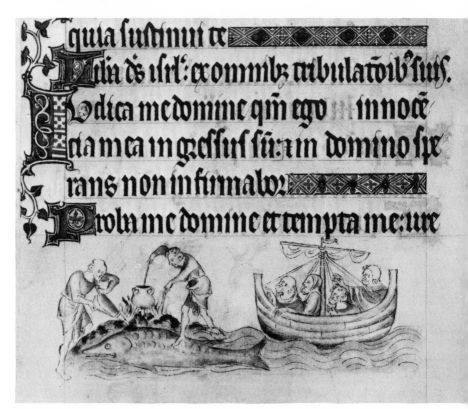

him firmly by the beard, while a pot, shown by the artist in mid-flight past the poor man's ear, testifies to female bad temper and worse aim.[4] When the vice of Discord was illustrated by the carvers of Notre Dame they merely showed a man and a woman squabbling. At Amiens Cathedral, whose thirteenth-century carvers drew inspiration for their own cycle of Vices and Virtues from Notre Dame, an overturned cooking pot has been added to the scene.[5] The kitchen was a classic battleground for the sexes, although which was regarded as the aggressor depended naturally on the point of view. A sequence of border scenes in the *Smithfield Decretals* shows a husband toiling to please, fetching water, washing dishes, grinding corn, baking bread, but beaten up after every task by an implacable wife.[6] In the fifteenth-century poem *A Young Husband's Complaint,* the henpecked victim is barked out of

3. Kitchen Flirtation.
*Smithfield Decretals,* illuminated in England, second quarter of the fourteenth century (London, British Museum, MS. Royal 10E. IV, fol. 109v). Courtesy of the British Library Board.

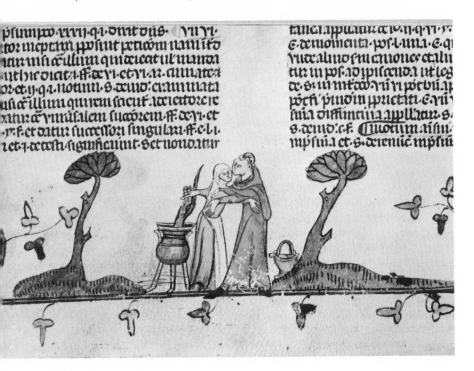

the kitchen in every verse, and hit on the head whenever he asks for dinner.[7] On the other hand, a twelfth-century celebration of virginity looks at life through a wife's jaundiced eye: "When she comes in she hears her child screaming, sees the cat at the flitch and the dog at the hide. Her cake is burning on the hearth stone, and her calf is drinking all the milk. The pot is boiling over into the fire, and her husband is grumbling."[8]

This particular treatise for women is a ringing call to celibacy, which grimly contrasts the horrors of home with the sweet serenity of monastic life. If other evidence is to be believed, however, bad temper could shatter the calm of a convent kitchen as easily as it soured the domestic scene. Indeed, when Langland wanted an appropriate setting for his personification of Wrath in *Piers Plowman,* he chose just such a kitchen, and made Wrath the convent cook. Predictably, the room seethes with malicious gossip, and the nuns are at each other's throats.[9] Tempers were not sweetened by the cook's traditional weakness for the bottle. In popular belief, cooks were expected to be drunk: the medieval phrase "a temperance of cooks" is heavy with sarcasm, and Chaucer's cook runs true to type by being so full of liquor that he falls off his horse.[10]

When not actually quarreling, cooks seem to have had an alarming sense of humor and plenty of time in which to indulge it. Among the stories written down in the twelfth century about the Saxon outlaw Hereward and his guerrilla warfare against the Norman conquerors, one tells how he slipped into the King's camp disguised as a potter. His first stop was at the kitchen, to show his wares. There the cooks, inevitably, were drinking on the job while they prepared the King's meal. As spirits rose, one of them had the brilliant idea of shaving off the potter's beard with his chopping knife. Hereward had to fight his way through a suddenly menacing circle of kitchen staff, armed to the teeth with razor-sharp equipment. Being no mere peddler but a hero in disguise, he not only escaped but left behind him several concussed cooks and, doubtless, one King crossly roaring for his ruined dinner.[11]

A misguided sense of humor brought these cooks nothing worse than sore heads and a dim sense of discomfiture; hasty temper proved fatal in another case. Matthew Paris records under the year 1238 the visit to Oxford of the papal legate Cardinal Otto. When a deputation of scholars came to his lodgings to pay their respects one of them combined business with pleasure and went round to the kitchen door to beg for food. There he was met by the master cook himself, who happened to be the legate's brother, prudently chosen for the job by Otto to make sure that "no poison might be given to him, which he, the legate, greatly feared."[12] Not only did the cook refuse to give any scraps to the student; for good measure he poured over him some of the greasy, boiling water from one of his cauldrons. It was, to be sure, an error of judgment. A second scholar saw what happened, drew his bow and shot him dead.

Not every cook had to take his place in the front line of battle, but each was expected to wage running warfare in his own kitchen against the hopeful hangers-on who drifted in and out. Olivier de la Marche, describing the role of the master cook at the court of Charles the Bold of Burgundy in the fifteenth century, said that his one essential piece of equipment was a long wooden ladle, to be used for two tasks: tasting his creations and whacking

4. The Tasting.
*Psalter*, Flemish, first quarter of the fourteenth century (Oxford, Bodleian Library, MS. Douce 6, fol. 139v).

5. Domestic Scene.
*Psalter*, Flemish, first quarter of the fourteenth century (Oxford, Bodleian Library, MS. Douce 6, fol. 22).

the boys who swarmed around his pots.[13] This determination to repel boarders did not prevent a cook from taking his own tasting duties very seriously. Like old soldiers, old jokes never die, and just as in Plautus' Roman comedy *Aulularia* the guests are said to fast while the cooks feast, so in a thirteenth-century French romance the hero hears the sound of cooks carving the joints and thinks: "they are cutting the best bits for themselves."[14] Figure 4 shows a cook thoughtfully sipping his soup.

The presence of a pair of stocks in a list of late fourteenth-century kitchen equipment[15] and a picture (fig. 6) of a three-tailed whip being cracked beside a cauldron strengthen the impression that passions ran high in many kitchens. Such scraps of evidence tend to confirm the truth of Lydgate's epigram: "Hoot ffir and smoke makith many an angry cook."[16] The tradition that cooks are by nature hot and crotchety flourished for many centuries. In Philip Massinger's play, *A New Way to Pay Old Debts* (1625), the cook's name is Furnace and his first words strike the keynote: "I'll be angry." A fellow-servant tries to smooth him down:

> Why fellow Furnace, 'tis not twelve a'clock yet,
> Nor dinner taking up, then 'tis allowed
> Cooks by their places may be choleric.

But Furnace scorns to keep bad temper within limits:

> At all hours, and all places I'll be angry;
> And thus provoked, when I am at my prayers,
> I will be angry.
>
> [1.2]

But it is possible to find more peaceful kitchen scenes, where cheerful calm prevails. Admittedly, these tend to show the cook alone, all irritants removed to a bearable distance. In certain Labors of the Months pictures for January or February he toasts his toes and some special tidbit over a winter fire; in some Nativities Joseph himself takes on the job and happily broods over his stewpot in a corner, while everyone else in the picture is occupied with the baby. Occasionally, even amiable cooperation is achieved. In a manuscript border, a woman cradles a baby in her arms while she stirs the pot and a boy blows up the fire (fig. 5); on a misericord, a man and a woman sit beside a cauldron, one flourishing the bellows and one ladling out the stew. On another, two women sit comfortably, plucking a goose together.[17]

There must have been periods in the day when even the most

bustling kitchen quieted down, tension relaxed, and tempers sweetened. Albertus Magnus hints at just such a moment in the account of his visit to Paris in 1245/48. The son of the King of Castile was in the city at the same time, and one day his cooks bought a large plaice for his dinner. When it was cleaned they found inside a most unusual oyster shell which they thought so interesting that they left their work and showed it to the prince. Impressed, he generously passed it on to Albertus, whose curiosity about strange natural phenomena was well-known. And so the plaice, the shell, the cooks, and their master all achieved an unexpected immortality in *De Mineralibus.*[18]

Possibly the first realistically depicted kitchen in medieval art catches that air of cosy well-being which all the best kitchens must possess. In the fresco of the *Last Supper* in the Lower Church at Assisi, painted by a close collaborator of Pietro Lorenzetti some time before 1330, a small kitchen is shown beside the dining room. A well-stocked cupboard, a blazing fire, two servants wiping dishes, one dog licking a plate, and one cat warming herself make up the tranquil scene.[19]

Medieval attitudes toward the cook and his staff were mixed. There was always a certain contempt for a man with an obviously messy job. Such scorn had deep roots and can be found expressed already in Roman times by Petronius: "A boy gorged on a diet like this can no more acquire taste than a cook can stop stinking."[20] In the early thirteenth century, the spiritual adviser to a well-born anchorite, writing on the need for humility, considered it an excellent discipline for her to swallow pride and accept impertinence from a kitchen boy: "If you incur disdain from Slurry, the cook's boy who washes and dries the dishes in the kitchen, you should be happy in your heart."[21] Richard de Bury, the fourteenth-century book collector, reeled back in horror at the thought of his precious treasure-trove being pawed over by "the smutty scullion reeking from his stewpots."[22]

The social gulf between the cook and the gentleman was wide and not easily crossed. In 1471, Richard, Duke of Gloucester, wanted to marry Anne Neville, but his brother, the Duke of Clarence, in whose house the girl was living, spitefully decided to prevent this for reasons of his own. He hit on the plan of disguising Anne as a maid and hiding her among the kitchen staff of one of his dependants. It seemed so unlikely that it would occur to Richard to look in such a quarter for his fiancée, that Clarence felt complacent. Satisfyingly, a rumor put just that idea into Richard's

mind, and he combed the kitchens of London until he rescued
Anne and triumphantly carried her off to be married.²³ Clarence
came to an unregretted though congenial end a few years later,
drowned in a vat of his favorite malmsey.

Some hint of the gentleman's attitude to the cook is suggested
by one detail of the ceremony of knighthood in England, as set
down in a fifteenth-century document. One of the two special
symbols of knighthood was the pair of gilt spurs, placed on a
man's heels as the king proclaimed him a knight. After this had
been done the new knight went to pray, and as he emerged from
the chapel he was met by the Master Cook, who claimed the spurs
as his own and carried them off. At first it seems extraordinary
that such a prized symbol should be handed over to a cook, but
the chronicler explains the significance of the scene: "The reson is
this, that in casse that the knyght do afftar eny thynge that be
defame or reproffe unto the ordre of knyghthode, the master
coke then with a gret knyfe, with whiche he dressethe his messes,
shall smyt of his spurrs from his heles; and therfore in remem-

6. Kitchen Discipline.
*Pattern Book,* early thirteenth century (Vienna,
Österreichische National-
bibliothek, codex 507, fol.
2v).

braunce of this thynge the spurrs of a new knyght . . . shall be fee unto the mastar coke."[24] The spurs are claimed by the cook, not for his own honor but as a reminder of what will be done to an unworthy knight: the symbol of his knighthood will be chopped off with a kitchen knife, the last disgrace and humiliation.

Social disdain was intensified by other considerations. Cooks ministered to bodily needs which by their very nature were inferior to spiritual ones. Jesus had been fond both of the housewife Martha and the contemplative Mary, but had made it quite clear where his preference lay: "Martha, thou art careful and troubled about many things. But one thing is needful, and Mary hath chosen that good part" (Luke 10:41–42). The sixth-century *Rule of St. Benedict,* the foundation stone of monasticism in the west, regards service in the kitchen as a useful spiritual discipline: "No one is exempt from duty in the kitchen. . . . From this service a monk learns charity and gains a greater degree of merit."[25] Any job connected with food had a certain taint for the spiritually fastidious. Ailred of Rievaulx, an austere and charming Cistercian in the first half of the twelfth century, looked back with deep embarrassment from the cloister to his early years as steward in the royal Scottish household, where he helped to plan the meals and waited at the dinner table. A contemporary biographer was careful to reassure his readers that while Ailred carved, "his thoughts would be in the other world."[26]

In the late fourteenth and fifteenth centuries in Holland groups of devout men, calling themselves the Brethren of the Common Life, lived together in small communities, spending part of their time in study and prayer, and part in manual labor. In theory, all members were on an equal footing, but even here the work most honored was book production, the least was cooking. Education of course played some part in this distinction, for only the literate could copy texts. The uneducated members were relegated to the kitchen, and while they were often treated with affection they felt themselves to be second-class citizens. One cook even ran away to a university to educate himself, but he could not cope with the courses and came home brokenhearted to his pots and pans.[27]

Despite the fact that the cook was not placed very high on the social scale, there was at least one situation in life where a man found no difficulty in swallowing his pride and claiming the title: when he held his lands by kitchen serjeanty.

The term *serjeanty* is derived from the Latin *servus,* from which also came *servitium* and *serviens.* One of the ways in which the king granted a piece of land to a man in return for some specific service was to offer him serjeanty tenure. The heyday of this practice in England was the late eleventh and twelfth centuries, when the shortage of ready money made it easier for the king to pay a man with land than with wages. The kinds of service so rewarded were exceedingly varied, from looking after the king's falcons to holding his head when he crossed the channel; from time to time certain kitchen jobs were paid for in this way.

In the Domesday Book of 1086, two cooks are mentioned by name and their serjeanty tenures recorded. One piece of land was granted to Walter in Essex, and another to Tezelin in Surrey. The history of both tenures shows how the service demanded for the land changed significantly in the course of time. Thus, Walter in Domesday is described as a cook, but by the early thirteenth century his successor's duties are more narrowly defined: he is to be the king's turnspit. A little later, he is merely expected to clock in for work in the royal kitchen on the three great feasts of the year, Christmas, Easter, and Whitsun. By the middle of the century, this humble labor was no longer required because some annual military service had taken its place. By 1294/95 he paid for his land each year with money. In this way the holder of the serjeanty gradually moved further and further from the kitchen, but his claim to the land was still based on his official title, "the King's Turnspit."[28]

The other Domesday cook, Tezelin, was granted the manor of Addington in Surrey. By the early thirteenth century, the only cooking required of his successor was the making of a single dish on Coronation day, a dish with two mysterious names, *Girunt* and *Malpigernoun*. By 1377 the holder no longer had to do his own cooking. A document of that year states that William Bardolf holds Addington by the service of "finding, on Coronation day, a man to make a dish called *dilgirunt*." At the very last coronation banquet ever held, in 1821, the holder of Addington was still doing his duty: "The Deputy appointed by his Grace the Archbishop of Canterbury, as Lord of the Manor of Bardolf, otherwise Addington, presented the mess of Dillegrout, prepared by the King's Master Cook." A recipe called *Bardolf* has been found in a fifteenth-century manuscript, and on the strength of the name it has been suggested that this may reveal the secret of Dillegrout. It is for chicken in a piquant sauce of vinegar, almond milk, sugar, and spices. A promising combination, but there is no evidence that any king found strength or time to taste it at his coronation

7. Preparing Sausage Skins.
*Psalter,* Flemish, first quarter of the fourteenth century (Oxford, Bodleian Library, MS. Douce 5, fol. 7r).

dinner, when his table groaned under similar tributes from every corner of the land. We are told only that Charles II took one look and "carefully abstained."[29]

In the case of both these serjeanties, the service required of the holder became in time more gentlemanly, as all traces of cooking disappeared, or permission was granted to appoint a deputy to take care of the work. Nevertheless, though the kitchen duties might be despised, the title "King's Turnspit" or "Master of the King's Dillegrout" was prized, because that alone established a man's right to the estate.

There is always a yawning gap between theory and practice, and whatever his official place on the social ladder, the cook had a shrewd idea of his actual worth. He knew he was indispensable, a magician with the power to make each day a hell or heaven for his master. Already by 191 B.C., the cook in Plautus' comedy *Pseudolus* had put the truth of the matter in a nutshell with his simple boast: "I am the savior of mankind."[30] Any self-respecting cook knew just how to make the weight of his displeasure felt when he considered himself put-upon. Francesco, a rich and powerful merchant in fourteenth-century Prato, soon regretted a rash, impromptu invitation: "I brought home to dinner the Mayor and Matteo d'Antonio. She [the cook] had no more to do, for the steak and the fish were already cooked. But because those two ate with me today, and because some fish was left over, and she has also got to cook two bowlsful of beans, she complains she has too much to do."[31]

The good cook charmed the appetite and called the tune, dazzling a docile household with firework displays of careless power:

Cookes with theire newe conceytes, choppynge, stampynge, and
    gryndynge,
Many new curies [recipes] alle day they ar contryvynge and
    fyndynge.[32]

He could also dazzle with the mysteries of his own special, technical vocabulary: "Just as one says 'fringed' with saffron, so doth one say 'garnished' with parsley; and it is the manner of speaking of cooks."[33]

Moralists, of course, disapproved, at least on paper. Livy traced the disastrous weakening of Rome's moral fiber to the year 187 B.C., when one of her armies returned victorious from an Asian campaign with some most undesirable new notions: "For the beginnings of foreign luxury were introduced into the City by the army from Asia. At that time the cook, to the ancient Romans the most worthless of slaves, both in their judgement of values and in the use they made of him, began to have value, and what had been merely a necessary service came to be regarded as an art."[34] There were plenty of medieval moralists to take up Livy's theme with gloomy gusto, but for the mass of mankind the truth of the matter was self-evident, and summed up in one pithy proverb: "God may send a man good meate, but the devyll sende an evyll cooke."[35] In the fourteenth-century romance *Sir Gawain and the Green Knight,* the hero is an appreciative guest at any number of elaborate and highly sophisticated dinner parties. When he has to journey reluctantly through the wilderness in search of his adventure, torn from the comforts of civilization, one of the hardships he has to endure is food below his usual standard: "Ther he fonde noght hym byfore the fare that he lyked."[36]

Only a saint can accept atrocious cooking in the proper spirit of humble fortitude, as this story about a desert hermit testifies. The holy old man became ill, and his disciple decided to make him some little cakes to tempt his appetite. Unfortunately, a life of self-denial does not develop skill in the finer points of cookery, and the young man poured linseed oil instead of honey into the mixture. His master let himself be coaxed into eating one bun, which he chewed in silence, and even submitted to a second. At the third he balked, and murmured firmly, "I cannot eat, my son." His companion then bit into one himself, realized with horror what he had done, and fell on his knees to beg pardon. The old man rallied him with these heroic words: "Vex not thyself, my son, because of it: for if God had willed that I should eat a good cake, thou wouldst have put in the honey, and not this that thou didst put in."[37] Whatever grimness might be detected by the cynic's ear in this sentence, it has to be conceded that few ordinary mortals could rise to these heights.

In Layamon's late twelfth-century history of Britain, the *Brut,* the glories of King Arthur's court are described. High on the list comes the proud boast: "Nefde he neuere naenne coc that he nes keppe swithe god [He (Arthur) had not a single cook who was not a very fine champion]."[38] This might be good enough for a court lost in the romantic mists of history, but what men wanted in their own kitchens was not a warrior but a wizard, ready to work his magic on a handful of ingredients and transform them into a dish fit for a king. Any cook who could do this named his own price, rested on his ladle, and waited to be wooed. In the fifteenth century, Sir John Fastolfe's cook retired to sleep under a coverlet provided by his attentive master, decorated with a startling pattern of roses and bloodhounds. In 1204, Queen Eleanor of England granted a plot of land for life to her faithful servant Adam the cook and his wife Joan. In 1284, Archbishop Pecham was accusing the Fellows of Merton College, Oxford, of paying their cook and brewer an "excessive and unstatutable" salary.[39] In 1390, the Earl of Derby gave Christmas presents to members of his household, including all those who helped to make his dinnertimes agreeable: the minstrels, the waferers, and the kitchen staff.

There is a note of kind concern in the official document which recorded that Thomas Beauchef, at one time cook to the Black Prince, was to be allowed to retire in 1383 on his full salary for life, because he was "an old man and not able to labour as he used to do." He was free "to go away for recreation and return when he pleases."[40]

The most genial treatment of a cook is in the romance *Havelok the Dane* (ca. 1300). At the nadir of his fortunes, Havelok has to serve as a kitchen hand. Bertram the cook is so kind to the shivering, starving boy, even buying him out of his own pocket "span new" clothes, that at the end of the story, when the hero has come into his own, Havelok rewards him with the earldom of Cornwall and affectionately addresses him as "Frend."[41] Here and there, an entry in a will suggests the same pleasant relationship between master and man: "I bequethe to Iohn Wylkynsone of the kechyn, VIs. VIIId . . . I bequethe to Ion of the kechyn, VIs. VIIId, And to be new arayd . . . Thomas my Cooke, oweth me, XXs, the whiche I pardon and forgeve hym."[42]

Even when there is no evidence of special merit or special reward, there are signs that a cook could hope for a life of quiet prosperity. The will of Walter Mangeard, "Citesen and koke of London," written in 1433, shows him able to provide for his wife, leave money to his church in Fleet Street, to the London Fraternity of Cooks, and to "Litill Watkyn, my Godsone and my servant." He forgave several debts, and made arrangements for some cattle he owned in the Sussex village of Hurstpierpoint to be sold and the money raised given to the parish church there. John Isabell, a cook in York who died in 1390, owned an eating house in the city's main street and a garden with two vineyards in the suburbs.[43]

In 1380, Thomas Walsingham compiled a book listing all the benefactors of the monastery of St. Albans, living as well as dead. After the contributions of kings, popes, lords, abbots, and knights have been acknowledged a group of humbler donors get their turn. Among these is Master Robert, cook to Abbot Thomas de la Mare (1349–96). Robert is described as a faithful servant, and shown holding up the heavy kitchen knife with which he labored for St. Albans (fig. 8). Beside him stands his wife Helena, a determined woman, who made sure that Robert's portrait would appear by giving three shillings and fourpence toward the cost of preparing the whole book. Another cook, Master John Brodeye, did not have to pay for immortality. His name was preserved in a

**8. Master Robert the Cook.**
*Liber Benefactorum,* St. Albans, 1380 (London, British Museum, MS. Cotton, Nero D. VII, fol. 109). Courtesy of the British Library Board.

chronicle because he caught the writer's eye by creating an intricate castle to decorate the royal table at the wedding of Edward I's daughter Margaret in 1290.[44]

Whether hot and harassed or cosseted and calm, the cook had the comfort of knowing that he was not alone; a certain amount of outside help might be summoned to smooth his path. For a fee, many services which demanded special equipment or special skills could be provided. Bread and ale, two staples of the medieval diet, were both made, for the most part, by professionals. A large household had its own teams, a modest one relied on the local bakehouse and aleshop. In Chaucer's *Reeve's Tale,* when unexpected company arrives at the mill, the miller sends his daughter out shopping:

> This millere into toun his doghter sende
> For ale and breed, and rosted hem a goos.[45]

The lines suggest that this household had a fire and a spit and could lay its hands on a goose, but had no equipment for baking or brewing.

Because most homes had no oven, the baker not only baked

9. Dinner Party.
*Queen Mary's Psalter,* English, first quarter of the fourteenth century (London, British Museum, MS. Royal 2B. VII, fol. 199v). Courtesy of the British Library Board.

bread but cooked pies. The prologue to the fifteenth-century *Tale of Beryn* is set in the Cheker of the Hope Inn at Canterbury, and there the barmaid is flirting with one of the guests. To please him, she pops into town for a little delicacy:

> She stert in to the town, and fet a py al hote
> And set to-fore the Pardoner.[46]

The accounts of two chantry priests at Bridport, Dorset, in the mid-fifteenth century show that in January 1455 they prepared an elaborate dinner party for several important guests. They listed everything bought for the occasion: best ale, a sucking pig, a goose, two cocks, eggs, raisins, and noted down a payment of five pence to William the Baker for flour, his labor, and the "pies made"[47](fig. 11).

Spices made the medieval heart beat faster, the medieval palate quiver with delight, and the medieval kitchen boy shudder with distaste. If bought in their natural state, much tedious pounding with pestle and mortar was needed to reduce them to precious, pungent dust. Edward IV's servants were expected, when necessary, to grind away at their spices through the dinner hour, munching a picnic meal as they worked.[48] Happy the household with a master rich and considerate enough to order his supplies ready prepared by the merchant. The steward of Bogo de Clare, an exceedingly wealthy churchman and brother of the Earl of Gloucester, kept accounts for the years 1284/86, which have survived, and these show that the spices ordered were pounded and sorted into sheepskin pouches before leaving the shop.[49] Apothecaries were well equipped to provide this service; indeed Ghent's Spice and Herb Merchant's Hall is decorated with the guild's characteristic crest of a mortar and two pestles.[50] They had a wider range of tools than most households aspired to, and sometimes even invested in a heavy pestle suspended from the ceiling to tackle the hardest jobs.[51]

Much pounding and chopping are needed to fill a sausage skin, and an elderly husband in late fourteenth-century Paris told his young wife the short cut to take: "When you have killed your pig, take the flesh of the ribs . . . and the best fat, as much of the one as of the other, in such quantity as you would make sausages; and cause it to be minced and hashed up very small by a pastry cook."[52] He expected his wife's cook to fill this mixture into the skins himself, but it was possible to buy the complete sausage. Fig. 7 shows butchers preparing the skins. Hulling wheat, by removing the first husk from the wheat grain, was another tedious chore which, in a city, could be farmed out for a fee to somebody else: "hulled wheat, the which is sometimes to be had from the spicers all ready hulled for a silver penny a pound."[53]

Sauces were as much enjoyed as spices, and while this particular husband carefully wrote down many recipes for different sauces, he knew that for a large dinner party the most sensible thing to do was to order them from a professional saucemaker: "From the sauce-maker, a quart of cameline for the dinner and for the supper two quarts of mustard."[54]

Festive occasions called for special dishes and special skills. A great household might have its own waferer and confectioner to create luxurious trifles, or follow the example of more modest establishments and buy them ready-made. Bogo de Clare's steward ordered sugar perfumed and flavored with roses and violets for the Ascension Day feast one year.[55] A bill sent by apothecaries

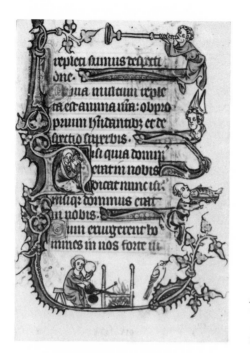

**10. Making Wafers.**
*Psalter*, Flemish, first quarter of the fourteenth century (Oxford, Bodleian Library, MS. Douce 6, fol. 119r).

**11. Baking Pies.**
*Psalter*, French, second quarter of the fourteenth century (Cambridge, University Library, MS. Dd. 5.5, fol. 280r). Courtesy of the Syndics of Cambridge University Library.

in Florence to Francesco, a wealthy merchant of Prato, in 1406, was for "a tart of marzipan."[56] In fig. 9, two guests are just about to break off pieces from a flowerlike object on the table, which may represent an elaborately molded cake or sweet bread prepared by a master confectioner.[57]

Of all delicacies, perhaps the most universally adored was the wafer, made of batter and cooked between two greased, heated iron molds to fragile, crisp perfection. In fig. 10 a woman beams with satisfaction as she holds up her finished wafer, just slipped from its irons. A wafer could be savory, with a cheese filling, or spicy with ginger, but the classic one was sweetened with sugar or honey. Its pet names suggest how dear it was to the medieval heart: *nebula,* the cloud, and angel's bread.[58] When learned discussion raged over the nature of the manna showered on the Israelites in the desert, the usual conclusion was that it must have been a wafer. The mind boggled at the thought of anything more truly heavenly: "The taste of it was lyke unto wafers made with honye."[59] The author of a fourteenth-century devotional treatise, *The Cloud of Unknowing,* caustically observed that novice mystics could be easily deceived by the devil into thinking that spiritual sweetness would actually drop down on them as manna, angel's food; "That is why it is their custom to sit gaping as though they wanted to catch flies."[60]

It was not hard to make wafers at home, but temptingly easy to buy them ready-made. John of Garland, in his thirteenth-century *Dictionary,* described the sights to be seen on a stroll through Paris, and mentions the waferer, his basket covered with a fresh white napkin, who offered customers a free sample, supremely confident that one taste would loosen purse strings and unleash desire.[61] For an elaborate wedding feast with forty guests, an interesting assortment of wafers might be ordered: "From the wafer-maker it behoves to order: . . . a dozen and a half of cheese gauffres . . . a dozen and a half of *gros batons* . . . a dozen and a half of *portes* . . . a dozen and a half of *estriers* . . . a hundred sugared *galettes.*"[62]

Arrangements could be made to have many more items delivered, to ease the pressure on one's own kitchen. For forty guests, a poulterer might be asked to supply "fifty young rabbits, to wit, forty for the dinner, which shall be roast, and ten for the jelly."[63] Figure 12 shows a spit load of fowls being roasted underneath a poulterer's shopsign. A pastry cook's delivery boys may be seen in fig. 14, carrying their trays of tarts over the Grand Pont of Paris.

Nor was such traffic all one-way. The cooks of many large house-holds liked to make a small profit on the side by selling their kitchen waste to bakers, who cheerfully carried off the odds and ends and popped them into pies. The trade became so brisk and produced so many tainted pies, that an ordinance forbidding it had to be passed in 1379: "Because that the Pastelers [pastry cooks] of the City of London have heretofore baked in pasties rabbits, geese, and garbage, not befitting, and sometimes stinking . . . it is ordered that . . . no one of the said trade shall buy . . . at the hostels of the great lords, of the cooks of such lords, any garbage from capons, hens, or geese, to bake in a pasty, and sell."[64]

The advantages of drawing on such a network of services were blissfully clear: convenience, the chance to enjoy the fruits of spe-

12. Cook Shop.
*Romance of Alexander*, Bruges, 1338–44 (Oxford, Bodleian Library, MS. 264, fol. 204 [detail]).

cial skills, and relief to one's own harassed, flustered kitchen. The hazards were less immediately obvious, but obligingly revealed themselves through bitter experience: incompetence, dishonesty, and expense.

Bread was one staple bought by every class of society (fig. 13), and a war of wits raged between the baker and his customer. Bakers, not unnaturally, rather preened themselves on their skills and their selfless service to the community. Certainly those of Chartres paid for several windows in the cathedral, which show them stirring their dough and reverently carrying their round white loaves to a grateful world. Gilbert de la Porrée, a twelfth-century chancellor of Chartres, remarked, however, to John of Salisbury, that in his experience all the incompetents and unemployed of the town tended to drift into the trade because it was

13. Bread Shop.
*Romance of Alexander,* Bruges, 1338–44 (Oxford, Bodleian Library, MS. 264, fol. 204 [detail]).

14. Tarts for Sale.
*La Vie de Saint Denis,* French, 1317 (Paris, Bibliothèque Nationale, MS. Fr. 2092, fol. 42r). Photo. Bibl. nat. Paris.

thought to be an easy one.[65] The results of such misplaced optimism showed all too often in the finished product, and matters did not improve noticeably over the centuries. The complaint in a medieval proverb, "in the oven of a lazy baker the dough freezes,"[66] is echoed in the mortified exclamation of an Elizabethan hostess: "Maistris, will you have some cake? Trulie it is but dow, I wold the baker had been baked when he did heate the oven."[67]

Incompetence may irritate, but cheating hurts the pride as well as pocket. Some ordered their spices ready-pounded and sorted, and were well-pleased with the whole transaction. Others were not so fortunate. In 1395 a merchant in Gloucestershire ordered from a London apothecary some powdered ginger, some wormseed, and some frankincense. Three neat little parcels were duly dispatched, but when they were opened it was found that certain substitutions had been made: rapeseed and radish root for ginger, tansy seed for wormseed, resin for frankincense. The customer was not amused.[68] Such episodes did not improve the spice merchants' image: "They care nothynge for the welth of ther soule, so they may be ryche."[69]

To slip out for a hot pie neatly solves the problem of the unexpected guest, but it is vexing to pay for one thing and eat another. A London ordinance had to be passed in 1379, forbidding the piebakers of the city to "bake beef in a pasty for sale, and sell it as venison."[70]

Only the humblest householder would dream of stepping out for food himself. Dignity must be maintained, and a servant sent forth with the shopping list. Cheating is a chameleon with an infinite variety of disguises, and one of its favorites is that of the fresh-faced page, earnest and eager to do his master's bidding. The thirteenth-century sermon writer Jacques de Vitry tells us just how the servant of four poor innocent students in Paris made a handsome profit for himself on every shopping expedition: "I buy mustard from the dealer who furnishes me with vegetables, candles, and so on for my masters, and every time I get mustard I divide a farthing's worth into four portions and set down each as a farthing. Then, as I am a regular customer, the dealer throws in a fifth portion, which I also reckon at a farthing, and so I gain four farthings for one."[71]

The baker provided an essential service because he possessed an oven, but many customers thought it prudent as well as economical to make up their own dough and bring it along to be baked. Such forethought was not enough when dealing with some bakers. In 1327 in London it was discovered that a certain John Brid asked his customers to place their loaves on his "molding-borde" to wait their turn in the oven. The board appeared to be a whole piece of wood, but in fact a circle had been cut out of it and then replaced as a lid. Hidden beneath sat a servant, and as each loaf landed on the circle he pulled down the loose wood and twisted off a piece of fresh dough. In the course of a hard morning's work a respectable pile of dough could be gathered together, ready to be given the touch of the master by Brid himself and sold as his own bread to a whole new crop of customers.[72]

Short-weight loaves, when discovered, outraged medieval house-keepers because a very precise relationship between the weight and the price was drawn up by the authorities. In fig. 15 a baker is shown weighing each piece of dough before it is formed into a loaf. One Stratford-at-Bow apprentice in 1387, knowing his master's loaves were too light, helpfully popped a small piece of iron into the test loaf before it was examined by a London official and passed for sale.[73] If caught and convicted, a faulty baker had to submit to the humiliation of being dragged on a hurdle from the Guildhall to his own house, "through the great streets that are most dirty," with a loaf hung round his neck (fig. 16). Though outraged victims frequently had the satisfaction of this spectacle, culprits learned to live with embarrassment; at the first opportunity they popped up again to flourish like the green bay tree.

Buying prepared dishes was hazardous. Not surprisingly, some people preferred to forgo convenience; they chose their raw ingredients and had them freshly cooked. There is a suggestion in the Prologue to Chaucer's *Canterbury Tales* that the gildsmen among the pilgrims had hired a cook to prepare their meals on the road from Southwark to Canterbury.[74] Chaucer's description of the man they picked inspires little confidence, but the company is too busy telling stories to put his powers to the test. In 1483, three German noblemen in a group of pilgrims traveling from Jerusalem to Mt. Sinai eased the rigors of the journey by taking with them John, their "accomplished cook."[75]

In many places, innkeepers were allowed to offer only lodgings to travelers; friendly neighborhood tradesmen kept a monopoly on food and drink. A manual of French conversation, written at Bury St. Edmund's in 1396, presents a traveler discussing the question of supper with his host. Perhaps made pensive by the army of rats and mice he has just noticed on maneuvers in his bedroom, he instructs the innkeeper to go out and buy some chickens for his own servant to prepare.[76]

When someone chose his own ingredients and took them to a

15. (*opposite*) Baking Bread.
*The Hours of Catherine of Cleves,* Flemish, mid-fifteenth century (New York, Pierpont Morgan Library, MS. M917, fol. 226).

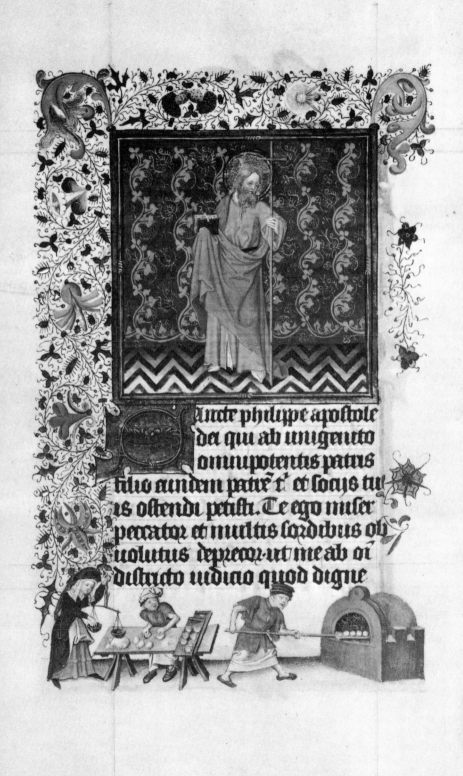

ancte phulippe apostole
dei qui ab unigenito
omnipotentis patris
filio aundem patre̅ t̅ et socijs tu
is oftendi petifti. Te ego miser
peccator et multis sordibus ob
uolutus deprecor ut me ab o̅i
diftricto iudicio quod digne

professional to be cooked, he had the double satisfaction of knowing, more or less, what he would be eating, and making his money
stretch a little further. A list of prices to be charged by pie bakers
in London in 1378 shows the difference in cost between a pie
made from scratch by the baker and one for which the customer
brought the filling: "The best capon baked in a pasty, 8d. . . . For
the paste, fire, and trouble [work] upon a capon, 1½d."[77]

Harassed hosts needed not only elaborate dishes to impress
their guests, but extra tablecloths and especially large saucepans.
In late fourteenth-century Paris, the accounts for a wedding feast
with forty guests show that the following items were rented:
"linen . . . for six tables; three large copper pots . . . sixteen bowls
. . . two boilers, two strainers, a mortar, a pestle, six large cloths
for the kitchen, three large earthenware pots for wine, a large
earthenware pot for pottage, four basins, four wooden spoons, an
iron pan, four large pails with handles, two trivets and a spoon of
pierced iron."[78] When the Brewers of London gave a dinner in
1423, they listed among the expenses payments "for hirynge of
spetes [spits], iiii d," and "for the hirynge of pewter vesselles,
vi d."[79]

It was also possible to hire pairs of hands to help. The Brewers'
dinner was planned with meticulous attention to detail; indeed,
even the sum spent on supper the day the accounts were made up
is recorded. The swarm of extras who insured its success included
"one minstrel called Percival," two turnspits, a laundress to wash
the tablecloths and napkins, and a man responsible for that indispensable service, "cariage of donge."[80]

For those too poor, mean, or improvident to make such careful
arrangements, nothing but trouble lay ahead. Matthew Paris records under the year 1251 that when the daughter of Henry III
was married to the King of Scotland at Christmas in York, the
guests were shuttled from one disorganized royal household to
another. The Archbishop of York had to bustle about in the background, papering over the cracks in the façade of hospitality, "at
one time by providing places of abode for the travellers, at
another by providing fodder for the horses, at other times by
supplying various household utensils, fuel for fires, and presents
of money."[81] Wolsey arranged matters much better in the late
1520s. When he was to entertain the French ambassadors at
Hampton Court, his officers from the beginning called in outside
help, and sent "for all the expertest cooks . . . that they could get
in all England . . . to serve to garnish this feast."[82]

16. Dishonest Baker's Punishment.
*Liber de Assisa Panis,* Paris, 1293 (London, Corporation of London Records Office, Guildhall, fol. 1). Courtesy of the Corporation of London.

For less exalted hosts, it was possible to hire a cook who specialized in grand dinner parties. The Brewers in 1423 not only paid to have one goose and two rabbits baked by a baker, but hired a cook, Thomas Bourne, as well.[83] The cook usually brought his own team of assistants and was expected to pay them out of his own exorbitant salary. When Francesco, the wealthy merchant of Prato, made a wedding feast for his daughter, the cook he engaged for this one occasion was paid half a maid's wages for a whole year.[84]

Householders clucked with horror at the expense of it all, but master cooks rested easy. Special occasions called for special dishes and only an expert could provide them. The Goodman of Paris wrote down one recipe for his wife, but at the end of his notes he gave a shrug of despair: "*Farced Chickens,* Colored or Glazed. They be first blown up and all the flesh within taken out, then filled up with other meat, then colored or glazed ... but there is too much to do, it is not work for a citizen's cook, nor even for a simple knight's—and therefore I leave it."[85] Once a man had learned to sigh over impossible dreams he was ripe for the most expensive cook he could afford at his next important dinner party: "That that my coke can nat doo, the towne coke shall fulfyll."[86]

No matter how wide the range of outside services might be, most of the work had to be done by the resident cook. To help or hinder him he had his team of assistants, and while he brooded over his sauces, they coped with all those laborious, repetitive jobs that must be done to keep things running smoothly. At the Hôtel Dieu, a hospital in Paris, the master cook had three assistants, to prepare the vegetables, turn the spits, and wash the dishes.[87] A fifteenth-century Latin-English vocabulary defines with brutal tidiness the kitchen hierarchy:

| | |
|---|---|
| Hic archimacherus | a master coke |
| Hic cocus | alle maner a cokys |
| Hic lixa | a swyllere [dishwasher].[88] |

To climb the ladder from bottom rung to top, skills had to be acquired. A kitchen boy with this ambition might be apprenticed to the cook and engaged on a long-term contract. One London merchant in the fifteenth century left a sum of money in his will "to lytell Jak of my kechyn, he to serve oute his termes."[89] The waferer at the court of Edward IV was expected to have an assistant already trained to make wafers himself.[90]

Many jobs, like washing-up, chopping wood, and drawing water, needed no special training but lots of energy and hard work. For these it was quite usual to hire casual labor to help the regular kitchen staff. In the romance of *Havelok*, the hero is one of a crowd of boys hanging round the castle gate in the hope of being taken on as extra hands. The cook is looking for porters to carry indoors the load of fish he has just bought. Havelok catches his eye by shouldering aside the opposition and striding easily into the castle with a gigantic basket full of fish on his head; after this demonstration of alacrity and strength, he is hired on the spot as a general odd-job man in the kitchen.[91] Havelok, being a hero in disguise, is treated with much affection by his master, the cook. The fate of other kitchen hands may have been less agreeable. Despite prohibitions by the Pope, many Christian merchants bought slaves in the east and brought them home for resale in Italy and Germany. In 1463 a pastry-cook in Vigevano acquired a girl in this way to help him in his business.[92]

In the accounts of Henry, Earl of Derby, for 1390/91 the Clerk of the Kitchen notes down a special payment to someone for making two hundred stockfish ready for cooking by beating them with a hammer: "pro verberacione iiC stokes, viii d."[93] The stockfish, or dried cod, was a necessary but unloved item in everybody's diet, and the tedium of its preparation is well described in this late fourteenth-century recipe:

> When it [cod] is taken in the far seas and it is desired to keep it for ten or twelve years, it is gutted and its head removed and it is dried in the air and sun and in no wise by a fire, or smoked; and when this is done it is called *stockfish*. And when it hath been kept a long time and it is desired to eat it, it behoves to beat it with a wooden hammer for a full hour, and then set it to soak in warm water for a full two hours or more, then cook and scour it very well like beef; then eat it with mustard or soaked in butter.[94]

There were many jobs like this to be done every day by those on the bottom rung of the kitchen ladder: turning spits, pounding spices, and churning butter. All were both tiresome and thankless; as the proverb put it: "He turns the spit who never tastes a morsel from it."[95] All were tasks to make a servant dream hopefully of spirits who, in the right mood, would do the work at night while the household slept. For a bowl of cream the Welsh Brownie would stir up a lump of butter; for even less the Finnish Para would steal one ready-made from someone else's churn. In one story, a Welsh housewife realized what was happening and economically dismissed all the maids in the belief that her Brownie would do everything and demand no wages. With an eye to social reform, the Brownie rose to the occasion and came out on strike until the maids got their jobs back.[96]

Such everyday drudgery with heavy equipment was physically demanding and this may be one reason why men and boys were preferred in the kitchen when it was possible to hire them. Sir Thomas More in his *Utopia* (1516) described an ideal society where some modifications would be introduced into the system: "all vyle service, all slaverie and drudgerye, with all laboursome toyle and busines, is done by bondemen. But the women of every famelie by course have the office and charge of cokerye . . . and orderyng al thinges thereto belonging."[97]

Of all tasks the most vital was to light the fire; without that, comfort died and dinner failed to appear. A nineteenth-century gourmet remarked with benign condescension: "The light of the kitchen fire was probably the brightest spot in the dark ages,"[98] and a hundred scattered hints betray medieval preoccupation with the problem of keeping it bright and glowing warmly. In the late thirteenth century Walter de Bibbesworth wrote a treatise for an English lady who wanted to improve her French, and to make his lessons more interesting he turned the vocabulary exercises into little vignettes of domestic life. When he came to fire-lighting he showed four kitchen boys in a bustle of activity, brushing the hearthstone, clearing away the cold ashes, and piling up a judicious mixture of oak, ash, and beech.[99] Each wood had its own special virtue, of catching quickly or burning steadily, and the skill lay in using each properly. Havelok boasts that he knows how to make and maintain a good fire.[100] In Chaucer's *Canon's Yeoman's Tale,* the alchemists' pot explodes while it is being heated, and amid the mutual recriminations there is much bad-tempered analysis of what had been wrong with the fire. One said the fire was just too hot, another that it was badly made to begin with, and a third, "By cause oure fir ne was nat maad of beech."[101]

To light the fire, Walter de Bibbesworth takes the coward's way out and suggests that a burning brand be brought from one already started, with a pot full of glowing embers to follow if the wood is green. Other writers believed in first principles: "It must be done with rubbynge of ii treen pecis [wood sticks] together."[102] Most households invested instead in fire irons, with which the first, essential spark could be struck. John of Garland describes a thirteenth-century market stall in Paris, where such fire irons could be found, next to needle cases, razors, whetstones, and mirrors.[103]

Once a spark was achieved, it had to be fostered instantly with kindling and transformed into a blaze strong enough to make the wood catch fire:

> Ac hew fyre at a flynte. fowre hundreth wyntre,
> Bot thow have towe to take it with. tondre or broches,
> Al thi laboure is loste. and al thi longe travaille.
> [You can strike sparks from a flint for four hundred years,
> but unless you have kindling, wood splinters, or tow to catch
> fire from it, all your work and long toil is wasted.] [104]

Everyone had his own pet kindling materials, from dry fern, straw, or rushes to tow, dried toadstools, and charred cloth.[105] Not one of these satisfied the Goodman of Paris, who drew up for his wife a daunting plan of campaign. The bark of an old nut tree was to be stripped off and boiled in a pot of lye or ashes for two days and one night "at the least." After that it was to be dried slowly in the sun or the chimney corner, beaten with a hammer "until it becometh like unto a sponge," and stored in a dry place. Mercifully, such patient preparations did not have to be repeated very often, for only the tiniest amount of the material was needed at one time: "When thou wouldst light a fire, then take a piece the size of a pea, and set it on thy flint and forthwith thou shalt have fire."[106]

To draw up the flames, a current of air had to be provided. If in luck, a kitchen boy was given a pair of bellows; if not, he blew: "I blowe the fir til that myn herte feynte."[107] When Chaucer's Host rudely asks the Canon's Yeoman why his face is such an odd color, the yeoman sighs and explains it is because of an occupational hazard:

> I am so used in the fyr to blowe
> that it hath chaunged my colour . . .
> . . . wher my colour was bothe fressh and reed,
> Now is it wan and of a leden hewe. . . . [108]

An illustration in the fourteenth-century *Holkham Bible Picture Book* shows a disciple on his knees, blowing up the fire to grill some fish for Jesus.

Because it took skill, good management, and a little luck to start a fire, many were reluctant to let theirs go out completely, and so the embers were banked up at night, and left dormant until morning. To lessen the dangers of burning down the kitchen by accident, a cover of rough pottery, with ventilation holes, was placed over the fire. It was called a *couvre-feu*, and in towns a special bell, the *couvre-feu*, or *curfew*, was rung at eight or nine o'clock in the evening, to announce the time when all fires had to be put out or covered up.[109]

Candles posed another fire hazard in the kitchen. As the main meal of the day was served about noon, cooks had to get busy early in the morning, and often worked by candlelight. Sometimes, indeed, they made their preparations the night before. The Knight of La Tour Landry tells an improving tale about a traveler who came home unexpectedly, late one evening, after many years abroad. He brought with him a splendid, fur-lined robe for each of his two nieces, but one forfeited her present by prinking too long at the mirror before sweeping out to meet him. The other was so happy to see her uncle again that she "lefte forthwith the tournyng and makynge of her breed, and with her handes yet full of paste came and embraced hym." The reward for such endearing impulsiveness was, quite properly, two furred gowns.[110]

The use of candles in the kitchen is sometimes noted in account rolls. They were required all the year round in the bakehouse at the court of Edward IV, and a chandler came to Bishop Swinfield's household one autumn to make eighty pounds of them from animal fat after the Martinmas slaughter of cattle. Much care was needed with such fire hazards: a cook at Goodrich Castle in 1299 set his candle safely inside a lantern in the kitchen window.[111] The fear of an accidental blaze was so great that some householders preferred to give up the convenience of an all-night fire, douse their embers, and go to bed in the comfortable knowledge that, ready to hand, lay twelve large sacks "to carry things away with," and a long rope down which to slide to safety in an emergency.[112]

After tending the fire, the most important, endlessly repeated job for a kitchen boy was washing-up (fig.17). The two, indeed, were intimately related, for the ashes from the fire were used to scour the spits and cooking pots: "Take a wyspe of strawe and asshes and scoure this potte."[113] The vessels were cleaned, of course, only where it mattered, on the inside; the outside was left blackened by the fire. Many such discolored pots have been dug up, including one, at Wareham Castle, which is completely black except for a clean band round its neck, suggesting that it had been hung up over the fire by a rope, like the cauldron shown in one scene of the Bayeux Tapestry.[114] In a tenth-century play, *Dulcitius,* by that formidable nun, Hroswitha, the villain arrests three Christian virgins and locks them up in a room near the kitchen. Late at night he steals back to molest them but gets into the store room by mistake and throws himself passionately on the pots and pans. He emerges discomfited, covered with soot from head to toe.[115]

Lots of hot water was needed to clean the equipment constantly in use. John of Garland in his *Dictionary* carefully describes the scene: "Cooks wash up in warm water cauldrons, brass pots, pans, frying pans, basins, ewers, flasks, mortars, platters, trenchers, sauceboats, spoons, bowls, gridirons, crumb graters and flesh hooks."[116] While cauldrons might stay black on the outside, crockery for the table had to be washed all over, not left "dirty on the underside, so as to stain the table cloth."[117]

Sharp knives are useful in the kitchen today; they were essential in the medieval period when so much heavy work was done at home. Not surprisingly, many whetstones, large and small, have been found in kitchen areas during archaeological excavations. The small ones have a little hole at the top and were probably hung on the belt, ready to hand whenever their owners wanted to strop a knife.[118]

A cook who is proud of his creations must work with clean tools, on clean surfaces, and medieval recipe books do their best to drive the point home: "lay it on a clene bord"; "Let the ovene be . . . clene swept"; "take a fayre Frying-panne"; "caste it on a fayre lynen clothe that is clene and drye."[119] Plenty of cloths and towels were kept in the kitchen for wiping dishes and hands. They were often made from table linen which had seen better days: "these raggis wyll serve for kytchyn clothes."[120] In the twelfth century, Alexander Neckam warned that they should not be left anywhere near the floor: "In the pantry let there be . . . an ordinary hand towel which shall hang from a pole to avoid mice."[121]

17. Washing Dishes.
*Smithfield Decretals*, illuminated in England, second quarter of the fourteenth century (London, British Museum, MS. Royal 10E. IV, fol. 144v). Courtesy of the British Library Board.

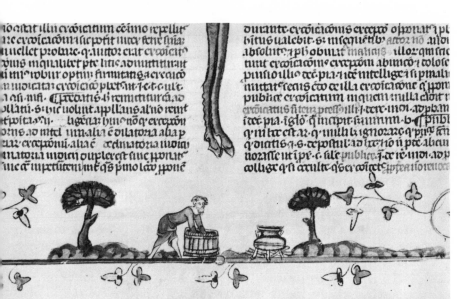

Mice posed a problem, and towels were not the only things hung high. Special shelves and brackets were sometimes made to keep bags of food out of harm's way.[122] A purposeful cat was an indispensable member of the staff. One picture in a late fifteenth-century manuscript made for a German patron shows a cat with a mouse in its jaws, while nearby lies proof of the culprit's crime, a half-gnawed pear.[123] Mousetraps also played a part in the kitchen's defenses. There is one carved on a bench end at North Cadbury, Somerset, and a thirteenth-century sermon recommends cheese as the bait, preferably roasted "to make it smell good."[124]

Flies were another nuisance. Meat was kept in safes with sides either pierced or made of mesh, to allow air to circulate.[125] In the summer these safes were draped with cloth, to prevent flies from slipping through the holes and spoiling the food.[126] To protect their clothes, everyone wore long aprons in the kitchen, and in large households linen to make new ones was issued four times a year, at All Hallow's (1 November), Christmas, Easter, and Whitsun.[127]

The concern for cleanliness went hand in hand with one for freshness. Ingredients were to be used with care. In frying, for example, the fastidious cook resisted all temptation to use the same fat again and again, and helped himself each time to "fressh grece."[128]

A sharp eye had to be kept on the larder shelves to make sure that nothing moldered away unnoticed in a corner. When food began to look unappetizing it had to be regretfully set aside: "Bacon which is fair and white is much better to be served up than that which is yellow, for however good be the yellow, it is too much condemned and discourages one to look upon it."[129] Food went bad with disconcerting speed; as a fifteenth-century housekeeper sighed, "To orrible it is to speke how sone it is defouled."[130] When it did so, it had to be written off as a complete loss, shameful proof of incompetence in the kitchen. Worry about waste haunted the dreams of prudent housekeepers, and an anchorite's carelessness in such matters was considered matter for the confessional: "Confess . . . all common sins . . . letting things become mouldy or rusty or rotten . . . not taking care of the things you use or things which you ought to attend to. . . ."[131]

To let food go rotten is one kind of wastefulness; to use precious ingredients inefficiently is another. Spices were the most expensive items in the kitchen cupboard, and cooks and their assistants were prodded to squeeze every drop of goodness out of them. A recipe that calls for the grinding of bread and spices in a mortar sensibly suggests that the spices be pounded first: "You should first bray the spices and take them out of the mortar, because the bread which you bray afterwards requires that which remaineth from the spices; thus nought is lost that would be lost if 'twere done otherwise."[132] Another, for hippocras, points out that spices which have been steeped in wine for several days to flavor it can still be fished out and used again in a stew: "And yiff thow cast hit [the spice sediment] awey, thow dost thy mastir no right."[133]

The medieval ideal of hospitality was lavish. In an early Welsh romance, the porter at Arthur's court promises the stranger "Meat for thy dogs and corn for thy horse, and hot peppered chops for thyself."[134] Openhanded generosity and careless abandon were the notes to be struck. The public performance was as richly festive as circumstances allowed, but behind the scenes stagehands were briskly practical and the manager kept a gimlet eye on the accounts.

Meticulously detailed records were kept of all expenses. Careful calculations went into the making of a successful dinner party, from the cost of hiring extra brooms to a decision on just how many wafers to allow for each guest. Day-to-day expenditure was noted down with similar precision. It was not the cook's task to write up the accounts himself, but he had to report what had been used and spent each day. Indeed, this was the only part of his job considered worthy of mention in a legal textbook of ca. 1290: "It is the cook's duty to render account each day to the steward for every course at table."[135] The book is believed to have been written by Matthew de Scaccario, a lawyer committed to comfortable confinement in the Fleet prison in London from 1290 to 1292. He was especially interested in accounts and administration, and so wrote entirely from the steward's point of view.[136] In a small household, the cook would speak directly to his master, in a large one to the clerk of the kitchen, who wrote down the expenses and then in turn reported to his own superior, the steward.

A daily record was the most approved, but sometimes a weekly account was considered acceptable. Two chantry priests in Bridport, Dorset, found it sufficient to add up their modest expenses at the end of each week in the 1450s. A typical entry is set out like this: "For bread, 5d. for ale, 8d. for meat, 9d. for fish, 3d. for beans and butter, 1d. for coarse salt, 2d. A workman ate in the

house one day. Total, 2s. 4d."[137] Master and man did not invariably see eye to eye on the virtues of day-by-day bookkeeping, and
in 1484 we find Margaret Paston sending an urgent appeal to her
husband for help: "I pray you that you will secure some man at
Caister to keep your buttery, for the man that you left with me
will not take upon him to make up accounts daily as you com-
manded. He says that he has not been used to giving a reckoning
either of bread or ale till the weekend."[138]

Consciousness of cost and worry about waste were the nagging
preoccupations of everyone who held the purse strings, but they
were special burdens for the steward of a large household. It was
painfully difficult to impose any kind of financial discipline on
such a heaving, changing crowd, never the same for two days
running. Great lords, ecclesiastical or lay, received streams of visitors, who had to be fed; indeed, they brought with them servants,
horses, and dogs, all hungry, all hopeful. The household of
Prince Edward of Carnarvon was swamped with unwelcome
guests during one week in 1292, and the daily accounts bristle
with indignant asides: "They are staying. . . . They are still here.
. . . Here they are still. . . . This day is burdensome."[139]

Great lords also moved from estate to estate throughout the
year, and dragged along a part of their household. The costs of
transportation, the ferreting out of provisions in local markets,
the constant replacements of equipment damaged on the way
easily sent daily expenses skyrocketing. They also helped to create
a fluid way of life, an ever-changing sea through which the steward had to steer his way, snatching advantage from every shift of
wind and wave.

If this posed problems for an administrator, it must have been a
nightmare for the cook, rattled from kitchen to kitchen, and still
expected to get his dinner to the table more or less on time. He
and his assistants were usually sent on ahead of the main party,
with a cartload of equipment. In Bishop Swinfield's thirteenth-
century household, one of the kitchen boys had the special task of
packing up the pots and pans for such journeys.[140] This life on
the road, the handling and hauling of goods and chattels, the
rough conditions on the way, all demanded strength, agility, and
freedom of movement. Such requirements help to explain why
the kitchen staff of a large household was made up of men and
boys, not women.

The kitchens where the cooks were supposed to work their
miracles might be solid, commodious, and well-planned, or flimsy,

makeshift shacks, blown together at high speed for a special occasion. A wooden kitchen of this kind was erected at Westminster in 1273 for the coronation feast of Edward I. Tempers cannot have been sweetened, or dinners improved, at Oxford in 1232 when the whole kitchen put up for the king's visit whirled away in a gale.[141]

Such premises were regarded as occupational hazards by peripatetic cooks. The kitchens to be hoped for were sensible buildings, designed with some understanding of the work done inside them. There are scraps of evidence to suggest that some, at least, were planned with care. A successful one might serve as a model for others. In 1386, the man responsible for a new kitchen at King's Hall in Cambridge specified that it was to be built "of the same excellent timber in quality and workmanship as that of the kitchen at the Friars Preachers." When the Merchant Tailors' Company in London decided to build a kitchen in 1425, they paid 7s. 4d. to Goldyng Mapylton, a carpenter, for drawing up a diagram, and thoughtfully provided wine and ale for him and his colleagues while they brooded over the details.[142]

Certain features were to be looked for in the well-made kitchen. In the first place, some provisions were needed for the disposal of endless quantities of waste. "Out of sight, out of mind" was the golden rule. The thirteenth-century abbey at Furness, in Lancashire, had a chute through which everything hurtled into the stream below, and most respectable establishments had a drain. It was prudent to fit a grate over this, to catch bones and so on. Those who economized at this point paid the penalty of constantly blocked passages. At the Tower of London in 1313 four men spent a week "working on clearing and mending a drain from the great kitchen, which receives all the refuse from the kitchen and was stopped up and blocked with the same refuse." The Fellows of Canterbury College, Oxford, obviously learned their lesson, for in 1440 they paid to have both their sink cleaned and an iron grate set over the opening.[143]

Most kitchens had just a trodden-earth floor; those with the rare luxury of paving were much easier to keep clean. At Eltham in 1393, the floor was covered with "1,100 feet of the . . . stone called 'urnel.' "[144]

To provide plenty of light, windows were set in the walls, often placed rather high, above the fireplace level. Usually they were quite plain and utilitarian, but in the fourteenth-century abbot's kitchen at Glastonbury they were traceried, while at the grand townhouse, Coldharbor, in London, Herman Glasyer was paid in 1485 for "iii panys of Venys glasse sete in the kytchin wyndowes."[145]

Cooking produces heat and smoke and a consequent need for ventilation. The simplest way to provide this was to knock a hole in the roof, and there are many references to such smoke-holes. A barrel with both ends pushed out might then be placed over the gap as a further improvement, but it remained a poor, crude solution to the problem. The well-appointed kitchen had its own elaborate louver to do the job. The word louver comes from the French *l'ouvert* ("the open one"), and the structure sat like a lantern over the roof-hole. It was closed at the top, and the smoke escaped through openings on its sides. These could be fitted with slats, kept open in fine weather or closed with a tug on a string to keep out rain and snow. Such "louverstrynges for the kitchen" were bought at Clipstone in 1370.[146]

An icy wind whistling through the louver could be very disagreeable, and in 1369 at Eltham a weathercock was set up on the kitchen roof "to know how the wind lies." After a glance at this it was easy to adjust the slats, and decide which to keep open and which to shut.[147]

These slatted louvers were made of wood, but there were also pottery ones which could not be opened and shut, but made up in fun and fantasy what they lacked in convenience. Many were shaped into heads: a king, with smoke pouring out through his eyes and mouth; an Oxford student sticking out his tongue.[148] The handsome fourteenth-century louver dug up at Great Easton in Essex looks like a little castle, crowned with finials.[149]

The louver sat in the center of the kitchen roof, and originally it was placed directly over the fire, which was piled up in the middle of the floor, to keep it as far as possible from the walls. This was only prudent when the building was of wood, but gradually it was realized that fires could be made along the sides or in the wall-angles as long as a stone hearth and a stone reredos, or fireback, were provided. With these precautions, a number of fires might be in use at the same time, while the center of the kitchen was kept clear for other work and hurryings to and fro.[150] The fourteenth-century abbot's kitchen at Glastonbury is square on the outside, but is inside transformed into an octagon by its four angle fireplaces. Each fire had its own chimney; occasionally it is possible to glimpse a surviving example today. A fine thirteenth-century one still stands at Abingdon Abbey in Berkshire.

At first these were built with reckless bravado out of wood, but in the end caution prevailed. An early fourteenth-century ordinance of the city of London stipulated that all chimneys must be made of stone, tile, or plaster.[151]

Kitchens continued to be built of wood throughout the period, but householders who could afford it chose stone or brick as the safer materials. At Gainsborough Old Hall in the late fifteenth century, the hall was made of timber, but the kitchen of brick. The abbot's kitchen at Glastonbury and the monastery kitchen at Durham, both of the fourteenth century, have stone roofs, while at Lincoln Palace the roof was timbered and covered with lead.[152]

In early times, one large room held both kitchen and dining hall, but by the thirteenth century it was the custom, when money and space allowed, to separate the two, and so reduce the danger of fire and the nuisance of noise and smell. The process must have started somewhat earlier, for the beautiful, portly kitchen at Fontevrault built at the end of the twelfth century not only stands apart from the refectory, but has an assured sophisticated design, which suggests that it represents an advanced stage in a series of experiments.

By the end of the Middle Ages, anyone sufficiently prosperous had his kitchen separated in some way from the main hall. Sometimes it was completely detached, a building standing on its own; sometimes it was built on the end of the house and entered from a courtyard where goods could be delivered. The larger the household, the greater was the cluster of rooms or outhouses to supplement the kitchen: scullery, bakehouse, brewery, store rooms, pens for livestock, like the "little mew to keep poultry in" owned by a London merchant in the fourteenth century, or rooms "where fish is washed."[153] A late medieval kitchen with just such a group of service rooms still survives at Haddon Hall in Derbyshire.

Even in the small, modest houses where parish and chantry priests lived, although the kitchen, for lack of space, might be a part of the main building, it was at least divided from the dining hall by some kind of service corridor, and sometimes by a buttery and pantry as well. Indeed, rooms in such houses still in existence, now tentatively labeled "kitchen" by archaeologists, may in fact have been storerooms, while the real kitchen once stood detached, only to be destroyed or incorporated into the main structure in the course of centuries.[154]

Inside the house, a corridor ran from kitchen to hall. If the kitchen stood outside, some kind of covered passageway sheltered the servants and, rather more importantly, the hot food from the cold and wet. Often a table was set up here for last-minute touches to the food. At Prestbury, Bishop Swinfield's bailiff ordered one to be made for his master's visit, and at Gillingham in 1261 there was "a certain bench between the King's hall and kitchen, to arrange the king's dinner on."[155] Serving hatches were sometimes opened up between the hall and corridor: they may be seen still at Durham Castle and Hampton Court, while in an old plan of Christ Church, Canterbury, two are marked, and labeled "the window where dishes are served out," and "the window through which plates are put out for washing."[156]

A sufficiently large and important household might well have two kitchens, one to serve the main company, and one to delight the head of the house and favored friends. The splendid kitchen at Glastonbury did not cater for the monastery as a whole, only for the abbot and his guests. In 1490 a "privy kitchen" at Westminster is described as "the place where the chief cooks prepared delicious and elaborate dishes."[157]

Such a division of labor strongly suggests that diners might sit down together on the same occasion but not to the same menu. Just what they ate and how it was cooked will be considered in the next chapter.

# 5

# Methods and Menus

The character of a meal is shaped by many things, and the degree of pleasure with which it is received depends on circumstance. After a hard day's journey, once settled in temporary lodgings, anyone will be thankful for a hunk of bread and a slice of meat. In his chronicle for the year 1327 Froissart noted that on their forays into England, Scottish soldiers never bothered with pots and pans, but seemed content to ride with a bag of oatmeal and a flat stone strapped between the saddle and the saddle cloth. When they got tired of a diet of stolen cattle, they mixed up a paste of oatmeal and water and made little cakes, cooked on the stone among the campfire embers.[1] Hildebert, a twelfth-century illuminator who decorated a manuscript of St. Augustine's *De Civitate Dei,* drew a picture of his own studio on the last page. The table is spread for a working dinner, a large mouse has just managed to knock over a dish of chicken as he nibbles at a bun, and a maddened Hildebert is about to hurl a sponge at him, exclaiming: "Damn you, wretched mouse, for irritating me so often" (fig. 18).

Such makeshift meals play no part in this chapter and, as so often, the unfortunate poor are left to forage for themselves in the shadows of history. Instead, the cook of a prosperous household steps to center stage, and we will consider how he tried to please an employer who had money in his purse and provisions in his larder. What sort of dishes did he prepare when coaxed to put his best foot forward?

As the pages are turned of the few surviving English and French recipe books, all from the late fourteenth or fifteenth century, the first hurried impression is of color, complication, and cost. A pork pie has its pastry painted with saffron and baked to a deep gold; when cut open, the meat filling is revealed, patterned with gleaming black prunes and bright disks of hardboiled egg.

18. Interrupted Meal.
St. Augustine, *De Civitate Dei*, Bohemian, ca. 1140 (Prague, University Library, MS. Kap. AXXI, fol. 133r).

Jellied beef broth is transformed into a heraldic shield, graceful compliment to an honored guest: "Get from the spicer two ounces of turnsole and set it to boil [with the jelly] until it be of a good color. And if you would make armorial bearings on the jelly, take gold or silver, whichsoever pleaseth you best, and trace [your design] with the white of an egg on a feather, and put the gold thereon with a brush."[2] The merest hint of a sauce brings out the madman lurking in the medieval cook. With wild bravado he tips into the brew everything he can lay his hands on, from honey to fish stock, and scatters over all a riot of spices for good measure.

Such exuberance has unnerved the critics, and unsettled many a scholarly digestion. Richard Warner, who edited some early recipes in 1791, dismissed the medieval cook with magisterial disapproval: "Even in his [Richard II's] time we find French cooks were in fashion; and they appear to have equalled their descendants of the present day, in the variety of their condiments and in their faculty of disguising nature, and metamorphosing simple food into complex and non-descript gallimaufries."[3]

As he deplores, Warner pinpoints the very quality on which the cooks most prided themselves, "their faculty of disguising nature." In a time of plenty, anyone with means could eat a roast chicken. That was not worthy of comment. The only question of interest was how that plain dish could be glorified. A twelfth-century commentator, Ralph Diceto, tells us the way the people of Poitou liked their beef prepared: "The men of Poitou love beef for daily fare. When the pepper and garlic have been mixed together in a mortar, the fresh meat needs as a condiment either the juice of wild apples or that of young vine shoots, or grapes."[4]

Like other artists of the time, the cook was proud to call himself a maker, a craftsman. The medieval pleasure in particular skills, technical mastery, and dazzling virtuosity colored the belief that complication was an essential ingredient in elegant cookery.

From time to time, of course, as in all ages, noble attempts were made to praise the simple things of life. When the passion for pastoral themes touched the French court in the fourteenth century, Philippe de Vitry, Bishop of Meaux, wrote an immensely popular poem, *Franc Gontier,* on the weary life of the courtier and the pleasures of being a peasant. The courtier wastes away with worry, while healthy, hearty, Gontier and his love picnic on fruit and nuts: "They had garlic and onions, and crushed shallots on crusty black bread, with coarse salt to give them a thirst." A hundred years later, François Villon rudely brought readers down to earth and back to reality with his *Reply to Franc Gontier*: "Let them live on coarse black bread made with barley and oats, and drink water the whole year round. All the birds from here to Babylon would not make me accept such a diet for a single day—no, not for a single morning!"[5]

The truth is that every effort was made to get as far away as possible from peasant life and peasant tastes. To prefer black bread to white, raw salad to rich sauce, is a very modern whim. In all the medieval arts, the quality of the materials used and the sophistication of the techniques proclaimed the importance of the subject and the occasion. Gold, fine pigments, jewels, enamel, and ivory added their own tribute of precious beauty to God, saint, or patron. Just so, the cook paid homage with rare, expensive ingredients, daring combinations of the familiar and the exotic, mysterious, bewitching sauces. His aim was to send to table a dish transformed, by taste, texture, and appearance, into a work of art. If he had ever stopped to consider the matter, he might well have taken as his example and inspiration the Eucharistic wafer, whose fragile perfection is an exquisite refinement of the humble, homely bread Jesus broke at the Last Supper.

In an age of connoisseurs, when sharp attention was paid to the proper way of doing things, whether the job in hand was the composition of a letter or the disemboweling of a deer, it comes as no surprise to find that the cook performed his conjuring tricks for an audience both alert and well-informed. Our knowledge of medieval cookery would be painfully impoverished were it not for the recipes and helpful hints written down for his young bride at the very end of the fourteenth century by the prosperous, elderly man known to us today only by the title of his book, *The Goodman of Paris.*[6] Even the grave, scholarly Grosseteste, Bishop of Lincoln in the first half of the thirteenth century, was heard to remark that "pure pepper was better than ginger in a sauce,"[7] while Henry, Duke of Lancaster, one of the most powerful English noblemen in the fourteenth century, introduced two detailed recipes, for chicken broth and rosewater, into the book, *Le Livre de Seyntz Medicines,* which he wrote in 1354.[8]

In this, he meditates on the seven deadly sins, with special and engaging reference to his own lapses. As he considers gluttony, he lifts a corner of the curtain which hides the Middle Ages, and allows us a glimpse of the pleasures given by a satisfactory dinner. Every sense is excited: he loves the smell as much as the taste of good food; his feet "run towards banquets," and when he has no invitation himself, he relishes a blow-by-blow account of the menu from some lucky guest. Delightful as it is to discuss other people's dinner parties, it is even more fun to plan his own, to order rich foods and invent new sauces.[9]

Much as he deplores his own greediness, Henry stops far short of suggesting a complete ban on banquets for his soul's health. That comfortable concept, the Golden Mean, is his answer to the problem, and he considers it only fitting that lords should continue to feast in moderation "as their estate demands."[10] The principle of hierarchy embodied in this disarming little phrase runs like an underground stream through the period's ideas about cookery, and rises to the surface every now and then in a recipe or a remark. Just as there might be in a great household two separate kitchens, one for the king or abbot and one for the rest of the company, so at any medieval dinner party some guests were more equal than others. Not everybody got a taste of the special delicacies provided. In the written instructions for the waferer at the court of Edward IV, a distinction is made between those great men who eat wafers every day, and those lower down the scale who enjoy them only at the principal feasts of the year.[11] Even when everyone present tastes the same dish, the size of the helping depended critically on the rank of the guest. The guidelines are laid down in several recipes: "Serve the hole pik [whole pike] for a lord and quarto of a pik for comons"; "Take chekine chapped [chopped] for comons, for a lord tak hole chekins."[12]

Rank helped to determine the choice of ingredients. According to one authority, a bishop had a solemn duty to his flock to avoid that plebeian, useful filler, the dried bean: "By oft use thereof the wits are dulled. . . . Therefore Varro saith that the bishop should not eat beans."[13]

Wealth proved an even more decisive factor. Copho, a twelfth-century physician in Salerno, advised his colleagues to make up medicines for the rich from expensive spices, and from everyday herbs for the poor. He added this bland explanation: "We usually give things for things, and words for words. For empty words we give herbs from the hills in exchange, but for precious money we give spices."[14]

The same principle was applied to cookery. The concept of understated elegance was not one which came easily to the medieval mind, and a host liked to use expensive ingredients, and be seen to use them, as a compliment to his guests and a proof of his own prosperity. For the purposes of conspicuous consumption, spices were a godsend.

In the first place, they were luxuries. They were brought to Europe from the East, and the long journey itself pushed up the price. Weight for weight, they were easily the most precious items in the kitchen, and they were carefully stored away in locked boxes, like one which may be seen beside the cook on a misericord in St. George's Chapel, Windsor.

Costliness alone would have given them a certain glamour, but the strange remoteness of the lands from which they came added a special magic. Many stories told how they grew in the Paradise Garden itself, and from there floated down the Nile, to be caught in nets: "And it is said that these things came from the earthly paradise, just as the wind blows down the dry wood in the forests of our own land; and the dry wood of the trees in paradise that thus falls into the river is sold to us by the merchants."[15] Bartholomeus Anglicus, in the thirteenth century, dismissed such flights of fancy with a dour footnote: "These men do feign, to make things dear and of great price."[16]

There might be skepticism about the origins of the spices haggled over in the marketplace, but no medieval writer could imagine a paradise without a spice plant. Whether his blissful garden were for saints or lovers, the air would be sweet with the delicate, tantalizing scents of cinnamon and nutmeg, ginger and clove.[17] Such associations made it possible for spices to be sent as tokens of special love between even the most austere and self-denying friends. So Lul, a missionary in Germany in the year 745/46, packed up some pieces of cinnamon for his affectionate correspondent, the Abbess of Thanet, far away in England.[18] It is unlikely that these ascetic, enthusiastic followers of St. Boniface ever thought of brightening their diet with the spice; probably it was to be used as incense, an offering to God and a reminder of human affection.

In more worldly circles, spice became the perfect symbol of luxury and lordly magnificence. Henry V was heavily in debt to Richard Whittington, but when Whittington was made Lord Mayor of London, he invited the king to a great feast and there before the assembled guests not only burned the bonds, but burned them with a fine abandon in a fire of cinnamon and cloves. The king was heard to murmur, with feeling, "Never king had such a subject."[19] In a fifteenth-century romance, *The Squire of Low Degree,* a king offers his daughter every luxury he can think of, including an incense burner for her bedroom, to fill the air with spices so "that whan ye slepe the taste may come."[20]

Pleasant as it may have been to savor spices in a dream, it was even more satisfying to enjoy them while awake. It was fashionable to serve them on their own after the main dinner had been cleared away. In a substantial household, lucky guests retired to a private room to take a cup of wine and choose a favorite morsel from a selection of comfits. Because sugar itself was considered in the same category, the heading "spices for the chamber" covered whole spices and such luxurious sweetmeats as crystallized ginger and perfumed sugar pieces. For forty guests, at a dinner in late fourteenth-century Paris, the following provisions were made, with the note, "little was left of the spices": "Spices for the chamber, to wit candied orange peel, 1 lb. . . . Citron, 1 lb. . . . Red anise, 1 lb. . . . Rose-sugar, 1 lb. . . . white comfits, 3 lbs."[21] Served with these tidbits was hippocras, a red wine heavily sweetened and spiced. The flavorings were first steeped in the wine, and then the whole mixture was heated and strained. A variety of ingredients might be used, but the Goodman of Paris had firm ideas about the final result: "the sugar and the cinnamon ought to predominate."[22] On such occasions, a spice would be sucked and nibbled as a candy, and the pleasure was one to be lingered over: "when anyone eats spice, she should keep her mouth closed, so that the sweet smell and savour remain in the mouth."[23]

The cook used spices as a painter might, to decorate his dishes and change or enhance their color. A white chicken stew might taste delicious but look insipid; the eye needed a touch of brightness to break the monotony: "When you have served it forth, powder thereon a spice that is light red coriander and set pomegranate seeds with comfits and fried almonds round the edge of each bowl."[24]

Of all the colors, a deep rich yellow was the one most gratifying to the medieval diner, and the spice which made it possible was saffron, the dried stamens of the crocus. "*Geneste* [the name of a dish] is called *geneste* because it is as yellow as the flowers of broom [*geneste*] and it is yellowed with yolk of eggs and saffron and this is done in summer."[25] Everybody loved saffron. Even Welsh fairies thrived on it, according to the twelfth-century Giraldus Cambrensis, who tells a story of a boy who was taken to a fairy palace and found that the whole court "neither ate flesh nor fish, but lived on a milk diet, made up into messes with saffron."[26] At the end of *The Testament of Cresseid,* the late fifteenth-century poem by Henryson, Cresseid, a destitute leper, looks back to her days of glory as Troilus' lover and sadly contrasts the moldy bread in her begging bowl with the clean plates and saffron sauces she had once taken for granted.[27]

The saffron crocus was first found in Greece and Asia Minor, and throughout the medieval period the Levant was one of the main sources of supply. Western Europe, however, discovered that the plant would grow comfortably in many places much closer to home. Parts of Spain and Italy produced large quantities and England built up a thriving business from the fourteenth century on, after an enterprising British pilgrim "purposing to do good to his country," had smuggled a bulb out of the Levant by hiding it in his pilgrim's staff which, with an eye more to the main chance than to spiritual profit, "he had made hollow before of purpose."[28] As its name suggests, the town of Saffron Walden was once the center of the industry in Essex, and in gratitude for the wealth brought by the plant to its citizens, there are saffron flowers on an arch and some roof bosses in the nave of its parish church, built around 1495.[29]

Even more important than the color spice gave to a dish was the zest it added to the taste. Medieval palates responded to the tang of ginger and the subtleties of cinnamon like flowers to summer rain. It is hard to judge from surviving recipes how much of any one spice was added to a particular dish. Directions are terse: "caste therto powder Pepyr [ground pepper], Canel [cinnamon], Gyngere, Clowys powther [ground cloves] ."[30] Much was left to the cook's discretion, but account books suggest that he added his "pinch of this and pinch of that" with a heavy hand when given half a chance. The Goodman of Paris noted down what had to be bought for a dinner party with forty guests, and even though certain sauces were ordered ready-made, the following quantities of spices were needed: "One lb. of powdered colombine ginger. . . . Half a lb. of ground cinnamon. . . . 2 lb. of lump sugar. . . . One oz. of saffron. . . . A quarter lb. of cloves and grain of Paradise mixed. . . . Half a quarter lb. of long pepper. . . . Half a quarter lb. of galingale. . . . Half a quarter lb. of mace. . . . Half a quarter lb. of green bay leaves."[31] In such amounts, it seems unlikely that any spice could sink without trace into the dish it was supposed to flavor, but the Goodman liked to make doubly sure that no pungency was lost in the cooking by adding spices to his soups at the last possible moment.[32]

Of all the spices available, pepper was one of the most popular and least expensive. It grew in India and Ceylon, and Europe could not get enough of it. Even the poor man dreamed of peppered chops, and no merchant ever had difficulty in getting rid of his stock. In the mid-fifteenth century an Italian guide for businessmen was drawn up, with the title "How to Know Many Wares." It listed the points to be looked for when picking out the best quality spices, and discussed the fine art of calculating the size of the market, to avoid the twin disasters of missed sales or expensive goods left on the shelf. Years of experience were needed to gauge the demand for rhubarb; pepper was the beginner's dream: "Of pepper, and other similar things that are easy to sell you can buy any quantity."[33] Some idea of the enthusiasm for this seasoning may be gathered from the fact that two fifteenth-century chantry priests in Bridport, Dorset, living modestly with a servant and one or two guests each week, were allowed half a pound of pepper as part of their annual salary, and yet sometimes had to buy more out of their own pockets.[34]

The tears pepper brought to the eyes could be produced just as enjoyably and even less expensively by the mustard seed. As the plant grew easily in Europe it was the poor man's spice, and used with a loving, lavish hand. Medieval palates were hardened but, as always, some were tougher than others. The French court poet Eustache Deschamps (1346–1407) wrote a passionate protest about the rigors of eating in Hainaut and Brabant. Mustard dogged his every mouthful: "I never ate or drank without it. They mix it with the water they boil the fish in, and I know that they have the dripping from the roast thrown into the mustard and mixed up with it . . . There you will have for your use, always— without asking—mustard."[35]

Even mustard might be beyond some pockets, but there was a large group of vegetables ready to satisfy the craving for strong flavor and bewitching smell. Onions, garlic, leeks, and chives were plentiful and cheap, and all did trojan service in medieval kitchens. Everyone could afford them and everyone used them, just as they are used today—fried, stewed, or eaten raw with cheese. So much pounding of garlic for sauces went on that it inspired a proverb, "the mortar always smells of garlic."[36]

Few could resist the familiar yet exciting taste. Cuthbert, the seventh-century Northumbrian saint, allowed himself to nibble raw onions during his last, severe fast. When his monks landed on the Farne island to find him dying, and were shocked to see no food of any kind lying in his room, he turned back the coverlet of his bed to show them his little hoard of five onions, one half-eaten, four still untouched.[37]

Self-denying saints are rarely gourmets; more sophisticated diners sometimes squirmed under the onion's tyranny. Francesco, a highly successful Italian merchant in fourteenth-century Avignon, wrote to his family in Prato, announcing his return and laying down a few ground rules for his welcome-home party: "Place not garlic before me, or leeks, or roots. Let it seem a Paradise to me. . . . "[38] In fifth-century France, Sidonius Apollinaris, a bishop who looked back with longing to the civilized life of Rome before her fall yet managed to make friends with the rough, half-savage Burgundians who overran his diocese, wrote a rueful poem on his new, large, onion-chewing masters:

> Wouldst know what terrifies my Muse,
> What is it she complains on?
> How can she write a six foot line
> With seven feet of patron?
> O happy eyes! O happy ears!
> Too happy, happy nose,
> That smells not onions all day long,
> For whom no garlic grows!"[39]

Such rebellious murmurs may be heard from time to time throughout the period, but the onion remained king of the kitchen garden.

More subtle smells and savors are added to a dish by herbs, and of these there was a very wide choice. Under the heading "Herbys to make bothe sauce and sewe [stew]" eighty-six plants are listed in an English mid-fifteenth-century treatise on gardening.[40] One or two of these, like lettuce and radish, would be placed now in a salad section; daffodils, roses, foxgloves, and lilies would be in the flower border. Such exclusions still leave a formidable selection, ranging from the familiar mint and thyme to mouse-ear, adder's-tongue, and the polypody fern. Moreover, the author clearly felt he could have added to his list, had there been space and time:

> Furthermore wul y noght go
> But here of herbys wul y ho.[41]

Many hints suggest the pleasure these plants gave, as their fragrances were enjoyed, their leaves nibbled and rubbed between the fingers. At the great mansion of Coldharbour in London, a workman was paid in 1485 to set up two iron stands for pots of herbs, not in the kitchen but in a private chamber.[42] Even St. Francis, that most austere of saints, suddenly took a fancy to a sprig of parsley as he lay dying, and permitted himself to ask for one.[43] Whether herbs lent much prestige to the table is another matter. In any competition with spices they suffered from being too common, too easily grown, too cheap. They flourished everywhere, and could be taken for granted. In his account of a luxurious feast enjoyed by the monks of Canterbury in Kent, in 1179, Giraldus Cambrensis describes the variety of drinks served, and makes an interesting comparison. There were "beverages so choice that beer, such as is made at its best in England and above all in Kent, found no place among them. There beer among other drinks is as potherbs are among made dishes."[44]

The wording here suggests that Giraldus was thinking of herbs as salad materials, and in this form they were at a special disadvantage in the eyes of the sophisticated: they were uncooked, and inevitably, therefore, less interesting than a "made dish." Salads were certainly eaten, and doubtless enjoyed, but may have seemed too close for comfort to peasant simplicities or monastic austerities. For most people, a little salad went a long way. Peter of Blois, expelled from Sicily in 1168, found the island's passion for raw vegetables deplorable: "Your people err in the meagreness of their diets; for they live on so much celery and fennel that it constitutes almost all their sustenance; and this generates a humour which putrefies the body and brings it to the extremes of sickness and death."[45] His suspicion is echoed by the proverb quoted in Cotgrave's *Dictionarie* (1611) under *salade,* "a Sallet without wine is raw, unwholesome, dangerous."

The best hope for turning such a simple dish into a connoisseur's delight was to make the combination of ingredients as interesting and unusual as possible and to concoct a delicious dressing. The choice of herbs and vegetables, as we have seen, was very wide, and the selection adventurous. One very pretty salad was made from violet petals, onions, and lettuce, while a fifteenth-century list of herbs "for a salade" includes parsley, mint, cress, primrose buds, daisies, dandelions, rocket, red nettles, borage flowers, red fennel, and chickweed.[46] It was considered polite to pool resources, and a twelfth-century English recluse, Christina of Markyate, was deeply offended by a neighbor's churlishness: "For a time she would eat nothing from the garden next door because the owner, out of miserliness, had denied her a sprig of chervil when she had recently asked for it."[47] A late fourteenth-century salad of parsley, sage, garlic, onions, leek, borage, mint, fennel, cress, rue, and rosemary was served with the classic dressing used today: oil, vinegar, and salt.[48]

In cooked dishes, herbs were used as a flavoring and for decoration. A favorite dish at Easter, when eggs came into their own again and plants were young and flourishing, was a tansy. For this, tansy leaves were pounded in a mortar and their juice added to beaten eggs to make an omelet with a tart, distinctive flavor.[49] Boiled pork might be served with a green sauce made from sage, hardboiled eggs, pepper, ginger, salt, and vinegar; a capon could be stuffed with parsley, sage, hyssop, rosemary, and thyme. An all-white pudding made from almond cream and sugar was decorated with borage leaves; meatballs were rolled in parsley to make them green.[50]

It is difficult and perhaps unnecessary to distinguish herbs from vegetables in medieval cookery. The demarcation lines were faint, and indeed all kinds of edible plants were gathered together under an umbrella noun, *wort*. Many satisfying dishes were created by combining every scrap of greenstuff that lay to hand. A mixture which included cabbage, beets, borage, violets, mallows, parsley, betony, the white part of leeks, and the tops of young nettles was blanched, drained, finely chopped, and added to a hare stew. The hare itself was optional; it was pointed out that the recipe would work just as well with a goose "or eny other fresh flessh."[51]

In many recipes there is heartening evidence of care to enrich the vegetables and get rid of as much water as possible. One, for "Buttered Wortes," calls for "al maner of good herbes that thou may gete," to be cooked in water and "clarefied buttur a grete quantite."[52] In another, for cabbages, the leaves are washed, blanched, drained, and chopped. After these preliminaries, the cooking is continued in meat broth, with one or two marrow bones added for extra succulence. Before serving, the purée is thickened with bread crumbs, salted, and colored with saffron.[53]

A list of seeds bought for King John of France in 1360 while he was a prisoner in England gives some idea of the plants considered to be necessary staples of a kitchen garden. It is headed by those standbys of every household, cabbage, onions, and leeks, and these are followed by lettuce, mountain spinach, and one or two herbs, parsley, hyssop, borage, purslain, and garden cress.[54] The only other vegetable on the list is beet, and it is probable that this was grown for its leaves rather than its root.[55] Other root vegetables—turnips, carrots, and radishes—were known and sometimes used, but probably did not appear on the table with the same regularity as cabbages and onions. One of the least familiar was the carrot, to judge by the explanatory note the Goodman of Paris felt it necessary to add for his young bride: "Carrots be red roots which be sold in handfuls in the market, for a silver penny a handful."[56] Radishes were eaten raw, with salt, while turnips were topped and tailed, then simmered slowly in water or broth, as they are today. To make them a little special, they might be sliced and fried after this first cooking, and flavored with spice, or preserved in honey.[57]

Flowers were used not only for decoration, but also for cooking. A dish of meatballs might be sent to table, each topped with a sprig of flowers; violet petals were first boiled, drained, and ground in a mortar and then stirred into a sweetened milk pudding. A more daring color combination was suggested in another recipe, when violet petals were added to a saffron-tinted pudding, and then fresh violets scattered over the golden surface. Roses, hawthorn, and primroses could be used in the same ways.[58]

Flower petals lent their own special fragrance to drinks. Carnations, with their delicious, spicy scent, were most often used like this; one of their pet names, indeed, was "sops in wine." They were associated with high festivity and flirtation, and in Spenser's *Shepheardes Calender* there is a call for

> ... Coronations, and Sops in Wine,
> worne of Paramoures.[59]

During a tavern scene in the fifteenth-century play *Mary Magdalen,* the heroine, naturally before her conversion, flirts with a dashing and deplorable young man called Curiosity, and as they dance he whispers in her ear, "Soppes in wyne, how love ye?" and she replies provocatively, "as ye don [do], so doth me."[60]

At more serious moments in life, herbs and flowers were valued for their medicinal properties and used in a whole series of cordials and syrups. In one manuscript of Froissart's *Chronicle* a story is told about the Siege of Rennes in 1357. The English, besieging the town, were camped in the countryside, matters were at a standstill, and everyone was bored. To while away an hour or two, a young knight, John of Bolton, challenged one of the town's defenders, Olivier de Mauny, to a duel. The fight began in high spirits, but ended with John defeated and taken into Rennes as a prisoner. His captor, Olivier, was himself seriously wounded and needed some herbs for medicines, but could not ride out beyond the city gate. He hit upon the idea of putting John on his horse and sending him back to the English camp to arrange a safe conduct. This was agreed to, so Olivier was carried out of Rennes, to be royally received and expertly nursed back to health by the English commander, Henry of Lancaster, with soldiers scouring the district for the necessary herbs. Everyone behaved beautifully, and the story ends with Olivier, restored to perfect health, riding back to Rennes without his prisoner; as a gesture of gratitude he had left John behind, a free man. Henry of Lancaster was heard to murmur that his guest was remarkable: "In return for my safe conduct and a few herbs he will give up a prisoner who could pay ransom of 10,000 moutons d'or."[61]

Dried peas and beans made substantial dishes. Like potatoes today, they added warm, comforting bulk to a meal, and were usually cooked slowly to a purée which might be thickened still more with bread crumbs or egg yolks. Crumbs, of course, were cheaper, and one cooking book gives two versions of the same recipe; "yonge pessene" (for every day) with bread, and "yonge pessen ryalle" (for a special occasion) with eggs. In the first, peas are simmered for a while in water and drained. One half is then set to cook in beef broth, while the other is pounded to pulp in a mortar, with bread, parsley, hyssop, and a dash of salt added to the pot. In the second, everything has become more expensive. Again the peas are divided, and while one half is pounded with herbs and a little bread, the other is cooked not just in a spoonful or two of broth but with a whole rabbit to add extra richness. The stew is then thickened with egg yolks, flavored with sugar or honey, and colored with saffron.[62]

Usually these vegetables are cooked in meat or fish broth, sometimes with a few onions added, but occasionally they are made into a sweet pudding. In one recipe, white beans were first steeped in water and then simmered in milk and honey. Salt was added before the dish was served, but perhaps only a touch, to sharpen the flavor.[63]

A favorite dish was peas or beans with bacon, made very much as it is today. The peas were first softened in water, then drained, and the cooking continued in bacon broth. Toward the end, a piece of bacon was added to the pot. In the final instructions, the medieval regard for finish and appearance peeps out: "When you take the bacon out of the peas, you ought to wash it in the sewe [broth] of the meat, so that it be . . . not covered with bits of the peas."[64]

Like herbs and vegetables, fruit was enjoyed but taken for granted in sophisticated circles. Native varieties were contentedly consumed without fanfare, being too abundant for their presence on the table to be noted with gratifying envy. Exotic and expensive fruits from far away were quite another matter. Dried currants, raisins, dates, and figs were fairly familiar because they were imported for winter and particularly for Lent, but oranges and lemons were rarities. The wife of Edward I, Eleanor of Castile, perhaps dreaming of home, bought fifteen lemons and seven oranges from a Spanish ship which docked in Portsmouth in 1290; Bishop Swinfield's steward solemnly recorded the purchase of lemons at Ledbury for the Christmas festivities of 1289.[65] They must have become a little more plentiful by the fifteenth century, because they entered into a disgruntled schoolboy's dream of revenge: "My Father sent my brother and me C C wardens [pears]. While I was absent my brother hath chosyn the beste and lefte me the worst. But I am sure my father wyll sende us pomgarnettes other orynges yf ther be eny to be solde. Then I shall serve hym lykewyse."[66] Even so they were still considered expensive luxuries. At the very end of the century a London draper courted a wealthy widow and was outraged when she still refused to marry him after three years of homage and an endless stream of presents. He brooded over his accounts and calculated that he had spent six pounds on the siege, frittered away on "diverse deyntees as ffiges & reisin, dates, almonds, prunes . . . pomegranats and orangs."[67]

The taste for fruit began in childhood. Henry of Lancaster only borrowed a comparison often drawn in devotional literature when he contrasted adult greed with the outlook of a child who "prefers a red apple to the riches of three kingdoms."[68] In the fifteenth century, the poet Lydgate looked back to his boyhood and remembered how he

> Ran into gardeynes, apples ther I stall [stole];
> To gadre frutes, spared nedir [neither] hegge nor wall,
> To plukke grapes in other mennes vynes
> Was more redy, than for to sey matynes.[69]

Walter of Bibbesworth in the thirteenth century provides a charming, step-by-step account of how to prepare an apple for a very small child. First the stalk is pulled off, then the skin peeled. After the flesh has been eaten, the pips are taken from the core and planted outside, just as they might be in a kindergarten class today.[70]

Fruit was associated with informal pleasures. Certain kinds of apple and pear could be kept for the winter, and one of the amusements on long, dark evenings was to roast them in the ashes of the fire: "Ye be welcome. Wyll it please youe to sytt or stonde be the fyre a litell while? The nyghtes be prety and colde now. A roste apple ye shall have, and fenell seede. Mor we wyl not promyse youe."[71] Chaucer evokes the irresistible fragrance of the storeroom when he describes the breath of Alison in *The Miller's Tale* as sweet as "hoord of apples leyd in hey."[72]

The account books of royal households indicate the determination of those who could afford it to gratify their taste for fruit. While Henry III traveled home to London across France in 1223, apples, pears, and nuts were delivered at every stop. In 1292/93 Edward I was at Berwick, and two cartloads of apples and pears were ordered for the King from Nicholas the fruiterer.[73] Among the duties of the officers in Edward IV's confectionery department in the fifteenth century was the organization of a steady flow of provisions from the royal gardens: "cheryez, perez, apples, nuttes, greete and smalle for somer season; and lenton wardens, quinces, and other."[74]

In this handful of references apples and pears are mentioned more often than any other kind of fruit. Only twentieth-century, urban man would leave the matter there; the medieval connoisseur would raise his eyebrows in disbelief at such crudity. His mind would turn to many beautiful types, each with its own season, its own special uses, its own special name. Among apples there were costards, pomewaters, ricardons, blaundrelles, and bittersweets; among pears, the caillou, the regul, pas-pucelles, and gold knopes.[75] Of all pears, the best-known was the wardon, a kind which ripened late, cooked well, and could be stored throughout the winter. Three gold pears on a silver field made up the arms of the Cistercian abbey of Wardon in Bedfordshire, and it has been suggested that the pear was first developed there, but no more than a heraldic pun may have been intended, just as the chantry chapel in Wells Cathedral, built in 1485–90 to honor Dr. Sugar, is decorated with shields bearing the device of three little sugar loaves under a doctor's cap.[76] The name may refer simply to the pear's keeping quality, and be derived from the verb *ward*, meaning to guard, protect, preserve.

Another standby of winter menus was the quince, but summer fruits do not appear often in the recipe books, although there are plenty of references to them elsewhere. Cherries were much loved, and Lydgate in one of his poems mentions the cry of strawberry-sellers in London.[77] Chaucer lists the plum among "homly" (familiar) trees in his translation of *The Romaunt of the Rose* (ll.1373–75). Medlars, mulberries, gooseberries, and peaches all crop up from time to time in a poem, an account book, or a garden list. In 1970, a kernel tentatively identified as that of a greengage was found embedded in a fifteenth-century building in Hereford. Before this discovery, it had been thought that the greengage was introduced to England from France at a much later date. The building where the stone was found stood next to the bishop's garden, and as several bishops of Hereford traveled to France on business in the fourteenth and fifteenth centuries, it may be that one of them brought back a slip of the tree from a host's garden.[78] The fifteenth-century garden of the Grocers' Hall in London contained one fig tree, some whortleberries, a small vineyard, and a melon bed, besides lavender bushes, roses, archery butts, and "six water potts of tyn for byrds to drynke of."[79] No wonder so many medieval gardens had pet names like "Le Joye."

The fact that many kinds of fruit are mentioned in records but used only rarely in recipe books suggests that people did not lose their childhood taste for raw fruit. Certainly happy greed shines through every line written on the subject by Friar Felix Fabri, a fifteenth-century pilgrim to the Holy Land from Ulm in Germany. On leaving Gaza, he and his companions sank their teeth into pomegranates, "big, and fresh as fresh"; in Cairo he discovered the banana: "The fruit does not grow each one by itself but twenty or more grow in one bunch like many grapes in one. They are pale gold in colour. . . . Of this fruit I ate to satiety."[80]

As in every period, those who wrote on the theory of diet took a gloomy pleasure in pointing out the dangers of this carefree approach. Raw fruit was unwholesome, the boiling of strawberries recommended.[81] Cotgrave in his *Dictionarie* (1611) records, under "*poire*," a proverb which sums up the prevailing view: "After a [cold] Peare Wine, or the Priest." There must have been much satisfied head-shaking by the experts over such incidents as the violent illness of King John after an orgy of peaches and ale.[82]

Although the references to fruit in recipes are infrequent, the uses found for them are varied. Rich, red mulberries often colored a dish. In one, a mixture of ground veal, bread crumbs, and egg yolks was flavored with sugar and spice and dipped in mulberry juice before serving.[83] The medieval palate enjoyed a sweet-sour tang to meat dishes, and many sauces and stuffings were devised to whet this appetite. A piece of fresh pork was simmered until tender, then skinned, boned, and chopped small. To this was added a handful of raisins, cut-up figs, bread crumbs, sugar, saffron, and salted pork fat. The mixture was bound together with egg yolks and milk and then stuffed into a whole pig, which was sewn up, roasted on a spit, and served with a ginger sauce.[84] A sauce for a young capon might be made in summer from cherries and quinces, simmered in mulberry wine with cinnamon, and thickened with bread crumbs or egg yolks; in late autumn, wild sloes were substituted for the cherries.[85]

Most recipes for fruit desserts call for long, slow stewing or baking, but in one or two fruit is fried or spit-roasted. To brighten a dull day in Lent, *Lente ffrutours* might be tried. Apples were peeled, sliced, dipped in batter, fried in oil, and sprinkled with sugar.[86] Spit-roasting demanded finer judgment. Dates, figs, raisins, and blanched almonds were strung alternately with a needle on to a thread "of a mannys length" and the string was wound round a spit and set over the fire. A batter spiced with ginger, sugar, saffron, and cloves was beaten up, not too thin, not too thick, but just so it would stick to the fruit. A dish was placed beneath the spit, to catch the drips, and then the cook was ready to begin. As the spit turned, the batter was poured over the fruit, spoon by spoon, "so longe til the frute be hidde in the batur." When crisp, golden perfection had been achieved, the string was removed from the spit and cut up into short lengths, of which one or two pieces were placed in each dish and served "al hote."[87]

Fruit baked whole in the oven was usually set not in a dish but a pastry case, referred to, disconcertingly, as a coffin. Quinces or pears were peeled, cored, and filled with sugar or honey and ground ginger, placed two or three to a coffin, and slipped into the oven.[88]

Apples might be simmered until tender and then sieved to make a fine, smooth purée which was mixed with almond milk, honey, and a dash of salt, thickened with bread crumbs, and colored with saffron and sandalwood. The whole was then quickly heated before serving. In another recipe, raw apple is chopped finely and added to a cooked rice pudding, which is sweetened, spiced, and colored with saffron.[89] Today, applesauce is eaten with meat and the contrasting flavors mingle in the mouth; in one medieval recipe the two are combined in the cooking itself. An apple purée is thinned with meat broth, to be served as a soup, colored with saffron and flavored with sugar and spice.[90]

A stiff quince preserve, called *cotignac,* is still made in France. It dates back at least to the medieval period, and recipes for it appear in the fourteenth- and fifteenth-century cookery books that have survived. Quinces were pared, cored, and simmered in red wine until quite soft. They were then pounded smooth in a mortar, mixed with honey, and set on the fire again to thicken. This stage was tiring, for the pot had to be stirred all the time to prevent sticking, and the mixture had to be so reduced that when cold it could be cut into slices. Once the right consistency had at last been reached, spices were added and the whole left to stiffen in a box. At this point the writer adds an approving note: "And hit is comfortable for a mannys body, and namely fore the Stomak."[91]

Wardon pears could be transformed into a very thick purée by cooking them in wine, straining away the liquid, and pounding the flesh in a mortar. This pulp was returned to the pot with sugar or honey and cinnamon and boiled for a while. After the mixture had cooled a little, it was thickened still more with egg yolks and given an extra bite with a touch of ginger. A note at the end of the recipe suggests the final consistency desired: "And serve hit forth in maner of Ryse [rice]." A simple recipe for stewed pears is still familiar today. Each fruit is cut in two and simmered in red wine with sugar, cinnamon, ginger, and a pinch of saffron for extra color. The writer's comment here sums up the aim of the medieval cook: "Loke that hit be poynante [sharp] and also doucet [sweet]."[92] A more festive treatment calls for whole pears, first cooked, then pared, and carefully cored from the base, leaving on the stalks. Each pear is filled with a mixture of spices, then the flesh is lightly scored, so that when the fruit is rolled in spice the powder will cling to the sides. After this the stalks are gilded with the finest gold leaf and the pears set upright in a coffin on a bed of thick almond cream.[93]

It may be gathered from this selection that most recipes used fruit available in the winter: apples, pears, quinces, raisins, figs, and dates. This suggests that summer varieties were treated very simply, perhaps eaten raw in defiance of the dietitians. When the officers of the London Goldsmiths' Company gave a select supper party in the summer of 1497, strawberries were on the menu; the entry reads "Strawberries with sugar."[94] Another recipe tells a different story. In this, the strawberries are washed in red wine and strained. Then they are simmered in almond milk thickened with flour, to which are added raisins, saffron, pepper, sugar, ginger, cinnamon, and galingale. A little fat is stirred in and the flavor sharpened with vinegar. The pudding is colored with alkanet (a red dye obtained from a plant root) and decorated with pomegranate seeds. Only then is it ready to be carried to the table, metamorphosis having been triumphantly achieved.[95] Strawberries were used as a sweet-sour grace note in a spiced custard tart with beef marrow and dates, "And streberies, if hit be in time of yere."[96]

The grape is in a category of its own for it is both eaten as a fruit and turned into wine. Its history in Britain is long but checkered. When the Romans first conquered the island they imported their wine, but in A.D. 280 the Emperor Probus gave permission for vines to be planted in Britain. Appropriately enough, in the early sixteenth century a terra cotta medallion bust of Probus was placed in the Vyne, a Tudor mansion built in a part of Hampshire called on Roman maps Vindomis, "the house of wine."[97] Lines of vine stalks have been found on a slope facing south and west near the Roman villa at Boxmoor in Hertfordshire. Interest in wine doubtless languished during the upheavals after the departure of the Romans, but the coming of Christianity in the sixth century brought with it a need of wine for mass. The Saxons planted many vineyards, and indeed Bede, in the eighth century, mentions grapes in his survey of Britain's natural resources.[98] Wealthy households drank wine regularly, long before the Conquest of 1066, while after that date the Normans brought with them fond memories of vineyards at home and a determination to plant new ones in Britain.

Right up to the fourteenth century the vine flourished in England, mainly in the south and west but also in one brave outpost as far north as Askham, near York. The vale of Gloucester was locally, if not internationally, famous for its grapes, and Ely was affectionately called by the Normans "*l'Isle des Vignes.*"[99]

For all this gallant show, Britain was situated very close to the northern limits of the region in which the vine could live comfortably. In the fourteenth century there was a slight but perceptible shift in climate, to colder and wetter summers, and the growing of vines on a large scale became a much less attractive proposition.[100]

The decision to let vineyards decay and disappear was made considerably less painful by the fact, plain to the knowledgeable for several hundred years, that from the British grape came only

British wine. Patriots like William of Malmesbury in the twelfth century might stoutly maintain that the wines of Gloucester "do not offend the mouth with sharpness since they do not yield to the French in sweetness";[101] foreigners had more stringent standards. Peter of Blois in the same century noted sourly that English wine "ought to be sieved rather than drunk," while in the next an Italian, Salimbene, kindly observed: "We must forgive the English if they are glad to drink good wine when they can, for they have but little wine in their own country."[102]

He was quite right. The English were indeed glad to drink good wine, and made every effort to do so. Native wines offered poor competition to foreign ones, and the owners of vineyards were the first to acknowledge it. In the early fourteenth century the Earl of Lincoln owned several plantations scattered over England, including one on his London estate at Holborn, but bought large quantities of wine for his own household from the Rhineland, Rochelle, and Gascony.[103] Wines had been imported into England from Roman times and their excellence was savored. Medieval palates loved the sweet, heavy wines from Greece and Cyprus, but the largest quantity of wine for England came from France, and in particular from Gascony, which had become, most conveniently, an English possession in 1152 and remained in English hands until 1453.

Despite vast expense, dangers and delays, interruptions by war, piracy, and bad weather, the trade was carried on with zeal. The arrangements for transportation from France to England were complicated enough, and even when the tuns had been safely landed the problems of distribution inland were still formidable. Carriage by cart over rough roads was slow, expensive, and hard on the wine, and so wherever possible a smoother ride by inland waterways was chosen. For example, wine shipped to Bristol would be unloaded and set on a boat to be taken by river as far as Worcester, and only then put on carts for the last stage to Warwick and Coventry. It is a measure of the enthusiast's determination that Richard Beauchamp, Earl of Warwick (1389–1439), once worked out a plan for making the river navigable right up to his own castle gate, to insure that supplies glided in for his banquets in the best condition possible.[104] Political distractions prevented him from perfecting the details and carrying out the scheme.

Foreign connoisseurs might sneer at British winemanship; native apologists could find a crumb of comfort in the knowledge that there was at least one country where palates were even less demanding. Wine shipped from Bristol to Ireland usually bore the label "not drinkable in England."[105] Stern measures were taken to make sure that standards were maintained if not improved. In 1364, a London taverner convicted of selling unsound wine was condemned to drink one beakerful from the barrel, have the rest poured over his head, and lose his license.[106]

Despite the decay of large vineyards in the fourteenth century, there were still plenty of grapes in church and private gardens throughout the rest of the medieval period. In the year 1395, Froissart strolled in Sir Richard Stury's garden at Eltham, down vine-shaded paths; in fifteenth-century London vines grew in that garden belonging to the Grocers' Company, mentioned earlier, and each liveryman was allowed two or three clusters of fruit a day while they were ripe.[107]

Grapes had varied uses in cooking, but all with one common purpose: to give a sweet-sharp piquancy to a dish. Grapes were often added to a stuffing. One, for a goose or capon, called for a mixture of parsley, sage, hyssop, and suet soaked for a short time in broth, combined with the yolks of hardboiled eggs, chopped onions, spices, salt, and grapes.[108] In this case the stuffed bird was roasted, but in another, chickens were stuffed simply, with herbs and grapes, and simmered in broth colored a rich gold with saffron.[109] In yet a third, the stuffing was transformed into a sauce. Parsley, grapes, garlic, and salt were put inside a goose, and once the bird was roasted these, by then deliciously flavored with meat juices, were drawn out, pounded in a mortar with three hardboiled egg yolks, thinned with verjuice, and spooned over the goose just before serving.[110]

Verjuice, as the word suggests, was the juice of green, unripe fruit, most often grapes but sometimes crabapples. It had a very sharp, tart, mouth-puckering taste and was one of the cook's most trusted standbys. Undrinkable on its own, in combination with bland ingredients it provided that undercurrent of tingling excitement which made the diner smile with satisfaction. It found its way into innumerable sauces, of which just one will stand as an example. A bream was grilled on a gridiron, and while it cooked a thin sauce was prepared from verjuice, wine, ginger, and salt, simmered together, and poured over the bream just as it was carried into the dining hall.[111]

Wine itself was very often used in cookery, and though careful emphasis was placed in recipes on the need for "good wine" it seems likely that the fine, expensive imports were kept firmly under the butler's eye and the native products considered quite satisfactory for the purpose. The celebration of mass also required wine made to the specifications of the Church rather than the connoisseur, and whenever possible this was supplied by British vineyards. Grapes were grown near the church of St. Mary at Westley Waterless in Cambridgeshire, and scrawled on a wall of the church is a note of the bunches of fruit harvested one year in the early fourteenth century: "From the clusters dedicated to God, first vine—8, second vine—2," and so on, down to the last, "eleventh vine—7."[112]

Nuts were used lavishly at every stage in a recipe. They yielded the oil in which other ingredients could be fried, and they decorated the finished masterpiece. A mock-hedgehog, ingeniously fashioned from a pig's belly, stuffed with meat and spice and roasted on a spit, made its appearance on the table bristling with fried almonds.[113] Less ambitiously, fried almonds, glistening brown, were scattered over a white rice pudding, but blanched almonds were specified for a pale purée of ground chicken and ground nuts.[114] In this case the cook may have been interested not so much in a contrast of color as in a change of texture between the soft meat pudding and the firm, crisp nut. Both effects were achieved in another recipe, this time for a pork pudding. After ground pork, ground blanched almonds, and rice flour had been simmered together, chopped fried almonds were stirred into the mixture, which was then spooned onto a dish and decorated with powdered ginger and more nuts.[115]

The same attention to contrasts of color and texture is shown in a recipe for a pork pie. The pastry case was filled with ground pork which was bound with egg and colored with saffron and other spices. Into this golden mixture were set black prunes, the bright yolks of hardboiled eggs, and dark brown, fried pine nuts and raisins. Before the pie was set in the oven its lid of pastry was painted a rich yellow with egg and saffron.[116]

The Goodman of Paris has an irresistible recipe for a nut sweetmeat. New nuts, picked before St. John's Day (24 June), were peeled, pricked, and set to soak in water for nine days, the water being changed each day. They were then drained and dried and the prick-holes filled with tiny scraps of ginger and cloves. After this they were boiled in honey and the whole sweet, sticky, fragrant mixture put in a pot and stored for some special occasion and very lucky guest.[117]

Ground nuts were sometimes used to give body to a sauce. That dreariest item on a Lent menu, the stockfish, was cheered up with a sauce made from ground walnuts, garlic, pepper, salt, and bread crumbs, thinned with the fish broth; for boiled capon a sauce of verjuice, ginger, and ground blanched almonds was suggested.[118]

Almonds formed the base of two items mentioned again and again in recipe books, almond cream and almond milk. To make the cream, blanched almonds were ground and some water added to them. One version of the recipe helpfully specifies that the mixture should be "akurd thick," as solid as milk curds. This was then put on the fire and stirred as it came to the boil and thickened. The pot was emptied on to an outstretched cloth held above a bowl, and the underside of the cloth stroked with a ladle, to draw off most of the excess liquid. Then the corners of the cloth were gathered up and this improvised bag hung up for an hour or two to allow the last drops to drain away. What remained was a pale, soft, plump sausage which might be sprinkled with sugar, decorated with red anise or green borage leaves, and carried in to the expectant guests.[119]

As the name suggests, almond milk was a thinner, less extravagant creation than the cream. The ground nuts were steeped in any liquid, water, wine, ale, broth of meat or fish, to make a "milk" whose consistency varied from "thryfty," or thin, to "good and styffe," depending on the amount of almonds used. This might be spiced or sugared and served on its own as a soup, with crisp, twice-toasted bread.[120] More often it was one of many ingredients in a recipe. A savory pudding might be made from ground capon, boiled rice, and almond milk, or spiced meatballs set in a sauce of almond milk thickened with rice. A sweet, spiced pudding of rice cooked in almond milk was first simmered and then divided into three parts: one left white, the next made yellow with saffron, and the third green with parsley. Spoonfuls from each were elegantly arranged on the serving plate.[121]

Nuts are nourishing as well as delicious, and this milk was a godsend during Lent. One recipe for soup, indeed, ends with the suggestion "And serve hit forth . . . namly [especially] in lenton tyme."[122] Lawrence Chateres, the kitchen officer of Croyland Abbey, was mentioned with special approval in the abbey's chronicle under the year 1405, because he "gave forty pounds to supply almond milk to refresh the convent on fish days."[123]

Dairy products were much liked. They were to be had in greatest abundance during late spring and early summer, that season of the year which followed hard on the heels of Lent, the long, six-week period when, in strict practice, they were forbidden. They were symbols of release from cramping rules and regulations, rewards for virtue, means for renewed self-indulgence:

> Soone at Easter cometh alleluya,
> With butter, chese and a tansay.[124]

They were also marvelously adaptable, good-tempered with other ingredients, and delicious on their own.

Of them all, the egg was the favorite. It was recommended for everyone and everything, even sick hounds which had lost their appetite: "buttered eggs doeth them much good."[125] They were boiled, fried, poached, scrambled, and used to bind a mixture or thicken a sauce. Only the art of whipping egg whites to a stiff foam lay hidden from the cook. He would have appreciated the theatrical magic of a soufflé, although it would have taxed his ingenuity to make sure it survived the long and drafty journey from kitchen to hall.

An elegant way to decorate a dish was to *endore* or paint it gold with egg yolks. Pastry would be brushed with egg before it was put into the oven to bake, a chicken roasted on a spit until it was just ready and then endored at the last minute to produce a crisp golden crust.[126] Eggs formed the base of all the much-loved wafers, pancakes, and omelets, but whereas a modern pancake batter uses the whole egg, at times a medieval recipe calls for only the whites.[127] Such ethereal pancakes were served with just a sprinkling of sugar; omelets were more substantial and filled with anything that lay to hand, raisins, fish, or ground meat.[128] One name for an omelet was *froise,* and Gower used it when he compared the little bubbling, sizzling snores of a man asleep to the noise of

> a monkes froise,
> Whanne it is throwe into the Panne.[129]

A pleasant, light dish could be made of beaten egg and bread crumbs, shaped together into dumplings, and simmered in chicken broth which was flavored with sage leaves and colored with saffron. A much more substantial boiled pudding consisted of eggs, cream, bread crumbs, and ground meat, peppered and spiced and put in a linen bag to be cooked in a cauldron of water. Once the mixture was ready it was taken out of the bag and quickly grilled on a gridiron to give it a brown crust.[130]

Custards made of yolks and milk were very popular. The method and the problem remain the same today: eggs and heated milk had to be cooked together to velvet smoothness, not lumpy disaster. To avoid this, "sette hit [the mixture] on the fire, and hete hit hote, and lete not boyle; and stirre it wel til hit be somwhat thik."[131]

In this recipe the custard was sugared, salted, and served as a soup, with fingers of fine bread, but in many instances it was used as the filling for a tart. Empty pastry cases were baked in the oven until almost done and then filled for the last few minutes of cooking time with a sweetened, saffron-colored custard. An expert cook with a steady hand did not have to draw the tarts out of the oven to do this; instead he had his mixture ready in a dish fastened to a *peel*, the long stick with which loaves were pushed in and out of the heart of the oven, and poured it into each case as it baked. Either honey or sugar could be used as a sweetener. Honey was cheap and plentiful because it was made by native bees, while sugar was an expensive import. Even so, by the mid-fifteenth century, when these recipes were written down, sugar is suggested frequently and honey sometimes regarded as second best, as in this particular one for the custard tarts: "Then take Sugre y-now [enough], & put ther-to, or ellys hony for defaute of sugre."[132]

Milk was enjoyed in moderation, often combined with eggs in custards and pancakes. It was supplied by sheep, goats, and cows, and while many recipes simply mention "milk," some are more specific: "Take cow's milk or ewe's milk," "take cow's milk very fresh," "give them [puppies] to eat flesh right small cut, and put in broth or goat's milk a little."[133] A man with his own cow knew exactly what went into his milk-jug; a town-dweller had to make it his business to find out: "Say to the woman who shall sell it to you that she give it not to you if she have put water therein, for often they add to their milk and it is not fresh if there be water in it, it will turn."[134]

Although it was irritating to find milk sold as fresh going "off" the moment money had changed hands, the curds formed in sour milk were, in fact, a favorite medieval delicacy. Often something acid, like verjuice, ale, or wine, was added deliberately to warmed milk to hasten the process. The curds were spooned into a linen bag and hung up for an hour or two over a bowl, to allow the whey to escape. After this the bag was emptied onto a dish and the curds served either very simply, perhaps with salt or a sprin-

kling of sugar and ginger, or more festively divided into parts
which were each given a different color, green from herbs, yellow
from saffron, red from sanders.[135]

If eggs are heated quickly with milk the mixture loses the satin
smoothness required for a custard and forms into a soft, fluffy
mass. Like curds, these scrambled eggs were versatile and very
popular. In one recipe bacon was added to the mixture:

> Take cow's milk or ewe's milk and set it to boil on the fire and
> cast in pieces of bacon and saffron: and take eggs, to wit whites
> and yolks, beat them well and cast them in all at once without
> stirring and boil all together; and after this take it off the fire
> and let it turn. . . . And when it has cooled, wrap it very tightly
> in a piece of linen or thin stuff and squeeze it into whatsoever
> shape you will, either flat or long, and weight it with a big stone,
> and let it cool on the dresser all night; and the next day cut it
> up and fry it in an iron pan, and it cooks by itself without other
> fat, or with fat if you will; and it is set in dishes or bowls like
> strips of bacon and stuck with cloves and pine-kernels.[136]

Butter is not mentioned very often in recipes, but it must have
been eaten quite simply and naturally with bread in butter-pro-
ducing countries. At the very end of the fifteenth century in
England a Venetian, who came from a country which mainly
used oil, noted down a little scene he had observed in London.
He mentioned that birds helped to keep the streets clean by
eating the refuse, and went on to say: "The kites are so tame,
that they often take out of the hands of little children the bread
smeared with butter in the Flemish fashion given to them by
their mothers."[137]

In cookery, butter was used for frying, particularly in egg recipes. For an onion omelet, the onions were cut up finely and
cooked in butter and the beaten eggs poured on top at the last
minute.[138]

*Pain perdu* is a delicious way to use up old bread, still made
today just as it was in the fifteenth century. Slices of bread are
dipped in beaten egg, fried in butter, and served with a sprinkling
of sugar.[139]

Bread and butter were combined in a more elaborate, baked
recipe. A sweet dough was kneaded and cooked, and after it had
cooled a little the top was cut off and laid aside. The inside of the
bottom half was carefully scooped out and made into crumbs,
leaving the crust walls quite intact. These crumbs were mixed with

clarified butter, replaced in the crust, and covered with the lid of bread. The whole cake was put back into the oven for a few minutes and then taken out to be served straightaway, "all hote," as a glorious surprise: crisp and brown on the outside, oozing with golden butter within.[140]

Most butter was made in the spring and summer months, and it was packed in salt to preserve it for the winter. To remove most of this salt, the butter was either washed and rubbed in fresh water or heated over the fire to clarify as is done today.[141]

If a saying in a fifteenth-century English-Latin vocabulary list is to be believed, cheese was popular: "Cheese and onions come often to table."[142] The munching of raw cheese was probably frowned on in polite society, as too close for comfort to peasant tastes and table manners. In the surviving recipe books it appears infrequently, mentioned only as one of many ingredients. It is there to add a hint of its own special flavor, as in several recipes for ground-meat pies which call for meat, dried fruit, nuts, eggs, sugar, and spices as well as a little grated cheese.[143]

Occasionally a savory egg custard might be made, with cheese and herbs,[144] but cheese came into its own as a principal ingredient only in tarts and wafers. For an open tart a pastry case was made and baked in the oven, care being taken to see that its sides were more than an inch in height as it was to be filled with a mixture that would puff up and rise. When cooked it was filled with a mixture of saffron-colored milk, grated cheese, and butter, and returned to the oven. Before serving the tart was sprinkled with sugar.[145] For wafers, either grated cheese was added to the batter before this was pressed between two greased wafer-irons or a slice of cheese was sandwiched between two layers of stiff batter.[146]

The crowning glories of the well-regulated dinner table, of course, were the meat, game, poultry, and fish which formed the main part of the meal. Tastes were eclectic, and everything that happened to be at hand could be pressed into service, from whelks to whale meat, the chicken's feet to the boar's head. As always, unusual tidbits and rare, expensive delicacies made greedy eyes sparkle with a special satisfaction. More than one head would have nodded in agreement with this confession by a spoiled fifteenth-century schoolboy: "I have no delyte in beffe and motyn and such daily metes. I wolde onys have a partrige set before us, or sum other such, and in especiall litell small birdes that I love passyngly well."[147] Connoisseurs would give up gladly their share of meat in return for one bone brimming with rich, succulent marrow ready to be scooped out, sucked, and savored. Rabelais noted that his dog shared the same taste: "Have you ever seen a dog fall on a marrow bone? . . . If you have seen my dog, you may recall . . . how fervently he clutches it, how warily he bites his way into it, how passionately he breaks it, how diligently he sucks it. What . . . moves him to act so? . . . Nothing but a little marrow. To be sure this little is more toothsome than large quantities of any other meat, for . . . marrow is the most perfect food elaborated by nature."[148]

Even the most exalted diner had to content himself for a large part of the time with the humdrum round of meat and fish. It was the cook's task to transform dullness into delectable surprise, charming the eye with color and decoration, tickling the palate with stuffings and sauces. The secret of roasting to perfection a plain joint of beef finds no place in the cookbooks, but recipe after recipe reveals, step by step, the art of making meatballs, each spiced, encased in crisp batter, and colored red, gold, or green.

It has been said that the passion for spices and sauces grew from a need to mask the flavor of slightly putrid meat. However, while medieval standards of freshness may have differed from our own, many hints indicate that people, then as now, recoiled from anything they considered to be stale and unwholesome, whether spiced or unspiced. Peter of Blois, an inveterate diner-out in the twelfth century, drew a pained comparison between the appetizing quality and variety of the food at Thomas Becket's table while he was Chancellor, and the repulsive squalor of Henry II's dinners, where the bread was half-baked, the meat taken from sick cattle, and the fish at least four days old.[149] When Montaigne in the sixteenth century remarks "many [meats] I like very high, even to the point of smelling," he implies that this is a personal idiosyncrasy, not shared by his friends.[150] In one of those splendid stories of heroic obstinacy so dear to the medieval heart, a father tries to force his daughter to marry a chosen suitor by clapping her in a dungeon and keeping her on a diet of bread and water. After a few days of this softening-up treatment, he decides to send in the suitor to plead with her, but first adds a cooked hen to her meager menu, to buoy her up and put some color back in her cheeks. Undaunted, the heroine whips two pieces of the bird from the plate and tucks them under her arms. When the young man finally arrives, the smell of rotting flesh fills the cell and he reels away to withdraw his suit, convinced the girl is on her deathbed.[151] The hero, waiting in the wings, knows better.

Scattered references like these suggest that the medieval diner was quite capable of detecting and disliking whatever he found unappetizing. On special occasions he preferred the cunningly spiced hamburger to the slice of rare beef because it was a work of art, meat glorified. This is not to say that there was no plain roasting or grilling, but that the emphasis in the recipe books is on the bewitching sauce or stuffing that will turn the familiar into the festive. Page after page is devoted to sauces for every conceivable kind of meat or fish, "for shulder of moton," "for capons," "for malardis [mallard ducks]," "for stokfysshe."[152] Sometimes the law is laid down firmly: for boiled crab or lobster, "his sauce is vinegre." Sometimes there is an indulgent pat on the head: for poached flounders, "no sauce but salt, or as a man luste [whatever you please]."[153] A slice of beef or venison is grilled on a gridiron and served up with a powdering of cinnamon and a spoonful of sauce made from a mixture of verjuice, wine, ginger, and pepper.[154] A turbot is tied to a spit and as it roasts it is sprinkled with salt and basted with a mixture of verjuice, wine, ginger, and cinnamon. A dish placed under the spit catches the drops, and at the end these are heated up and poured over the fish in the serving plate.[155]

Every part of meat or fish was used. Meat dripping was the principal cooking-fat; meat and fish stocks formed the base of innumerable dishes. Fish roe, liver, stomach, and head were cleaned and gently stewed, then cut up small and spiced.[156] The entrails of a sheep were simmered, chopped up, seasoned, thickened with bread, and bound together with milk and egg yolks. This mixture was filled into a sheep's stomach, which was sewn up and cooked in a cauldron of water to make the dish called a *haggis.*[157] A stew could be made from the feet, heads, livers, and gizzards of chickens cooked in meat broth, thickened with crumbs, salted, and sharpened with a dash of verjuice.[158]

Marrow, that special delicacy, enriched innumerable tarts. In one recipe, small pastry cases are baked, then filled with cooked ground pork or chicken, mixed with pieces of marrow, sugar, and spices and put back into the oven. In another, the marrow is picked out of the bones, which are then simmered in water to make a rich broth that is used as a base for almond milk. Pieces of marrow, raisins, and chopped dates are placed in baked pastry cases and over them is poured a custard of the sugared, spiced almond milk and egg yolks. Back into the oven go the tarts, until the filling has puffed up and set: "whan yt A-rysith, it is y-now [enough]; then serve forth."[159]

The enclosing of meat and fish in pastry was popular. In some instances the pastry itself was not eaten but used merely as a container. A recipe for baked lamprey states explicitly that the fish is lifted out of its pastry case to be eaten, while the gravy which remains in the pie is to be mopped up with slices of bread, not pieces of the crust.[160] Today, fine pastry is the chief glory of a pie, but the medieval kind must have been on the hard side because it often contained no fat. It might be flavored and colored with sugar and spice but it was mixed only with water. "Take and make faire paste of floure, water, saffron, and salt."[161] Fat adds richness but also fragility, whereas the walls of a large medieval pie had to be solid: "take stronge Dow [dough]."[162]

An elaborate, multicolored tart could be made equally well with meat or fish. A square case was baked while four pancakes were made. In the meat version, ground chicken and pork were mixed with bread crumbs, cheese, salt, and eggs, divided into four parts, and colored white, yellow, green, and black. Spoonfuls of each were arranged in the case like the squares on a checkerboard. The pancakes served as dividers, to separate one layer from the next.[163]

Stuffings were much used to add interest and surprise to a familiar roast. Lean fillets of beef might be filled with suet, herbs, salt, and pepper, then rolled up, cooked on a spit and, as a last refinement, painted with egg yolk.[164] A capon was boned, stuffed with a combination of pork, chicken, and spices, simmered for a while, then finished off on a spit, where it was coated with a saffron-colored batter.[165] A stuffing of suet, bread crumbs, salt, pepper, and saffron, bound together with egg yolks, was made for a pig.[166]

Such mixtures were also served on their own. Boiled, ground pork was combined with salt, spices, bread crumbs, cheese, and raw egg yolks and filled into a long earthen pitcher. The mouth of this was covered tightly with canvas, and the container was hung in a cauldron to simmer until the stuffing was cooked through. The pitcher was fished out and broken open to reveal a long, firm sausage. As a last step, this was put on a spit and roasted while it was basted with a sweet, spicy batter. Then, crisp and golden on the outside and soft within, it was carried off to the dining table.[167]

This method of cooking in a tightly closed container produces deliciously succulent meat with all its juices preserved. A capon was filled with parsley, sage, hyssop, rosemary, and thyme and painted with saffron. Then it was placed inside a pot, laid to rest on splints of wood so that it did not touch the sides, and surrounded by more herbs and "the best wyne [wine] that thou may gete." The lid was sealed on the pot with a thick paste of flour and water as an extra precaution, and the pot placed on a stand over a charcoal fire. When the chicken was thought to be ready, the pot was taken away from the heat and laid on straw so that it would not crack on contact with the cold floor. Once it had cooled, the lid was taken off and the chicken lifted out. The fat was skimmed off the fragrant broth in the pot, a syrup of wine, sugar, currants, and spices poured in as a final enrichment, and the whole spooned over the chicken.[168]

Many different kinds of stew were made. Venison might be simmered quite simply in water, then cut into slices and served with *furmenty*, a much-loved dish of hulled, boiled wheat cooked very slowly in milk, sweetened, colored with saffron, and thickened at the last moment with egg yolks.[169] Pieces of beef were simmered in broth with chopped onions, spices, parsley, and sage, and this stew was thickened with bread crumbs steeped in broth and vinegar. At the final tasting, salt and vinegar were recommended with that anxious warning which must have echoed in the cook's uneasy dreams: "Loke that it be poynaunt y-now [sharp enough]."[170] A hare or a goose could be cooked in meat broth with a few marrow bones, chopped cabbage, and leeks, with some oatmeal to thicken the stew.[171] The rabbit was an expensive luxury until well into the fifteenth century in England because it began to become established there only in the late twelfth century. To own a rabbit warren was a mark of distinction; indeed, in the mid-fourteenth century the design on the seal of Thomas, Lord Holand and Wake, showed a tree with his crowned helm in its branches and its roots growing out of a warren.[172] In consequence, not many recipes for rabbit find their way into the cookery books, but in one it is stewed in broth and served with a fittingly expensive sauce of almond milk made with broth and wine and flavored with cloves, mace, ginger, and sugar.[173]

Spiced meatballs were exceedingly popular. Sometimes they were simply simmered in broth, but the favorite method was to shape them "round as an Appil," dip them in a batter of flour, sugar, and almond milk, and roast them on a spit.[174] Brawn, the flesh of both the wild boar and the domestic pig, was often chopped up small, mixed with spices and almond milk, and set to cook in a pot until the mixture had thickened. It was then put into a linen cloth, tied up tightly, and left to cool. Once unwrapped, the long sausage was cut into thick slices. With the medieval flair for presentation, it was suggested that these should be arranged on a dish with the bare, gleaming ribs of the boar laid amongst them.[175] For "Brawn Royal" the slices were colored: green with ground leek leaves, brown with cinnamon and ginger, blue with the plant turnsole.[176]

An elegant way to serve both meat and fish was to present them shimmering in their own jelly. This was particularly effective with fish, as they seemed to be swimming in their natural element. A "crystal jelly" was made simply by poaching a fish in white wine and allowing the liquid to set in a cool place. In a more elaborate treatment, a tench was simmered in red wine and then lifted out of the pan, to be skinned and boned. The skin was put back to boil in the liquid, spices and verjuice were added to give a proper tingle to the taste, and the whole was strained and poured round the fish to set. One or two blanched almonds planted in the tench added the finishing touch.[177] A meat jelly might be made from calves' feet and veal hocks simmered in wine. Once these were removed, pieces of pork and chicken were simmered in the broth. These too were taken out and the liquid was strained several times through a cloth until quite clear. Salt, spices, and vinegar were added to taste, and enough saffron to give a "faire Ambur colour." Slices of meat were arranged on a dish and the jelly was poured round them to set "on a colde place." This golden creation was decorated with blanched almonds and slices of ginger.[178]

Undoubtedly the most spectacular meat dishes, reserved for the grandest parties and most dauntless cooks, were the fantastic monsters specially fabricated for the occasion. A capon and a pig were each cut in half, boned, and then sewn together, the forepart of the one with the hindquarters of the other, and vice-versa. The bodies were filled with stuffing, roasted on a spit, and painted with egg yolks, saffron, ginger, and streaks of green parsley juice. No wonder the recipe ends on a hushed note of reverence: "than serve it forth for a ryal [royal] mete."[179]

The methods which made these recipes possible were baking, roasting, frying, boiling, simmering, and poaching. All depended for success on the skillful management of the fire. For baking, a

Si dirons dalixandre / ꝯment il esploita
Molt fu rois alixandꝰ / ꝟolans ⁊ iraſcus
⁊ phelippes ſes peres / li anchyens kenus
Quant il ot atendu · uꝯ · ſemaines ou plus
⁊ il ꟙit que ſes lettres / neſtoit point reuenus
Si penſa quil eſtoit / occhis ⁊ retenus
Ses homes fiſt mander / quant il les ot eſmus
Sor le califfe ala / iꝛes ⁊ fourmeus
A terre ligaſta / par armes ⁊ ꝑ fus
Li califfes ꟙint outre / o toutes ſes uertus
Aymon fiſt ceꟙalier / qui ert grans ⁊ corſſus
⁊ li bien ſe prouꟙoit / ⁊ eſtoit ſi cremus
Qua ſenſeigne porter / fu ſor tous eſleus
⁊ aymes lenkierka / qui niert mie eſpdus
Tant itrencha de hyaumes / tant iꝑcha deſcus

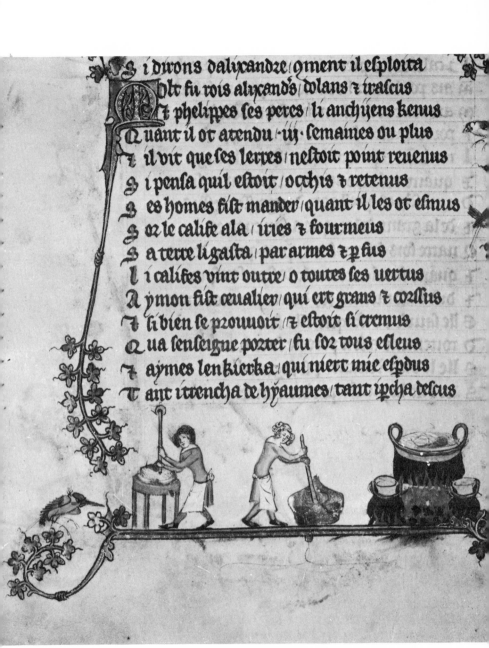

9. Kitchen Activities.
*Romance of Alexander,* Bruges, 1338–44 (Oxford, Bodleian Library,
MS. 264, fol. 170v).

olt ot emenidus
le cuer cortois z sage
Briement por abregier
le gros de nostre ouurage
Cascune des parties
le tenoit a si sage
Que il les acorda z hst le mariage
R ices furent les noches z de noble barnage
T eles qua alixandre afferoit par vsage
E n fin quant repairier vaut a son herbergage
I e boin duc enmena si fu de son manage
A rchade li donna quil tenoit sans seruiage
z li dus le serui sans vilce z sans outrage

fire had to be made inside the oven and then cleared away once the oven had been heated right through. Walter of Bibbesworth in the thirteenth century recommended the use of bracken or straw from the stables for a quick blaze.[180] Every now and again in a recipe there is a reminder that the sweeping-out of the oven must be done properly, to leave the baking surface clean: "Let the ovene be heet [heated] and clene swept."[181] The oven lost its heat gradually, and the experienced cook made full use of its warmth after his batch of pies had been baked. A pear dish, for example, was cooked and then finished off in a cooling oven: "aftur the bred is out of the ovene, then set it [the pear dish] ther in and it shalle . . . be hard [become set]."[182]

For all cooking it was important to regulate the fire with care, to achieve just the right conditions for a particular dish. When meat-balls are to be roasted, "make fyre with-owte smoke," when an omelet is fried, "sette a panne with grece over the fyre, & be-war that thin grece be nowt to hote."[183] On a broad hearthstone it was possible to move cooking pots from place to place, from the heart of the fire to the very edge, depending on the needs of the moment. When wheat had been slowly cooked with milk to make furmenty, sugar, salt, and egg yolks were added. At this stage, the dish had to be kept warm, waiting for the venison stew with which it was going to be served, but it was important that it should not get too hot in case the yolks curdled. To prevent this, a tiny fire was made specially for the pot, by drawing one or two coals or brands to the side of the hearth: "Late it boile no more then, but sette it on fewe coles, lest the licoure wax colde." In the same way, once a fish soup had been cooked it was left to thicken by itself over its own small fire: "thanne take it fro the fyre, an sette the vesselle on a fewe colys, an late it wexe styf be hys owne acord."[184]

Pots and frying pans were not set right on the fire; instead they might be made with their own built-in legs or placed on a portable trivet. Such legs and stands reduced the danger of accidents by cradling the pan firmly, and prevented the burning of ingredients by keeping the bottom away from the direct blaze. In fig. 19 three cauldrons are bubbling on the hearth, each raised up from the flames; in fig. 5 the stand can be seen more easily.

20. (*opposite*) Turnspit Boy.
*The Hours of Catherine of Cleves,* Flemish, mid-fifteenth century (New York, Pierpont Morgan Library, MS. M917, fol. 101).

Another way to control the heat was to suspend the food over the fire at just the right height. Sometimes a pot had its own handle, sometimes it was hung up by a rope. In the kitchen area of Wareham Castle Keep in Dorset, a large cauldron has been dug up and its outside found to be blackened by smoke except for a clean band round the neck, where the rope was tied.[185] In the eleventh-century Bayeux Tapestry, a stewpot is lashed by rope to a pole held up by stakes, but in more sophisticated kitchens the pot hung from an adjustable hook or a notched chain, so that its distance from the fire could be regulated.[186] A Last Judgment scene in the fourteenth-century *Holkham Bible Picture Book* splendidly demonstrates both methods of cooking: one cauldron full of damned souls bubbles on a stand, while another, loaded with a dishonest baker and an ale-wife, swings from a chain as bustling devil cooks give expert prods and pokes.[187]

When a cauldron was large and roomy, it was economical to cook in it several separate items at the same time. One recipe for a rich meat sausage gives instructions for the mixture to be sealed inside an earthenware pitcher and then adds this note: "caste hym to sethe [simmer] with thin [thine] grete Fleysshe . . . in Cauderoun."[188]

21. Spit-Roasting.
*Book of Hours*, Flemish, early fourteenth century (Cambridge, Trinity College, MS. B 11.22, fol. 159). Courtesy of the Master and Fellows.

Many delicious dishes can come out of a bubbling stew pot, but closer to most men's hearts than any of these was a piece of meat roasted on the spit and served with its own special sauce. Indeed, Charlemagne's ninth-century biographer records the irritation with which the emperor reacted to a suggested change in diet: "He came positively to dislike [his doctors] after they advised him to stop eating the roast meat to which he was accustomed and to live on stewed dishes."[189] To achieve perfection in roasting it was necessary to adjust the height of the spit, and in well-equipped kitchens the jack or support on which the spit rested had several notches, from which to choose the best for each occasion (fig. 21). The other essential pieces of equipment, besides the boy turning the spit, were the pan to catch the juices and the long basting spoon. Both can be seen very well in fig. 20, where the boy looks away from the fire and holds up his hand to shield his face from the heat. Many spits were of iron, but sometimes wood is recommended. When making meatballs, "gif hem a fayre spete of haselle [hazelwood]."[190]

Another technique was to contrive a small, makeshift oven and bury it in the embers of the fire. This scarcely rates a mention in the cookery books but was probably used quite often, particularly in households with no proper oven of their own. One recipe gives

22. Cooks at Work.
*The Luttrell Psalter,* East Anglian, ca. 1340 (London, British Museum, MS. Add. 42130, fol. 207r). Courtesy of the British Library Board.

23. Kitchen Inventory.
*Statuta Collegii Sapientiae,* Freiburg im Breisgau, 1497 (Freiburg, Universitätsbibliothek, fol. 47v).

some idea of the method. Two earthenware dishes were greased and put down on the hearth to warm. A batter was poured into one, the other was placed over it as a lid, and coals were piled on top, so heat was coming from above and below. When the batter had begun to set, the cover was removed, a meat mixture added, and the process repeated. Finally, flavored, beaten eggs were poured on top and the cover was replaced for the last time until these too had cooked.[191]

In fig. 23 an inventory of household equipment is being made. Dishes, frying-pans, a spit, a pot with legs, and a trivet can be seen, but the picture gives no hint of those thousand and one little gadgets which made the cook's work possible. His insignia, or cards of identity, were the flesh-hook and the ladle, and he is shown holding them up to view in representations as far apart as a thirteenth-century manuscript now in Vienna (fig. 6) and a fifteenth- or sixteenth-century misericord in Maidstone, Kent. [192] In fig. 22 he is armed with both as he hovers over three pots. Kitchen boys pound and grind (fig. 19), while a rather more exalted cook, King Wenceslas I, who established Christianity in Bohemia, carefully sieves the flour for his eucharistic wafers in fig.

24. That indispensable piece of equipment, the salt-box, appears in a fifteenth-century German engraving and its faithful copy, a sixteenth-century misericord in Manchester Cathedral. The title of the scene is *The Rabbits' Revenge,* and its theme the triumphant reversal of the natural order, with a huntsman roasting on a spit while his hounds simmer in a row of pots, and a rabbit cook takes a pinch of salt from the box hanging nearby.[193]

No picture offers more than a faint idea of the equipment used, but written records are more helpful. The accounts of Henry, Earl of Derby, for the year 1390/91 give a vivid impression of a sophisticated kitchen's resources. Nothing escapes notice, from jacks, spits, and cauldrons at the top to cloths for draining curds at the bottom. There are knives, ladles, skimmers, bread graters, pestles and mortars, weights and measures, hammers for stockfish, sieves for flour, gridirons and frying pans. Provisions are stored in sacks, baskets, leather bags, and barrels; dishes of every shape and size are made of metal, earthenware, and wood. The list is all the more remarkable because it is for a household on the move, as Henry was making a leisurely pilgrimage from England to Jerusalem during this year.[194]

The modern heart sinks in the empty, drafty shell of an abandoned kitchen; it falters at the sight of blackened shards from

24. Sieving Flour; Making Wafers.
*Velislav Picture Bible,* Bohemian, ca. 1340 (Prague, University Library, MS. XXIIIC.124, fol. 184a).

some forgotten, cast-out pot. Everything seems alien to its own experience until a picture or a chance remark touches this long-lost world to life again.

In manuscript borders there are many illustrations of roasting, boiling, and baking, with every conceivable kind of cook in attendance, from devils to griffins, but now and again it is possible to catch a glimpse of some other kitchen activities. In fig. 26 dough is kneaded in a trough, and the cook tells her companion to pour in a little more water; in fig. 25 sauces are added at the last minute to roast joints, just before they are carried into the dining hall.

Occasionally, some sharp-eyed observer sketches in a kitchen vignette. Dante describes two sinners in hell,

> sitting, propped like a couple of pans
> Set to warm by the fireside, back to back.

25. Dishing Up.
*The Luttrell Psalter,* East Anglian, ca. 1340 (London, British Museum, MS. Add. 42130, fol. 207v). Courtesy of the British Library Board.

Others, diseased with sin, are frantically scratching themselves:

> The nail went stripping down the scurfy shales,
> Just as a scullion's knife will strip a bream,
> Or any other fish with great coarse scales.[195]

When fairy bakers suddenly catch sight of a visitor to their kitchen in the romance *Huon of Burdeux,* their reaction is just the same as any mortal cook's would be: they become conscious of their sticky hands and begin to rub the dough off their fingers.[196]

On the whole, it is the recipe books themselves which make us feel at ease in the past. Some crumb of advice, some recommended shortcut, will make cook smile to cook across the centuries, in understanding of a shared problem, approval of a shared solution.

When a meat jelly is to be decorated with blanched almonds there is the reminder that they must be arranged in position "er hit kele [before it cools]."[197] To prevent that common calamity, the jelly's refusal to become firm at all, "set it for a night to get cold in the cellar."[198] Once something has consented to set, how is it to be removed intact from its container? "Chauf the vesselle with out with hoote water or againste the fyere [warm the outside of the pot with hot water, or put it near the fire]."[199]

Some ingredients easily burn or stick as they cook, particularly if the pan is allowed to get too hot. To prevent this, they must be stirred frequently and thoroughly:

> Wot you well that pea or bean pottages or others burn easily, if the burning brands touch the bottom of the pot when it is on the fire. Item, before your pottage burns and in order that it burn not, stir it often in the bottom of the pot, and turn your spoon in the bottom so that the pottage may not take hold there. And *note* as soon as thou shalt perceive that thy pottage burneth, move it not, but straightway take it off the fire and put it in another pot.[200]

While some things catch in the pan, others boil over into the fire. For this hazard, prevention is considerably less messy than cure: "Note that commonly all pottages that be on the fire boil over, and fall onto the said fire, until salt and grease be put into the pot, and afterwards they do not so."[201]

Different experts have different remedies: "Yf the potte renne over: alaye it with a lytel colde water." When disaster calls for drastic remedies, "pulle awey the stickis: and the boylyng wyl abate."[202]

Nothing shows better the tiny threads of common practice that link the cooks of today and yesterday than the medieval treatment of the egg as a thickening agent. From the combination of milk and eggs can come, in a moment, a perfect custard or a vexing failure, depending entirely on the experience of the maker. Then as now, the secret lay in warming the eggs with the milk slowly enough to ensure that the yolks would not curdle in the sudden heat: "The safest way is to take a little (warm) milk and moisten the eggs in the bowl and then do so again and again, until the yolks be well mixed with plenty of milk by the spoon; then put it into a pot away from the fire and the pottage will not turn."[203] Then as now, at the first sign of trouble, the only thing to do was to lower the temperature of the mixture as quickly as possible: "If you see that it is likely to turn, put the pot in a pailful of water."[204]

Another simple, satisfying dish, a favorite through the centuries, is the cheese omelet. The recipe is easy and presents only one problem: how to prevent the melted cheese from sticking and burning in the pan:

> First you shall heat your frying-pan very well with oil, butter or such other fat as you will, and when it is very hot all over . . . mingle and spread your eggs over the pan and turn them often over and over with a flat palette, then cast good grated cheese on the top; and know that it is so done, because if you grate cheese with the herbs and the eggs, when you come to fry your omelette, the cheese at the bottom will stick to the pan; and thus it befalls with an egg omelette if you mix the eggs with the cheese. Wherefore you should first put the eggs in the pan, and put the cheese on the top and then cover the edges with eggs; and otherwise it will cling to the pan.[205]

Where the medieval recipe seems disconcertingly unfamiliar is in its directions on quantities and timing. There were of course official liquid and dry weights and measures used in buying and selling, and most households possessed their own containers, of a given, known capacity. One fifteenth-century will mentions "a bras pot of a galon"; another "a posnet [pot] of a potell [two quarts] and a posnet of a quarte [one quart]"; a third, "a potel pot of peuwter."[206] Occasionally, a recipe will reflect this awareness of amounts and quantities: "and [if] the pot be of iiii galons put ther to XII yolks of egge rawe"; "bette [beat] the yolks of XL eggs in a mortair . . . put ther to . . . an unce [ounce] of sugar and an unce of canelles [cinnamon]."[207] More often, and far more characteris-

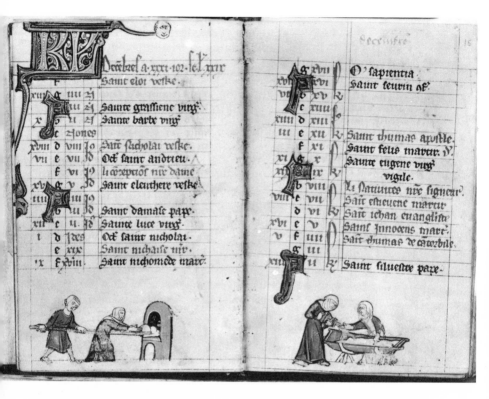

**26. Baking; Making Dough.**
*Book of Hours,* Franco-Flemish, early fourteenth century (Baltimore, Walters Art Gallery, MS. W88, fol. 15). Courtesy of the Walters Art Gallery.

tically, the recipe lays all responsibility in the lap of the cook: "Take yolkys of Eyroun [eggs] nowt to fewe, ne noght to many."[208] To a rice and vegetable dish add an unspecified amount of honey, the only guide being the caution "nowt to moche [not too much] that it be not to swete."[209]

In the same way, a standard length measurement may be used now and again. Pastry is to be cut into pieces, "evry pece ii enche [two inches] square."[210] Much more often, the practiced eye is left to make its own judgment, helped by a suggested comparison with some familiar, everyday object. Pieces of pastry must be fashioned "of the brod [of the width] of a saucere as thyn as ye may dryf [roll] them."[211] Mixtures must be shaped into little balls "like an hassille nott [hazel nut]," "as gret as plomes [plums]," "as it were

Applys," "like to the pastilles of wood [balls of woad]."[212] Fat is to be chopped "as small as dice"; apples for fritters cut "like obleies [sacramental wafers]."[213]

As for timing, by the period when these recipes were written down, in the late fourteenth and the fifteenth centuries, public clocks had begun to be a part of the city scene, and reckoning by hours had become a possibility: "Let the water droppe owt to [two] or iii owrys."[214] Far more often, however, the measurement of time was made in the old, traditional way by a comparison between the job in hand and some familiar, everyday activity, like reciting a certain prayer, or walking a certain distance. The very recipe which reckons in hours at one point, suggests at another that the mixture be left to rest "a forlongwey [the time it takes to walk a furlong]," with the airy afterthought, "or to [two]." Such careless confidence peeps out again and again. A batter must be beaten up "long enough to weary one person or two"; nuts boiled "for the space of time wherein you can say a *Miserere,*" with the eminently sensible qualification, "or as long as you shall see is needful."[215]

Success depended not on precise instructions but the eye or judgment of the experienced cook. Even the medieval beginner probably followed such cryptic hints with more assurance than his modern counterpart because he was used to timing all his activities in the same way. Craftsmen at work on York Minster in 1370 were allowed a break for drinks after noon which was to last "the time of half a mileway [the time it takes to walk half a mile]."[216] A Master of Game blew his horn at the end of a hunt for the time it took to say "half an *Ave Maria.*"[217] In a disarming reversal of the cookbook comparisons just noted, a printer in Parma in 1473 forestalled the critics with this publisher's puff for his new edition: "Should you find any blots on this work . . . lay scorn aside; for Stephanus Corallus of Lyons, provoked by the ill will of certain envious folk who tried to print the same book, finished it more quickly than asparagus is cooked."[218]

A study of the recipe books seems to bring us closer to the medieval cook, and yet it has to be admitted that little or nothing is known of the way he handled these aids. Did he read them himself, or were they read to him? The recipes are filled with practical hints and knowledgeable asides, and this suggests that they were intended for use in the kitchen, not the study, but how closely they were followed remains a mystery. Many recipes are common to the handful of cookery books which has survived in

England and France from this late medieval period, so the manuscripts seem to preserve a central tradition of acceptable practice in "Gentyll manly cokere," as one puts it, rather than the idiosyncracies and private tastes of any particular household.[219]

All that can be said with any certainty is that the cook did not decide on the day's menu by himself. In a small household he discussed the details with his master or mistress, and in a large one with the officer in charge of such matters. When the Goodman of Paris wrote a book for his young bride on the duties of a wife, he devoted one section to the art of ordering supplies and dinners and one to cookery, so that she might learn to become an experienced housewife who knew exactly how to instruct her staff: "The fourth article is that you, as sovereign mistress of your house, know how to order dinners, suppers, dishes and courses, and be wise in that which concerns the butcher and the poulterer, and have knowledge of spices. The fifth article is that you know how to order, ordain, devise and have made all manner of pottages . . . sauces and all other meats. . . . "[220]

Turning to the royal household of Edward IV in the third quarter of the fifteenth century, we find an officer, the surveyor, who has overall responsibility for the preparation and serving of food. His job is "to oversee, with the master cooke . . . all maner of stuf of vytale [foodstuffs], wich is best and most holsom [wholesome] . . . with all the honest maner of clenly handling and dylygence of keping and covering."[221] The officer who supervised the service in the dinner hall had to ask the surveyor and the cook each day what they had prepared for the meal, "What metes & how many disches."[222]

When the cook and his mentors sat down to plan a party for guests there was no argument about the overall plan of campaign. Lavish abundance was the note to be struck, with as many different dishes as possible following each other to the table, until the dazzled diner was forced to admit: "ofte tymes in grete festes and dyners . . . we be fylde wyth the sight of the noble and lichorous [delicious] metis, and whan we wolde ete [would like to eat] we ben saciat [sated] and fild."[223]

The past master in the art of creating successful dinners showed his mettle in the choice of dishes which would impress the guests without exhausting his kitchen staff or emptying his treasure-chest. When Francesco, the rich merchant in fourteenth-century Prato, expected company one day he decided on pork jelly as one of the main dishes, "to do honour to all these folk without too much trouble."[224] The Goodman of Paris begins to tell his wife how to make mock-hedgehogs, but decides the game is not worth the candle: "Hedgehogs can be made out of mutton tripe and it is a great expense and a great labour and little honour and profit, wherefor *nichil hic*."[225]

The arrangement of a medieval menu differs sharply from a modern one. In the latter, ideally, a certain attempt is made to balance the flavors and textures of the different items, and each course of the meal is planned as part of a whole. In the former, there is simply a profusion of dishes, each regarded as an isolated, self-contained unit, served with its own sauce or accompaniments and judged on its own merits. To take a very simple example, for the supper party given by the four wardens of the London Goldsmiths' Company in the summer of 1497, the following menu was chosen: for the first course, roast capon, pike, and baked venison; for the second, cream of almonds, rabbit with chicken, turbot, pigeons, tarts. With each, strawberries and sugar also appeared.[226]

The great advantage of this approach was its flexibility. Anything could be added or subtracted at a moment's notice without wrecking the delicate balance of the dinner. As gifts, rents, and tithes might all be presented in the form of food—a pot of ginger, one hen, three piglets, a clutch of eggs—the housekeeper could not be always sure what would appear on the table. An incident in the romance of *Eustace the Monk* illustrates this well. Eustace, disguised as a merchant, pays a visit to a wicked count, and, pretending to bribe him in a forthcoming lawsuit, humbly presents a basket of freshly baked pies. The greedy count accepts, the pies duly appear on the dinner table that very day, and, to the satisfaction of the heroes and chagrin of the villains, they are found at the first bite to be filled with tow, pitch, and wax.[227]

Even when provisions were bought in the marketplace, there could be no certainty that a hoped-for delicacy would be for sale on the right day. As the Goodman of Paris tersely notes in his account of a wedding-feast in May, "Item, cherries, none, because none were to be had."[228] Despite such crises and calamities, dinner was served, somehow, every day. Just what the table looked like as the guests hopefully took up their positions will be considered in the next chapter.

# 6

# Laying the Table

Whether dinner was served in the great hall or a private chamber, that room did not stand empty for the rest of the day. If small, it might double as sitting-room or bedroom; if large, it hummed with the business and pleasure of the whole household. Space was precious, and dining tables are bulky objects. For this reason they were made of separate parts, trestles and boards, easy to set up just before a meal and clear away when it was over.

Only occasionally is mention made of a "table dormant," a permanent fixture. Chaucer's Franklin had one standing in his hall, and Froissart refers to another that belonged to the King of France: "the great marble table which is always in the Palace and is never moved."[1]

Few references suggest tables made of fine materials. Froissart's example was of marble, and so was one used by the Emperor Frederick II in the first half of the thirteenth century, in his hunting lodge at Ferentino. Frederick, so often denounced as Antichrist in person during his endless battles with the pope, might be amused to see his table today, demurely doing duty as the high altar of Lucera Cathedral.[2]

On the whole, the table was regarded as just a simple, practical scaffolding of no particular importance. Perhaps because of the dust raised as it was banged together and pulled apart each day, there are many instructions to servants to see that its surface is wiped down before it is set for dinner: "And whan ye laye the clothe, wype the borde clene with a cloute, than [then] laye a cloth."[3] After this ritual gesture, no further attention was lavished on the table itself. It hardly mattered whether it was smooth or scratched, as in any respectable household it was decently shrouded in white linen at mealtimes. Indeed, Chaucer's Franklin did even better than this, for his table "stood redy covered al the longe day."[4]

Pride in highly polished mahogany had not yet been cultivated, and a bare surface, however handsome, stirred none but disapproving thoughts of peasant crudity. In the fifteenth-century romance *Sir Degrevant,* Myldore entertains the hero in her bedroom. A table made of ivory is set up before him, but there is not a moment to admire such elegance before it is lost to view: "Clothus keverede that ovur [cloths covered it up]."[5]

Fine linen was the badge of breeding. Even in the open air the rule held firm. It was a poor picnic that took place without a snow-white cloth laid carefully on the ground. Lovers eloping from enraged parents found time to pause for a light meal of wine, bread, and chicken pasties, served on a napkin under the trees.[6] Huntsmen enjoying a break in the day's sport looked on expectantly as their servants laid "the towels and board cloths all about upon the green grass, and set divers meats upon a great platter."[7] At the end of his forty-day fast in the wilderness, Jesus is shown in a fourteenth-century illustration, sitting on the ground while angels arrange his dinner in front of him on a neat, fringed tablecloth (fig. 27).

Society approved of table linen, and only those beyond the pale, peasants and barbarians, could be comfortable without it. The fourteenth-century writer of *Mandeville's Travels* was severe about the standards of behavior at the Great Khan's court in Cathay, and linked the lack of napkins there with the nasty habits this led to: "All the comouns there eten withouten cloth upon here [their] knees. ... And after mete thei wypen here hondes upon here skyrtes."[8]

It was usual to buy linen in bulk and cut it up for tablecloths, napkins, and handtowels as they were needed. Listed among the goods belonging to Richard de Blountesham in 1317 are "one piece of tablecloth containing 10 ells ... and one piece of towelling containing 14 ells."[9] Although there were many exceptions, depending on type, the breadth of a standard piece of cloth was sixty-three inches, rather too narrow to cover a table generously, particularly as the fashion of letting the cloth hang down to the ground was much admired.[10] This may be one reason why instructions to servants often include the advice to spread out two or three cloths overlapping each other on the table.[11]

27. (*opposite*) Angels serve Jesus in the Wilderness.
*Meditations on the Life of Christ,* Italian, fourteenth century (Paris, Bibliothèque Nationale, MS. ital. 115, fol. 71v). Photo. Bibl. nat. Paris.

loro; Claltro sue al pane, laltro al uino, laltro liappa
richia liperscitelli. elluali catcuno d'aitte syon. e locddano
edu difcsta fino dinati alsigre. Clmate addue elliato e
mercpiati elloro ista fcsta dua passica gradissima plugle e
come losignore magia elli agli losuerno

noi dourremo puigere riguardalo reuereteinte e esserui
col sigre. e dio loro. elo catore dituitol modo. loqua da e
sca atog cume. cosi humiluato e abbicognute disostatimie
dicibo coporale. e magiare come tutti lialtri al ipo. lissi
muoueno acopassia. Clusi dirietemte iudica temedi
ano. Et creto se calcuse usiteroso loponessi miete uisssie
e amuelo alquito pfote espassice gricaresti edurest. oli

Naturally, the master and his favored guests enjoyed fresher, finer linen than that allotted to dependents and servants. A careful inventory distinguishes between the different grades: "i gud borte cloyth [tablecloth] for the hey bord [high table], another for the secunde borde, and the thredde [third] for the meny borde [retainers' table]."[12]

Linen has a long life, and the best tablecloth worked its way gradually down the social scale, to end its days polishing the silver or wiping dishes dry: "These raggis wyll serve for kytchyn clothes."[13] In the fifteenth century, one sharp-eyed officer in Edward IV's household had the job of inspecting the royal linen throughout the year, to decide what could still appear in public and what had to be whisked out of sight and put to use behind the scenes.[14]

Cloth might be plain or "of work," that is, decorated in the weave or with ornamental borders. *Diaper* was the term for a fabric with a repeated pattern, and many charming effects could be achieved. One fifteenth-century tablecloth is described as "unam mappam . . . diaperd cum rosis."[15] In the picture of the Duke de Berry's feast (fig. 28), the tablecloth has a continuous lozenge motif, while the attendant's towel is fringed, with a double row of decoration at the end.

Certain centers in Europe were known for their cloth, and the phrases "of Paris," "of Avignon," "of Champagne," "of Rennes" dot the inventories. Aylsham in Norfolk was an English town noted for its linen, and when Sir Degrevant sits down to Myldore's elegant little supper he is offered

> Towellus of Eylyssham,
> Whyght as the seeys fame [sea-foam].[16]

Table linen was a valuable item in any household, carefully graded and handed on after the owner's death to lucky relatives and friends. It could also be given as surety for a loan. Margherita Di Marco Datini, wife of a wealthy merchant in fourteenth-century Prato, listed among her supplies two tablecloths left in pawn to her husband.[17]

However proud a housewife might be of her private store, it is unlikely that she could find there the number of cloths, napkins,

28. (*opposite*) New Year Feast.
*Très Riches Heures of Jean, Duke de Berry,* Paris, 1413–16 (Chantilly, Musée Condé, MS. Lat. 1284, fol. 2r). Photo. Bibl. nat. Paris.

and towels needed for a special occasion. Borrowing from friends was one answer and, in a city, renting was another. The detailed accounts for two Parisian weddings in the late fourteenth century each include a note about the problem: "*Item* . . . two helpers for the service of the kitchen, one of whom shall go bargain for the kitchen things, pastry and linen for six tables. . . . *Item* . . . For the hire of linen, to wit, for six tables."[18]

Snowy, crisp, and gleaming, a cloth adds its own grace note to the well-appointed table as the guests arrive. As they leave, few sights are more disheartening than its ruin, few thoughts more daunting than how to get it clean again. It would be rash to assume that the question ever troubled the dreams of the Duke de Berry and his peers, but it must have haunted their household officers. The problem was aggravated in the period by the custom of several people helping themselves from a common dish, and by the fact that food was eaten so often with the fingers. What place was more likely for the careless guest to wipe them than the table-cloth?

Napkins provided a partial answer. Late in the sixteenth century, Montaigne's words suggest just how useful they might be: "I could dine without a tablecloth, but to dine in the German fashion, without a clean napkin, I should find very uncomfortable. I soil them more than the Germans or Italians, as I make very little use of either spoon or fork."[19]

While easier to wash than a tablecloth, because so much smaller, a heavily stained napkin is still a problem. It is significant that in the linen chest belonging to Margherita Di Marco Datini are "twelve old napkins to keep before one when eating."[20] This suggests that older napkins were provided for everyday use, and splendid ones for ceremony and show. In rather the same way, a London will of 1424/25 lists "wasshyng-towels, bothe for before mete and after."[21] It was the custom to wash hands at the beginning and end of a meal, but whereas the first occasion was a polite formality, the second was a necessity. How sensible to reserve the best towels for the ritual, while battle-scarred veterans of a hundred dinners coped with the messy ending.

After the napkin and the towel, the last lines of defense for the tablecloth were careful management and fastidious behavior. In these matters, the monasteries pointed the way for the rest of society. Though individual monks might glory in bad manners as evidence that their minds were set on higher things, the monastic orders in general were guardians of decorum and the social decencies. In the statutes of the Carthusians the kitchener is instructed to see "that the vessels for food and drink are carefully washed and wiped outside so that they do not spot the tablecloth."[22] The Cistercians were expected "not to wipe their hands or knives on the tablecloth unless they had first cleaned them with bread."[23]

In Portugal at least, the Church lent some moral support to the harassed laundress by teaching that any man sinned when "he became repulsive in eating or in drinking . . . vilely dirtying the cloth."[24] In polite society everywhere, for laymen and monks alike, delicacy and dexterity were the ideals to be aimed for; food was to be dipped into sauces and then lifted to the mouth without leaving behind a trail of spots on cloth or clothes: "Youre mastir may take with ii fyngurs in his sawce dippynge, and so no napkin, brest [breast], ne borclothe [tablecloth] . . . enbrowynge [staining]."[25]

Good advice and good intentions are of little comfort in the aftermath of even the best-regulated party, and medieval diners must have left in their wake a great deal of clearing-up to be done. In the fifteenth-century accounts kept by the Brewers' Guild in London for two of their dinners are entries of payments to launderers: "Item, for washynge of naperie, VI d. . . . Item, for wasshyng of dyverse naprie. . . . XII d."[26]

The temptation to use stained linen again was hard to resist, as may be gathered from two small crumbs of evidence. The first is in some thirteenth-century Anglo-Norman lines on good housekeeping: "If the cloth is too dirty, do not allow it to come into the hall. A well-worn white cloth is much better than a dirty new one."[27] The second is in a contemporary description of the magnificence of Richard I's Christmas feast at Messina in 1190. As incontrovertible proof of its splendor, the writer says that every dish was of gold or silver, and there was not a dirty tablecloth in the hall.[28]

The gap between everyday reality and the ideal may have been wide, but the ideal remained constant: "If you give a feast . . . give them clean seats and a fresh tablecloth."[29] So, in the fourteenth-century romance *Sir Gawain and the Green Knight,* when the hero finds shelter in a strange castle, any fears he may have about his host are put to rest by the sight of the table set up for his first meal, "clad wyth a clene clothe that cler quyt [white] schewed."[30]

Modern taste finds little satisfaction in a clean cloth if it is merely rough-dried; to delight both sight and touch it must be crisp and freshly ironed as well. Medieval feelings about the matter are lost in time. There are countless references to "washing and care of the nappery or table linen," but the evidence for smoothing and pressing the fabric is, to say the least, scanty. It is hard to believe, however, that such connoisseurs of life's pleasures as the Duke de Berry and the Emperor Frederick II would have been indifferent to the sight of creased and crumpled linen, accustomed as they were to fine food served on magnificent dishes. They appreciated beauty in their table arrangements, and it seems fairly safe to assume that their cloths and napkins were expected to provide a fitting background. How launderers may have achieved this goal remains a vexed and clouded question.

There were several possibilities. Cloth newly woven for the market was stretched while still wet on tenter frames, and the tautness thus achieved helped to eliminate some of the wrinkles as it dried. It could also be calendered, or passed between two heavy rollers. The first person listed in the *Middle English Dictionary* as a calendrer is, very fittingly, Robert le Kalender, living in 1278. Both these methods used by cloth workers could have been adapted by the launderers. A third approach was to fold the dampened cloth and flatten it in a screw-press. The fifteenth-century Latin word list, *Promptorium Parvulorum,* has the entry: "Pyle of clothys . . . on a presse, *panniplicium.*"[31] Linenfold paneling, fashionable in the Tudor period, borrows its characteristic pattern from the narrow pleats into which material was pressed by this technique. It is interesting in this connection that a late fifteenth-century courtesy book advises the attendant who is to lay the table to "brynge forthe . . . fayre applyed [pleated] Tabill-clothis."[32]

All three methods could have been used both by the finishers of new cloth and the launderers, but for each quite large pieces of machinery and a certain amount of room were needed. As has been shown, there are indications that table linen could be rented for special occasions, and launderers hired. One of the advantages of this service for all but the wealthiest and most self-sufficient households may have been that the professionals not only did the hard work but provided the equipment. In a late fourteenth-century list of expenses for a wedding in Paris there is a payment to a laundress for "folding."[33] It is possible that she was engaged to flatten linen in a screw-press.

For those who had not the space, the equipment, nor the wherewithal to call on outside help, the slickstone may have been the answer. The slickstone was a smooth stone, held in the hand

and passed over the surface of a material to press and polish it. It was used by many different craftsmen, goldsmiths and workers with paper and leather as well as cloth, but because it was small and inexpensive it was well adapted for the home. Indeed, in the sixteenth century Lyly suggests that it was easy for anyone to improvise a substitute for such a simple tool: "She that wanteth a sleekstone to smooth hir linnen, wil take a pebble."[34] The clearest indication that the slickstone was used by medieval launderers comes in a French-English phrase book of ca. 1415: "Go ye to the slykestere with the slykston And pray that dame that she thy coyfe slyke [Go to the sleekster with the slickstone, and ask her to smooth your cap]."[35]

Starch adds a certain finish to the cloth's appearance, and records of its use go back to the fourteenth century. It was often made from the roots of the arum flower. John Gerard, in his *Herball* (1597), mentions several of its popular, country names, and in the list are Cuckowpint and Starchwort. He adds: "The most pure and white starch is made of the roots of Cuckowpint."[36]

If there were no other evidence for medieval pleasure in fine linen, pictures of feasts would be proof enough. There may be little in the way of crockery or cutlery, but there is always a splendid expanse of white cloth. This was the stage on which the drama of the meal was played.

Of all the props that set the scene and helped along the action, bread was first in importance. A proverb sums up medieval feelings on the matter: "Without bread, wine and ale there would be no delightful feast."[37] A second, "Hunger makes men inventive," is illustrated in one text by a picture of a man gloomily stuffing himself with apples and pears because there is no bread to be had.[38] In fig. 29 the table is being laid for dinner, with knives, tumblers, and bread rolls, brought by basket to the dining room.

Not only was bread the backbone of a meal; it might do trojan service as plate, spoon, saltcellar, and towel. Even more important, any diner, as he sat down, could gauge his importance and the friendliness of his host's feelings toward him by a glance at the bread laid in his place. Quality, quantity, freshness—all sent out their silent, sometimes disconcerting, signals.

Flour came in many different grades, from finest wheat, through mixtures of wheat with rye, to barley, rye, and oats, and so down to gritty combinations of beans, peas, and bran, the desperate scrapings of the agricultural barrel. Colors ranged from white through varying shades of gray and brown. Wheat was the

titi elli gia era que: Ila sc̃da p q̃llo lapossiamo cp̃tedere
gouine sappartchia le noṡṡe:

po ch̃lla puofouĩte lo difecto ol uino. Onte era fi come

uni oi oifciepli . q̃ficome pt̃e aui mane iDauino

most admired grain, of which, whenever possible, the Eucharistic wafers were made. When circumstances forced the use of mixed grain for these, Aquinas had decreed that wheat must predominate.[39] Bede, in his entry under the year 616, describes the greedy interest with which some pagan Saxon princes watched the shining white wafers handed out by a Christian bishop to his congregation. Though longing to have a mouthful, they were very indignant when told that to get one they must consent to conversion. In high dudgeon, they banished the bishop and his tantalizing wafers from the kingdom.[40] Their desire foreshadowed future attitudes. Everyone who could afford it wanted wheat bread, as white and as carefully sifted as possible, and it became a mark of social consequence to serve or receive it. Significantly, one of the names for white bread of the finest quality was *paindemaine,* from the medieval Latin *panis dominicus,* Lord's bread.

The privilege of eating good bread was jealously guarded and zealously angled for. Francesco, the merchant husband of Margherita, worked in Florence, fifteen miles from Prato, but had his bread baked at home and sent to him. One day there was a terrible mistake: the bread he received had been made from flour intended for the servants. A brisk letter was dispatched immediately: "Bid Nanni take a sack to the miller and say that it serves for making bread for *me*—wherefore he must grind it as fine as he can."[41]

Large households, both lay and monastic, kept careful note of the grades of bread they used: "monks' bread," "servants' bread," "alms bread." In the register of Worcester priory, dating from 1240, there is recorded the pleasant custom of celebrating the major festivals by moving everybody one step up on the bread scale.[42] To put peasants in a good mood when they were called on for extra work at busy times of the year, a master might supply better than usual bread for their dinner. Thomas Waleys, a Dominican preacher in England in the fourteenth century, tells a story of some peasants who rejected the wheat bread kindly offered by their bishop in favor of bean bread, with the sturdy cry: "Let bean bread be given us and then we shall be able to work."[43] It must be suspected, however, that this was a story told

29. (*opposite*) Laying the Table; Eating the Meal.
*Meditations on the Life of Christ,* Italian, fourteenth century (Paris, Bibliothèque Nationale, MS. ital. 115, fol. 79v). Photo. Bibl. nat. Paris.

to gladden the hearts of employers nostalgic for the good old days when everybody knew his place. Certainly, Langland's less amenable peasants, in the same century, are always getting ideas above their station and clamoring for better bread, while his Piers Plowman makes a tender promise to each crippled, broken beggar around him, that one day: "He shal ete whete bred. and drynke with my-selve."[44]

Conversely, as a deliberate act of penance the Carthusians every day received a tort, the much-despised rye loaf of the poorest quality, to remind them that they were "Christ's beggars."[45] The tort was indeed a cross to bear, a social humiliation and a mortification for the digestive system. It was notoriously hard. One sermon tells the story of Perys, the meanest man in the village, who never gave a penny to the poor. A beggar, having made a bet that he would squeeze something out of the old miser, stood in his path just as he was carrying rye loaves from the oven to the pantry. Exasperated, Perys looked round for the nearest stone but, finding none, snatched up the equivalent and hurled a loaf "to have broken his heued [head]." The beggar ducked in time, and so collared the bread and won his wager.[46]

These distinctions left their mark on the dinner table. The most important person present found in his place the best and freshest bread available, in the largest quantity. Eight little white rolls might be laid before the lord of a great establishment, only four before a guest.[47] Further down the scale, the rolls were replaced by household bread, defined as "for the most part finer than browne, and browner than wheaten."[48] At Edward IV's court, one loaf was allowed between two people.[49]

The bread coarsened on the downward path, and unwanted visitors could find something very nasty in their place. When Patience and the Dreamer attend a dinner in *Piers Plowman,* they are shunted off to a table by themselves and given one "soure lof" to brood over. Patience, very properly and allegorically, exclaims: "ther fareth no prynce bettere," but the Dreamer fails to reach these heights: "I morned [mourned] evere."[50] A man who ate rye bread when there was no financial reason to do so was considered so eccentric that he had to have an explanation ready: "I yete [eat] rye bredde for no nyggyshenesse [meanness]; but for a poynte of physycke."[51]

Bread also perceptibly aged: the master's bread had to be new, the next°grade one day old, all household bread three days old.[52] Freshness could be a compensation for other deficiencies in the meal. The early fifteenth-century accounts of Syon Abbey state that new bread is to be served at least once a week, on days when the only drink permitted is water.[53]

Etiquette demanded that God should be served before man, and a loaf be placed in the alms dish before the master's rolls were presented. As everyone knows, in gift-giving it is the thought that counts, and this graceful gesture must be considered only slightly marred by the fact that the head of the house munched on manchet, the best bread, while God received chet, a second-class loaf.[54] In monastic accounts, too, "monks' bread" and "alms bread" are placed at opposite ends of the scale.[55]

The meal, however, offered brighter prospects for the poor, as it was the custom to pile into the alms dish not only the "official" contribution but the bread parings that had accumulated during dinner. The outer crust of a loaf was trimmed off for reasons both practical and aesthetic. Paring removed any traces of ash still streaking the surface, and created an elegant new shape. Dough was formed with the hands into a ball and so set to bake. Naturally, the finished bread was also round, and can be seen often in pictures, tucked under the arm of someone in the act of cutting off a slice. Grandeur demanded grander treatment, and there are elaborate instructions on how to square a loaf and range it with its fellows on the table: "Ye muste square and proporcyon your brede, and se that no lofe be more than an other."[56] In the process, at the hands of a dedicated artist, quite a lot of the original could be whittled away, and there are many anxious footnotes by economical stewards: "See that theie be not parde to ny the crome [see that not too much bread is cut away with the crust]."[57] Such warnings were particularly necessary when the parings were not given away to the poor, but regarded as part of the wages of the man wielding the knife.[58]

Fingers of bread were used to sop up sauces and gravies. Indeed, the adjective "soppy," used of someone who is foolish, or "wet," is derived from this bread sop. To ensure that a great lord's food had not been poisoned, it was "assayed" by an official taster, who nibbled a morsel of everything solid, and dipped a sliver of bread into everything liquid, a pleasant if precarious occupation. The ordinary man used his bread as a supplementary spoon. Because so many kinds of food came to the table in dishes from which at least two people, and often more, were to help themselves, and because the loaf itself was often shared, there were the sternest instructions that the slice of bread used must be cut, or at least broken, from the loaf, never bitten off. Once enjoyed, it could not go back to the dish for a second dip; a fresh one had to be prepared. Loud sucking noises were discouraged.[59] Sometimes wine was not drunk, but sopped up with bread. The thirteenth-century hero, Aucassin, with a lover's enthusiasm, thought Nicolette "sweeter than a sop in a cup of wine."[60] A later writer, who did not have the advantage of being in love, found the habit irritating:

> Thou must not dip bread into wine
> If Fra Bonvicino has to drink out of the same bowl with thee.
> He who *will* fish in the wine, drinking in one bowl with me,
> I for my own liking, if so I could, would not drink with him.[61]

The little heaps of neat, fingerlike objects which often appear on dinner tables, as in the frontispiece, possibly represent supplies of bread slivers, prepared in advance for the meal to come.

Bread had several other, minor uses. When not doing duty as a spoon, it might double as a towel or even an oven cloth. To clean a knife for the next dish, the diner was expected not to lick it, but to wipe it neatly on a piece of bread.[62] Many serving dishes were of metal, and so very hot to handle; a slice of bread in each hand made the carrying bearable. The servant is warned to keep the bread well out of sight, and the writer, suddenly remembering that he is writing a *Boke of Curtasye*, ends with a conspirator's aside:

> I teche hit for no curtasye,
> But for thyn ese.[63]

After its importance as food, the most useful role bread played at table was as a plate, or trencher. A trencher could be made of many different materials, earthenware, wood, or metal, but well into the sixteenth century it was very often made of bread. The word is derived from the French verb *trenchier* or *trancher*, to cut, and the plate was made freshly for each meal by cutting off a slice from the loaf. It soaked up gravy, and could be eaten by the diner, tossed to a favorite dog, or tidied away with all the other remains and given to the poor. A clean trencher was prepared once or twice during an elaborate meal as the table was swept clean between each course, the servants removing "all broke cromys, bonys and trenchours before the secunde cours and servise be served."[64]

Any man who ate his own trencher must have been particularly hungry, as the bread used was rather coarse and stale, to make it solid enough for the purpose. The flour was unbolted and the loaf itself several days old: "trencher bred iiii dayes [old] is convenyent and agreable."[65] The Goodman of Paris adds the information that a trencher should be "half a foot wide and four inches high."[66] In texture it was close and firm enough to be used sometimes as a candle holder.[67]

An ordinary diner made his own trencher after he sat down at the table, by cutting off a slice from the nearest loaf, but the most important people present expected to be served. Once again, the bread bore silent witness to their status. One manual suggests three trenchers for the master of the household, two for his son, and one for the least distinguished at the table. Another, more lavish, proposes four for the lord, "and soo iii or ii after her [their] degree."[68]

To prepare a trencher for someone else was a courtesy. In the *Holkham Bible Picture Book,* Jesus may be seen, as a young boy, cutting bread for Mary and Joseph. A person sufficiently distinguished to receive several trenchers would find them presented to him on the blade of the server's knife and then ranged before him, sometimes side by side or in a square, sometimes in a little pile. One might be set out on its own to act as a personal saltcellar.[69] In fig. 30 the attendant is just building up an elegant pyramid before his master.

If at no other stage in the meal, a clean trencher was expected at the very end, when cheese and little delicacies were brought in. The child addressed in *The Babees Book* is given this advice: "Whanne chese ys brouhte, A trenchoure ha [have] ye clene On whiche withe clene knyf ye your chese mowe kerve."[70] From these "dessert" trenchers developed miniature wooden plates, charmingly decorated on one side with flowers and improving texts, of which a few sixteenth- and seventeenth-century examples still survive.[71]

Salt is an essential ingredient in a savory dish and, because no cook can calculate the amount to please each exacting guest, an essential part of every table setting: "The feast that wanteth salt is fit for devils."[72]

As with bread, the appearance of the salt gave some clue to the state of the host's finances and his opinion of the guests. Quality, and consequently cost, varied according to the production methods used. The best salt was made either by boiling down brine water from wells, or by burning peat impregnated with seawater.

30. Table Service.
*Schatzbehalter*, Nuremberg, 1491 (Baltimore, Walters Art Gallery, page aeiiiiv). Courtesy of the Walters Art Gallery.

The peat was dried, then burned, and the salt ash was left behind, to be dissolved in water and evaporated by boiling. At the end emerged a fair, delicate white salt. This was much prized, but the process itself was unpleasant and tedious.

In the fourteenth and fifteenth centuries a new salt appeared on the scene, produced with a most agreeable minimum of effort and expense. It came from the Bay of Bourgneuf, on the west coast of France, where seawater was collected in shallow pools or basins and there evaporated by the sun during the long hot summers. Enraptured entrepreneurs called this salt "manna from heaven," exported it all over Europe, and rubbed their hands over the profits.

There were, however, minor disadvantages. As little or no attempt was made to purify the salt from dirt and débris collected in the basins, its appearance left something to be desired. The

adjectives "black," "grey," and "green" crop up ominously in contemporary descriptions of Bay salt. Evaporation did not leave behind salt of as fine a grain as boiling did, and again the adjectives
tell the story, ranging from "great" through "rough" to "gross."[73]

The careful housekeeper therefore made a practice of buying
different salts for different purposes: cheap salt for use in the
kitchen, for the servants, for the unregarded guest; fine salt for
the important dinner party. The accounts of the Priory of St.
Mary de Pré in Hertfordshire for the years 1341 through 1357
show that the wardens bought "salt for the larder and white salt
for the household."[74] These considerations of quality, color, and
texture explain this advice on what to put into a lord's saltcellar:
"Loke thy salte be sutille, whyte, fayre and drye."[75]

The budget-conscious soon found ways to do their own
refining: "To make white salt: take a pint of coarse salt and three
pints of water, and set them on the fire until the salt is melted in
the water, then strain it through a cloth, towel, or sifter, then set it
on the fire and boil it well and skim it, and let it go on boiling
until it is quite dry and the little grains that have been throwing
up water be quite dry; then turn the salt out of the pan and
spread it on a cloth to dry in the sun."[76]

Just as medieval refinement required bread to be squared, so it
expected salt to be smoothed. One writer recommended for the
purpose the use of an ivory spatula, two inches broad and three
inches long.[77] If a host had taken the trouble to provide a shapely
little mound of fine white salt he certainly did not wish to see it
sullied. Rules for helping oneself were very firm: no food was to
be poked into the salt:

> In salt saler yf that thou pit
> Other fisshe or flesshe . . .
> That ys a vyce.[78]

Instead, salt was to be taken on the point of a knife, laid on the
guest's own trencher and dipped into at will:

> . . . . lay it honestly
> On youre Trenchoure, for that is curtesy.[79]

A surviving wooden trencher, ca. 1600, has in one corner a small
depression, hollowed out to hold the salt.[80]

Sometimes an extra bread trencher would be sliced off especially to act as an improvised saltcellar: "Dresse it [salt] aparte
upon a clene trencher."[81] One manual advises a servant to pile up

three trenchers in his master's place and set a fourth a little to one side: "for to lay uppon salte."[82] To ensure the saltcellar remained pristine, economical excesses had to be discouraged: "Let the servants avoid putting into the salt cellars the salt lying scattered on the table, soiled by the meats."[83]

Because salt was used by everyone, it was provided on each table. The principal saltcellar, however, had a symbolic as well as a practical function. Brought in with some ceremony it was set directly by the master's seat and marked for all to see the place of honor and the center of the feast. Other salts were cleared away in the course of the meal when no longer needed, but the Great Salt remained on the table from beginning to end.[84]

Always on display, salts were intended to delight the eye and confirm their owner's dignity. They were made of the most costly materials possible and decorated accordingly. Silver, silver gilt, and gold were much enjoyed. William Bird, a great Bristol merchant of the fifteenth century, owned one silver salt and "2 of the best gilt."[85] As a New Year's Day present in 1415, the Duke de Berry accepted from one of his favorite artists, Paul de Limbourg, a little agate salt with a gold lid whose knob was decorated with one sapphire and four pearls.[86]

A splendid specimen was a financial asset, an insurance against a rainy day, its weight and price carefully recorded. Too valuable to be discarded, old salts never died; to satisfy a new owner or a new fashion they were simply melted down and remodeled.[87]

Faithful to the cherished medieval axiom that plainness is prosaic, fantasy is fun, the salt appeared on the table in every possible disguise. It might be a lion, it might be a whelk shell with not a whelk but a dragon climbing out of it[88]—biologically unsound, but aesthetically inspired. The most popular form on the continent, though not found so often in England, was the ship, or *nef*. One may be found at the Duke de Berry's elbow in fig. 28, and three in the frontispiece. The *nef* was an irresistibly elaborate confection, offering the craftsman unlimited opportunities to show off, with spider's webs of rigging, lilliputian anchors, diminutive cannon, microscopic bags and bales. Sometimes large enough to hold its owner's napkin and cutlery as well as salt, it had all the charm of a doll's house. Richard II owned one whose forecastle was crowded with eight tiny men holding up the banners of France.[89] Awkward pauses in a feast could be eased when a nef was trundled in a stately progress along the table. The 1329 inventory of the English Royal Plate lists "a silver nef with four wheels and a gilt head of a dragon at either end of the said ship."[90]

Of all the implements brought to the table, fingers were the most helpful. Everybody had them, everybody used them. Because they were constantly on display, dipping busily into shared dishes, heavy emphasis was laid on keeping them clean. Licking was not encouraged:

> Thou must not lick thy fingers.
> He who thrusts his fingers into his mouth cleans them
>     nastily . . .
> The fingers are none the cleaner, but rather the nastier.[91]

Instead, they were to be washed at the beginning and end of every meal. Servers whose hands became splashed with gravy were advised to wash them "in some unobtrusive way" between courses; boys were to sit down to table with clean hands and nails; page boys must stand before their master "withe clene handes Ay Redy him to serve."[92]

Not everyone, of course, lived up to these high standards. Lydgate, in the fifteenth century, looking back to his boyhood, remembered himself "with unwasshe hondes redy to dyner."[93] One of the pet aversions of the fourteenth-century book-collector Richard de Bury was the man who went straight to the library after dinner and proceeded to paw the books with sticky fingers: "It is part of the decency of scholars that whenever they return from meals to their study, washing should invariably precede reading, and that no grease-stained fingers should unfasten the clasps, or turn the leaves of a book . . . the cleanliness of decent hands would be of great benefit to books as well as scholars."[94]

Indifference to clean hands was regarded as the sure sign of the unschooled and the uncouth. The ceremony of hand-washing came immediately before or immediately after the saying of grace, and acquired a certain spiritual overtone through the association. Each act was a preparation for the meal and a cleansing at its conclusion; the two together framed it with decent decorum. William Horman, in his *Vulgaria* (1519), provides a one-line definition of the greedy man: "He is so gredy on his meate: that he wyll nat abyde wasshynge and grace."[95] By contrast Jesus, whose table manners were of course impeccable, is shown patiently waiting to begin his dinner after the forty-day fast until an angel has fluttered down through the air with a towel and a jug of water for his hands (fig. 27). Even the mice in a late fifteenth-century re-telling of an Aesop fable are sufficiently well-bred to wash before their meal, although, not being human, they are excused the prayer:

> quhen [when] thay disposit wer to dyne,
> Withowtin grace thay wesche and went to meit.[96]

The ceremony itself posed certain delicate problems for the anxious diner. Beginners were instructed not to splash water over their neighbors, and never, in an excess of zeal, to spit into the basin.[97] The sophisticated could afford perhaps to laugh at such basic rules, but had their own distracting worries. When the same basin and towel were used by several people, how dirty could one decently make them and, if a choice had to be made, which should turn gray, the water or the towel? Caxton in his *Book of Curtesye* advises thoroughness at the basin:

> Wasshe with water your hondes so cleene
> That in the towel shal no spotte be sene.[98]

Others preferred the towel, and prudent housekeepers, as we have noted, kept better ones for use at the beginning of the meal and older ones for heavy duty at the end.

Either method left one open to the sniggers and raised eyebrows of uncharitable observers. Safety lay in guile. Women in particular, on important occasions, preferred to enjoy a sustaining meal in private before making an appearance at the dinner table, radiant, refined, and merely toying with a morsel. At the critical moment they could then dip their fingers confidently in the water and leave it sparkling, touch the towel and leave no stain.[99]

Servants had their own worries. They must make sure that the towel on its first appearance was invitingly clean, the basin freshly scoured.[100] In freezing weather no one liked the shock of ice-cold water, so warm must be provided. In summer they had to remember that guests enjoyed lots of water, in winter that a drop sufficed.[101] Metal chafing dishes were sometimes used to keep water hot at the table. One of the officers in Edward IV's household had the job of looking after "the chaufirs with water, and, in tyme of yere, to see hit hote after the noble old custume."[102] A few of these dishes still survive, including a late fifteenth-century example that belonged to William Catesby, Richard III's Chancellor of the Exchequer.[103]

Scented water gave special pleasure, and there were many recipes for making some: "To Prepare Water for Washing Hands at

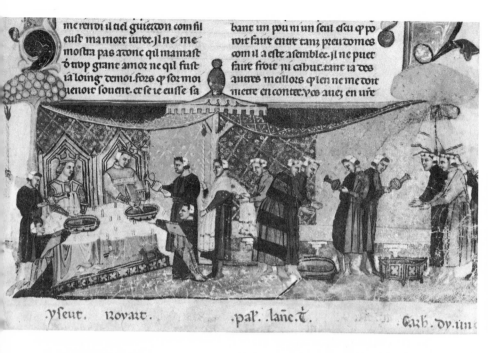

me renoi il ael guiecton com fil
euft ma more wire. jl ne me
moftra pas acone qil mamaft
ó trop grant amoz ne qil fuft
ia loing cenoi.foze cp formoi
uenoic fouent. et fe te euffe fa

banc un pou ni un feul efai cp po
roit faire entre canz prei comes
com il a efte afemblee. jl ne puet
faire froit ni cabut. tant ia des
autres meillots cp len ne me woit
mettre en contte. Yos auez en une

yfeut.    novait.            ·pal·.lanc.t̃.                    ẽub. ov.iiii

**31. Washing Hands.**
*Prose Tristan*, Italian, ca. 1320–50 (Paris, Bibliothèque Nationale, MS. Fr.
755, fol. 115). Photo. Bibl. nat. Paris.

Table: Set sage to boil, then pour out the water and let it cool
until it is just warm. Or you may instead use camomile or marjo-
ram, or you may put in rosemary; and boil them with orange peel.
And bay leaves too are good."[104]

Sometimes hands were actually plunged into the water, sometimes they were held out above the basin while water was poured
over them from above (fig. 31). Froissart describes the dramatic
death of Gaston de Foix at such a moment: "The Count rose from
his seat and stretched out his hands to be washed. As soon as the
cold water fell on his fingers . . . his face turned white, his heart
throbbed violently, his legs failed him, and he fell back on to the
chair, exclaiming 'I am dying. Lord God have mercy!' "[105]
Horrified, the two knights who had served him drank the water
on the spot, to forestall any suspicion that they had poisoned it.

The disadvantage of this method was that water poured too
exuberantly could splash the diner's clothes and spoil the festive

mood. It was considered advisable for two attendants to shield the sleeves of someone really important with a towel.[106]

The tablecloth itself, at least for the principal guests, was protected by a *sanap*. This name, derived from the Old French *sauvenape*, save-cloth, was given to a long wad, made up of several thicknesses of linen and toweling and stretched with much ceremonial along the table's edge, under the diners' hands before washing commenced, and afterward removed. In fig. 32 a folded cloth which may be the sanap can be seen running the whole length of the table.[107]

The kinds of hand-washing so far considered have been somewhat formal, taking place in the dining room. On everyday occasions there was less ritual and, perhaps, more actual washing. Evidence of built-in washbasins and cisterns is quite often found in passages leading to the main refectory in monasteries and large secular houses; sometimes there was a drain to lead off the water and sometimes water was piped in from a cistern. At Battle Hall near Leeds in Kent, built ca. 1330, there is, still intact, a handsome laver and cistern. The cistern is designed as a castle with two round, battlemented towers, each with a lion's head spout.[108]

Handwashing was a time not merely for the display of good manners but of enviable possessions. Towels, basins, and jugs had to be as fine and plentiful as money could buy. Most people took great pride and pleasure in the choice, even though St. Bernard of Clairvaux, whose table manners were as eccentric as only a saint's could safely be, sighed impatiently: "Is it quite impossible to wash one's hands in, and drink from, the same vessel?"[109]

Hints in wills suggest that it was considered elegant to match tablecloth and towel in a set, either in actual design or in quality: "To Anneys Tukkysworth my best bordclothe and the Towayle; and Richard Gery the nexte bordcloth and Towayle."[110]

Basins and jugs were made of the best materials available to the owner, and exuberantly decorated. When, in the fourteenth century, Sir Ralph Hastings washed his hands, he had the satisfaction of glimpsing his own crest, a bull's head, glimmering through the water at the bottom of his silver basin.[111] Because made, originally, only for the greatest lords as a protection against poison, jugs fitted with lids were coveted status symbols, which provided yet another surface begging for decoration. Richard II had such an ewer, with birds engraved and enameled all over the body and a tiny woman perched on the knob of the lid.[112]

Quite the most charming and elaborate of all water-containers are the *aquamaniles,* in which the jug is not merely covered with fantastic creatures but itself transformed into one: a lion, a griffin, or a rider on horseback. These little figures were very fashionable from the twelfth century, and they are thought to have come originally from the East.[113] Every subprior of the monastery at Durham had the pleasant privilege of using one at dinner: " . . . the Ewer purtrayed like unto a horse and a man sitting on his back as if he had been riding a hunting, which served the Subprior to wash at the aforesaid table, where he did sitt as chief."[114]

The main European center for their production was Dinand in Belgium, and the materials used were brass, copper, and bronze. These metals can be shaped easily by craftsmen but, as Albertus Magnus pointed out in the thirteenth century, they have one grave disadvantage: "If wine or any other liquid except water is poured into a brazen vessel, it is immediately spoilt, with such a loathsome bitter taste that it can hardly be drunk. But water is not immediately spoilt . . . if water stands there for a long time . . . then water, too, has its taste and odour spoilt."[115] Prudent servants must have taken care to fill the aquamaniles only just before they were used. There would have been little point in making perfumed water if its fragrance was to be overwhelmed by the smell of metal.

Cups, serving-plates, and saucers, the little dishes for sauces, were chosen with the same care as the salts and ewers and gave even more satisfaction. The cup in particular was a very personal possession, regarded with a special affection. Gold, silver, and silver gilt were, as usual, most prized; vessels made of less expensive materials were often trimmed and embellished with these precious metals. A drinking horn given in 1347 to the Gild of Corpus Christi in Cambridge has silver gilt additions: legs on which it could be rested between drinks and, as its finial, a tiny watchman looking out from a battlemented turret.[116] More popular than the horn after the Norman Conquest was the *mazer,* a finely turned wooden bowl which might be banded with silver or set on a metal foot. An early fourteenth-century mazer which has survived is decorated with a silver gilt medallion of Guy of Warwick killing his dragon.[117]

An occasional coconut or ostrich egg strayed into Europe from the East, to be mounted as a cup and transformed into an enviable conversation piece. Nicholas Sturgeon, a priest, had two ostrich egg cups to leave in his will in 1454, and the Master of Sherborne Hospital in the previous century gave his niece a cup

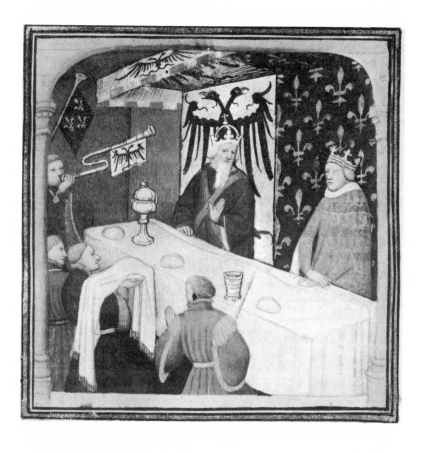

**32. Waiting to Begin.**
*Les Grandes Chroniques de France,* Paris, ca. 1414 (London, British Museum, MS. Cotton Nero EII, vol. 2, fol. 229v). Courtesy of the British Library Board.

of "Indian nut," which was probably a coconut.[118] Glass was rarely used until the end of the Middle Ages, but there are a few references to it. In the *Grandes Heures* of the Duke de Berry the guests at the Marriage at Cana enjoy red wine glowing in transparent goblets.[119]

Pottery, when sufficiently fine and elaborately decorated, was also coveted. One great center of production was Saintonge in southwest France, making very thin white polychrome ware, patterned with bold brown. In England, Saintonge pottery has been found most frequently in ports like Southampton, where several

33. St. Louis feeds the Poor.
*La Vie de St. Louis par le confesseur de la reine Marguerite*, Paris, thirteenth century (Paris, Bibliothèque Nationale, MS. Fr. 5716, fol. 213). Photo. Bibl. nat. Paris.

jugs have been unearthed in the early fourteenth-century cellar of a merchant's house.[120] The pottery most admired all over Europe from the thirteenth century to the end of the fifteenth was the lusterware made in Spain by Arab craftsmen, at first near Malaga in Andalusia and then near Valencia in Aragon. This had rich, intricate designs, combining Moslem and Christian motifs, and the characteristic colors used were dark blue and copper.[121] Customers might choose one of the stock patterns and have their own heraldic devices added as a personal touch. Francesco, the merchant in fourteenth-century Prato, was so delighted with his first set that three years later he ordered another, only to find to his intense irritation that his business partner in Valencia, who was supervising the transaction, had forgotten what the coat of arms looked like and had to write to Prato for a model.[122] In a Book of Hours made for Engelbert of Nassau in the late fifteenth century, two borders are painted as open shelves, on which is arranged a splendid collection of Valencian dishes and jars.[123]

Loving care was lavished on these precious cups and plates. Large medieval households were on the move throughout the year, traveling from one estate to another, and the master had no intention of leaving behind his most prized possessions. Henry, Earl of Derby, who became Henry IV, in the 1390s not only had a special *cuphous,* a trunk for his gold and silver plate, but a special horse to carry it. His silver cups were packed in leather bags, and his four ostrich egg cups rested in a case designed for them.[124]

When at home, valuable tableware was kept under lock and key and issued as needed for particular meals. In Edward IV's household some spice plates were stored in the counting house, but the grandest, which appeared only on the most festive occasions, were guarded in the jewel house. A groom in the "Office of Picher-house and Cuphouse" was appointed to care for the plate: "to waysshe and wype and gader home the plates of sylver and peauter into the office dayly."[125] In fig. 34, he is on his knees, polishing up a large serving dish.

Intended to impress the guest and gratify the host, such valuable objects were not always placed on the table for actual use. Instead they were set out in a blaze of glory on a special stand called the cup board, which had a series of shelves arranged in tiers. Before a feast began the butler was instructed to spread over these shelves a fine cloth and then, as one writer magnificently puts it, to "emperialle thy Cuppeborde with silver and gild fulle gay."[126] To do this he must arrange his splendid pieces to the best advantage: "the largest firste, the richest in the myddis, the lighteste before."[127]

Such a cup board was a star attraction at a feast. Froissart describes the stand of royal plate at a dinner given to celebrate the entry of Queen Isabella into Paris in 1389, and adds: "Many an eye looked covetously at it on that day."[128] It was a favorite amusement for guests to file past the display, taking surreptitious note of cost, quantity, new additions, and mysterious disappearances. Sad to say, disagreeable necessity sometimes forced an owner to sell a piece or use one as a bribe. Cups and dishes were financial assets, whose weight and value were carefully recorded. Even when battered and broken, they were still precious, to be hoarded for a rainy day. So Thomas Bath of Bristol in 1420 listed the following in his will: "A becure of selver I-keveryd, and a branche of the covercle y-broke away, that weyyth XVI ounsus [A covered silver beaker, weighing 16 ounces, with part of the cover broken off]."[129]

34. Polishing the Silver. *De Buz Book of Hours,* French, early fifteenth century (Cambridge, Mass., The Houghton Library, Harvard University, MS. Richardson 42, fol. 1).

An old-fashioned piece might be put to other uses, melted down and remodeled to satisfy a modern taste. In the thirteenth century, Bogo de Clare used up nine silver dishes in the making of eight new ones.[130] Most, however, were expected to become cherished heirlooms, passed on from one generation to the next. In his will of 1424/25, Roger Flore speaks of "my maser of a vine rote, the which was my faders," and leaves it to his heir with the words: "for the terme of his life, and so from heir to heyr."[131] Such objects were rarely thrown away when broken, but mended and so brought back to life. In the thirteenth century, the Bishop of Hereford spent tenpence to have his mazer repaired.[132]

Dishes were regarded with complacent pride; special, personal cups with affection. Little pet names for them pop out of the records: "the grete grubbe," "Peregrin," "Christmas," "Benison," "Crumpledud."[133] Happy memories faintly warm a sentence in a will: "a covered cuppe of silver, the wich I was wont to drynk of"; "my horn with cover of silver and gilt in which I was accustomed to drink at the Feast of the Nativity of Our Lord."[134]

Metal was always the coveted material. As the social scale was descended, gold and silver faded from the picture and brass and pewter took their place, to be cared for with the same proud pleasure. Roger Elmesby, a wax-chandler's servant in London, left to his godson Robert Sharp in 1434 two pewter saucers which had been lovingly marked with the boy's own initials.[135]

Not even the grandest household, however, had every table shimmering with well-polished dishes. At Edward IV's court, the chief yeoman in the "Offyce of Picherhouse and Cuphouse" was responsible not only for all the silver but also for "pottes of lether, tankardes of yerthe [pottery], asshin [ashwood] cuppis."[136] Such humble materials were undoubtedly useful but not highly regarded, particularly by those who felt themselves entitled to better. An ordinary mortal could become pettish if expected to eat off plates beneath his dignity; a saint might choose to do so as a deliberate penance. When he had to spend some time away from home on business Francesco wrote to his wife: "I eat naught that pleases me, and they are not things to my liking, and the bowls are coarse."[137] In his fifth-century biography of Augustine, Possidius describes how the saint and his companions ate off simple crockery, adding a careful explanation: "not because they were too poor, but on purpose."[138] Augustine, who enjoyed his food, wisely tempered austerity by allowing himself a silver spoon.

In contrast to the cosseting attention paid to special cups and plates, ordinary pottery was bought, smashed, and bought again with startling ebullience. It has been noted already that grand households were peripatetic and carried much domestic bag and baggage with them. Whereas the best tableware traveled in its own containers, everyday equipment rattled along, roughly packed in carts or slung here and there amid the other luggage. This carefree approach was fraught with possibilities of disaster for breakable pots. In Bishop Swinfield's household accounts for 24 January 1290 it is noted that the cook's cart overturned on the road; on 27 January are listed all the cups, dishes, plates, and saucers which had to be bought as replacements by the cook at a nearby market.[139]

Even when there was no accident on the way it was often necessary to rustle up large numbers of pots from local potters, particularly for the great feasts of Christmas, Easter, and Whitsun when the household would be swamped with hopeful visitors. Such supplies must have been regarded as expendable, to be broken during the feast or abandoned when the lord's party had moved away, because the orders are repeated year after year. Sometimes the call for crockery would go out in plenty of time for potters to make them especially for the occasion. On 15 March 1265 an order for five hundred pitchers was sent to the potters of Kingston on Thames, to be delivered to the King's butler at Westminster in nineteen days' time.[140] Other households lived in a state of perpetual crisis. On 1 April 1290, Easter Saturday, Bishop Swinfield's unfortunate cook was buying large quantities of cups, plates, and dishes at Worcester, in preparation for the great Easter celebrations which were to begin the very next day.[141] The potter must have been a familiar and welcome figure to harassed stewards. No wonder that when Hereward the Wake needed a disguise which would ensure him safe passage through enemy lines and right into the heart of the Norman camp, he chose to be a potter and headed for the kitchen.[142]

As always, manners were shaped by table equipment and arrangements. In his own home a man might hope to have his own cup, from which he alone would drink; as a guest he was resigned to sharing on many occasions. From this grew the insistent emphasis in all books of etiquette on wiping the mouth before drinking, holding the cup from below so that fingers did not dip into the wine, keeping hands clean anyway as a precaution:

> If thou offerest the cup,
> Never touch with the thumb the upper edge of the bowl.
> Hold the bowl at the under end . . .
> He who holds it otherwise may be called boorish.[143]

An early fifteenth-century manual gives crystal-clear advice:

> The bowl should be held between two fingers:
> The thumb should not touch the sweet wine.
> A man's beard should not be immersed in the wine . . .
> Drink and then turn the bowl to thy neighbour,
> So that his lips are not placed where thine were.[144]

A very important person might eat alone, but most guests were expected to eat with their immediate neighbors on the table (fig. 29). One man was said to mess with another, and the dishes they shared were their mess for the meal. There still survives the menu of a supper given by the four wardens of the Goldsmiths' Company in London in 1497. This lists the names of the guests and indicates the seating-plan by grouping them into six messes of different sizes.[145]

The number of people who helped themselves to a mess and the number of separate dishes covered by that term varied according to rank, the magnificence of the household, the importance of the occasion, and the generosity of the host. Thus, at Edward III's court, on an ordinary day, the King himself had eight dishes set before him, his "lordes in hall and chamber" five, his gentlemen, three, plus soup, and his grooms had two. In 1478, the servants of Edward IV's household were expected to share one gallon of ale between four men, one meat dish between three, and one loaf between two.[146] In the more lavish world of romance, King Arthur once provided at a New Year feast twelve different dishes for every pair of guests, thus causing such delightful confusion that it was hard to find room for everything on the table.[147]

Such arrangements inevitably led to much dipping of companionable fingers into a common bowl. The pleasure of the occasion, therefore, depended both on the state of one's neighbor's hands, a matter which has been considered already, and his frame of mind. Two habits were found specially irritating; the descriptions are self-explanatory:

> Ill does the hand which hurries
> To take a larger help out of a dish in common . . .
> Do not poke about everywhere . . .
> He who turns and pokes about on the platter, searching,
> Is unpleasant, and annoys his companion at dinner.[148]

Pent-up fury with the impossible behavior of a friend bursts out in the words of a fifteenth-century schoolboy: "I wyll never sytt agayn with the at an mease [mess] while I lyff . . . for thou art a lurcher and a gloton. Lurchers I call suche as devoure all the beste musselys [morsels] . . . I forsake thy company forever, nor we wyll never drynke together agayne."[149]

Of the different kinds of cutlery, the knife was the most familiar and most often used. Guests could be expected to possess one, and usually brought their own with them when they went out to dinner. There is a story about some girls who, flustered and late for a wedding feast, took a shortcut across a meadow and in no time found themselves plastered with mud. Undaunted, "they made clene their hosen and gownes with theyr knyves the best they couthe" and pressed on to the roast beef.[150]

Tiny details tend to confirm that the knife came to table as the diner's personal possession. In his advice on good manners, Lydgate tells his reader not to bring a dirty one into the hall, implying that the knife is his responsibility.[151] The reader of another courtesy book is expected to keep his knife sharp as well as clean, so that he will be able to carve his own meat neatly when the time comes.[152] An Italian treatise encourages the faint-hearted with these bracing words:

Put not back thy knife into the sheath before the time . . .
Perhaps something else is coming to table which thou dost not reckon for.[153]

In an Elizabethan conversation piece, a forgetful man appeals to his friends: "He which hath two knives, let him lend me one."[154]

If friends proved indifferent, or funds ran low, improvisation was the answer. Attempts to spread butter on bread with the thumb were discouraged, and a crust was recommended as the substitute knife.[155] A fried egg might be attempted with a straw or a blade of grass.[156] Even worms must turn, and rebellion among the readers is suspected when this point in the etiquette book was reached.

Rank has its privileges, and if the diner were sufficiently important he had no need to remember what to bring or resign himself to making-do; a knife would be included in his place-setting. Certainly the lord of the household could expect to find one waiting for him. He was allotted a spoon, a napkin, and a knife, while only the first two were issued to his guests.[157] It is just possible to see the small knife the Duke de Berry holds in his hand while waiting expectantly for dinner to begin (fig. 28). As a mark of special consideration, a knife might be laid for a favored guest. In the Last Supper scene on the twelfth-century *Pala d'Oro* in St. Mark's in Venice, the only knives on the table are beside Jesus and Peter, seated opposite his master in the place of honor.[158]

Compliments make complacent guests, but must be skillfully paid if they are not to lead to social disaster. In the late thirteenth-century play *Le Jeu de la Feuillée*, three fairies pay a call on the town of Arras. A table is prepared for such distinguished visitors and they are ushered to their places. Two sit down, wreathed in smiles, but the third becomes distinctly moody. Only two knives are on the table, one for Arsile, one for Morgue, and none for Maglore. Her temper is hardly sweetened by the tactless exclamations of the others about the elegance of the cutlery, and she begins to brood over curses appropriate for careless hosts.[159]

Italy, being wealthier, more sophisticated, and more closely in touch with refined Byzantine society than the rest of Europe, was the first to expect the host to supply his guests with dinner knives as a matter of course. A whole line of them is being laid on the table in fig. 29, a fourteenth-century illustration. In an Italian courtesy book of the same period there is the implication that one knife between two guests has become the accepted allowance, with a rule for precedence already established:

> With thine equal begin,
> If the knife lies at thy right hand;
> If not, leave it to him.[160]

On the whole, however, it seems to be the general rule that throughout the Middle Ages knives were personal property, brought to the table by all but the grandest lords and most important guests. If the company could muster only a few, then these were shared for the occasion. To share a knife was a sign of confidence and trust. The phrase "au pain et au cousteau avec" was translated by Cotgrave as to be "verie familiar, verie much conversant, at bed and at board, as a companion, or haile-fellow well met."[161] The possibility of sharing may have been one of the factors that made experts on etiquette frown on certain practices. Using a knife at table to pare nails, pick teeth, or push food into the mouth was discouraged.[162] To go to the other extreme was equally disliked: "It is not polite to gnaw a bone like a dog."[163] Rules were relaxed for the deserving poor entertained by the pious St. Louis (fig. 33).

The proper use for a knife was to cut meat from the bone into manageable pieces which could then be picked up by hand. It might also serve as a fork, to prong a juicy morsel from a serving dish. This could be dangerous:

> If the dish . . . be fleshe, ten knives shall thou see
> Mangling the flesh, and in the platter flee:
> To put there thy hands is perill without fayle,
> Without a gauntlet or els a glove of mayle.[164]

The knife and not the fingers scooped up salt from the salt-cellar.[165] Unanimity is never easy to achieve, and one writer makes a niggling exception to this general rule:

> At the dinner, let salt be taken with the fingers, not by the knife
> When it is necessary to salt fresh fish.[166]

Large, heavy carving knives were in a class by themselves, necessities at every meal where whole joints and carcasses had to be dismembered. One or two are usually to be seen in pictures, scattered haphazardly on the tablecloth. They were provided by the host and common property for the meal. It was a mark of courtesy, a polite attention, to carve for someone else. A well-bred man would do the honors for the woman sitting next to him.[167]

Great lords and distinguished guests were cossetted at every turn, and the official carver in a large household had the prized but nerve-racking job of ministering to their every whim. Ladies were notoriously hard to please, as they never knew what they wanted for two minutes together.[168] Volumes were written to help the carver cope with every imaginable bird and beast, to "lyfte that swanne," "unlace that cony," "mynce that plover."[169] The importance attached to the job may be gauged by the attention lavished on it and the enervating enthusiasm displayed by all writers when they reach this section—their promised land—in the courtesy books.

Reduced to its essence, the carver's task was to make everything easy and agreeable for his master. Bones were extracted, fat pared away, and a perfect portion shaped. Before this was presented it was cut into three or four slivers, each just large enough to be dipped with two fingers into the appropriate sauce.[170] Once a course had been cleared away, the knife could be used to tidy up the table, sweeping together the crumbs and débris into some container.[171]

Whereas personal knives were sharp and pointed, carving knives had broad, heavy blades for dealing with the sturdiest carcass. In the late Middle Ages a third knife was developed. Called in French a *présentoir,* as the name implies it was used not for cutting but for presentation. Having prepared a portion, the carver would offer it on this to his lord, and lay it on the trencher. The presenter was wide, with a rounded end, as can be seen in fig. 30, where a slice of bread is handed to an inattentive king.

Blades and handles were made in many centers: Paris, Beauvais, Langres, Périgueux. For English cutlery Sheffield, then as now, had pride of place. Chaucer says of a miller in the *Reeve's Tale*: "A Sheffield thwitel [knife] baar he in his hose."[172] Handles were as beautiful and elaborate as the owner could afford, ranging from the modesty of wood, horn, and brass to the splendors of ivory, silver, and gilt enamel. The guildsmen and their wives in the Prologue to the *Canterbury Tales* have social pretensions and the money to back them. Their knives are mounted "noght with bras/But al with silver."[173] For those lucky enough to have them, coats of arms made a gratifying flourish on the handle. In 1352, King John II of France proved he was a worthy father of the Duke de Berry by combining refinement with piety and ordering one pair of carving knives with ebony handles for use during Lent, one pair with ivory for Easter, and one pair checkered with ivory and ebony for Pentecost.[174]

An important and unpopular man might insist on handles of unicorn horn, for this material was believed to be a sure antidote to any poison slipped into the dish. Valiant spadework by Sir Thomas Browne in the seventeenth century uncovered the melancholy truth that early authorities had praised not the unicorn but the Indian ass for the virtues of its horn. Moreover, what passed for the horn of a unicorn in the markets of Europe was in fact the tooth of the narwhal, a very different matter: "And thus, though the description of the Unicorn be very ancient, yet was there of old no vertue ascribed unto it; and although this amongst us receive the opinion of the same vertue, yet it is not the same Horn whereunto the Antients ascribed it."[175] Sad to say, such comments came too late to disturb the dreams of medieval tyrants.

Spoons have been used from very early times. The English word is derived from the Anglo-Saxon *spon,* a chip; the Latin, *coclear,* from *coclea,* a snail or snail shell. Both roots suggest the improvisations from which the finished article evolved. To the medieval cook with his passion for broths, gravies, soups, and sauces, the spoon was a necessity. In many a Nativity scene Joseph can be found stirring some nourishing stew for Mary, while on the door of the thirteenth-century Sainte-Chapelle in Paris Adam fondly does the same for Eve after the birth of Abel. For the medieval diner there were certain alternatives. Fishing with fingers for the vegetables in a broth was one possibility, often practiced though always deplored. Sopping up the soup with pieces of bread was another. Tipping the bowl and drinking directly from it was a third (fig. 33).

Teeth and fingers, however, are better substitutes for a knife than for a spoon, and so the latter was always a welcome addition to the table. In the Hôtel Dieu, a hospital in Paris, no patient was allowed a knife but each was issued with a spoon.[176] In the *Chester Shepherds' Play,* when one of the shepherds offers a soup flask as a present to the baby Jesus he is thoughtful enough to hand over his own spoon as well:

35. Storing the Spoons.
*Statuta Collegii Sapientiae*, Freiburg im Breisgau, 1497 (Freiburg, Universitätsbibliothek, fol. 31r).

> to eate thy potage withall . . .
> as I my selfe full oft hath done.[177]

The spoon was a personal possession, often brought by the guest and not supplied by the host. An early sixteenth-century carving in Vanaja Church, in Finland, shows a shepherd arriving at the stable in Bethlehem with a spoon tucked into his cap.[178] To confirm this as an international custom and convention, the contemporary English poet Alexander Barclay, describing yet another shepherd, picks out the same detail: "In the side of his felte [hat], there stacke a spone of tree [wood]."[179]

When they were provided, spoons sometimes glittered too temptingly for weaker brethren. In the twelfth-century *Roman de Rou*, a knight cannot resist the impulse to slip one up his sleeve.[180] Disillusioned stewards liked to sweep the spoons from the table after the main course and count their stock before the guests had flown.[181] The fifteenth-century statutes of a German college made it very plain that any student who failed to hand in his beaker and spoon after a meal would be docked of a day's ration of bread and wine.[182] A whole chapter is devoted to the subject, headed by a picture of the steward stowing away the valuables in his special

eusmaduito
uummeanni

cupboard (fig. 35). Prevention being better than cure, in fig. 36, where St. Louis is shown doing good works among the sick, the selected patient is allowed to clutch a knife, but Louis holds the spoon. Even in the most trusting household, only one was issued for a meal. The veteran of many dinner parties never left his spoon in a dish, for fear it would be carried off to the kitchen. Instead he retrieved it, wiped it carefully on his bread, and waited hopefully for the next course.[183]

Everyday spoons were made of simple materials, wood, metal, or horn. Of the three, horn was the favorite: "being neither so churlish in weight as mettall . . . nor yet so soiling in use ne rough to the lips as wood is, but lyght plyaunt and smooth, that with a little licking will always be kept as clean as a dy."[184]

A silver spoon was in a class of its own, and the possession of even a single one could be noted with pride in a will or an inventory. It was probably used only on special occasions and valued mainly for its weight, as a good investment. Thomas Bath of Bristol in 1420 listed in his will: "halfe a dosyn off silver sponys . . . that weyyth V ounsus I quarter and halfe [5 ¾ ounces]."[185] Like other pieces of precious tableware, spoons were kept in circulation for a long time. The thirteenth-century accounts of the Countess of Leicester contain an entry about eight silver pennies melted down to mend four broken spoons.[186]

The bowl of a medieval spoon was fig-shaped, broad at the edge and tapering to the shaft. Sometimes the handle ended in an ornamental top, a gilded acorn, a strawberry, a woman's head, or a "wild man" motif. Sometimes it displayed its owner's arms. The Mercers' Company in London still has in its possession four silver spoons of the early fifteenth century, marked with the arms of Dick Whittington, the famous Lord Mayor.

Expensive, beautiful, agreeable to sight and touch, the silver spoon gratified many senses when it made its rare appearances. In fig. 37 the witch of Endor has managed to produce a handsome one for Saul. The dinner she had prepared for him did not actually demand one, consisting as it did of "a fat calf . . . and unleavened bread" (1 Sam. 28:24), but perhaps the illustrator felt that Saul needed something to cheer him after the grim vision of

36. (*opposite*) Spoon Feeding.
*The Hours of Jeanne d'Evreux,* Paris, ca. 1326 (New York, The Metropolitan Museum of Art, The Cloisters Collection, Purchase 1954, fol. 123v).

death and destruction conjured up by his hostess. For a man eating his last meal on earth, Saul looks remarkably pleased with life and very happy with his spoon.

The third and last implement familiar today, the fork, was conspicuous by its absence in the Middle Ages. It seems to have been an elusive, easily forgotten tool, with a habit of slipping in and out of history. Its basic shape and usefulness for spearing objects were known from very early times, but it was one of those inventions that the human imagination found hard to accept and adapt for

37. Saul and the Witch of Endor.
*The Tickhill Psalter*, English, early fourteenth century (New York Public Library, Spencer Collection, Astor, Lenox and Tilden Foundations, MS. 26, fol. 44r).

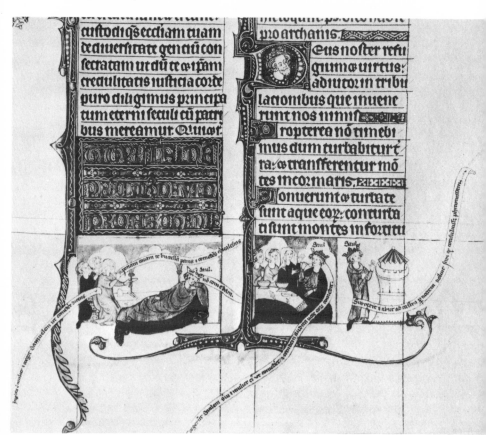

different purposes. In particular, its progress from the kitchen to the dining table was exceedingly slow and erratic.

The fork is mentioned in the Old Testament: "And the priests' custom with the people was, that when any man offered sacrifice, the priests' servant came, while the flesh was in seething, with a fleshhook of three teeth in his hand, And he struck it into the pot . . . all that the fleshhook brought up the priest took for himself" (1 Sam. 2:13–14). This claw-like fork was used by cooks in the same way in the Middle Ages, to fish meat out of a cauldron. Quite often it appears in kitchen scenes, as in fig. 38, which illustrates the Old Testament passage just quoted.

There are two passages in the *Satyricon* by Petronius which show that the fork was known in the Roman kitchen. In one, an angry cook, "snatching a fork from a bureau, stood *en garde* like a gladiator." In the other, a witch "with a long fork took down from the cupboard an old sack in which she kept her stock of beans."[187] Both references suggest a tool with a long reach. Just such a long-handled fork was used by medieval kitchen boys to pile logs on to a fire while standing at a safe distance from the blaze (fig. 39), and by huntsmen to offer choice morsels from a slain deer to their hounds as a reward.[188]

The table fork may have appeared occasionally at elegant Byzantine dinner parties; a fourth-century silver one survives, in the Dumbarton Oaks Collection.[189] It is suspected that the idea of eating with a fork at the table reached Byzantium from the East rather than from Rome, as so little evidence of Roman use has been found. One or two Roman forks have been dug up, including some stems with a fork at one end and a spatula at the other, but so far no literary or pictorial evidence to explain or confirm their use has been uncovered.[190] In rather the same way, a few small Anglo-Saxon forks, again including some double-ended ones, have been discovered, but their purpose remains a mystery.[191]

Even if it be conceded that the fork might have made an occasional appearance on Roman or early medieval tables, it cannot have been widely known, since it caused a sensation when used in Venice in the eleventh century. A Byzantine princess came to marry the future Doge, Domenico Selvo, and at one of the celebrations she scandalized society by refusing to eat with her hands like any ordinary mortal. Instead, after the food had been cut up into little pieces by her eunuchs, she fastidiously popped them one by one into her mouth with a golden fork. Total decadence. Peter Damian, hermit and Cardinal Bishop of Ostia, denounced the whole appalling scene in a passage splendidly entitled: "Of the Venetian Doge's wife, whose body, after her excessive delicacy, entirely rotted away."[192]

Despite this foray into Italy, the table fork still failed to capture the imagination of the West. For the next few centuries the fork appears only in Byzantine art, where one may be spotted from time to time in representations of Abraham entertaining the angels, the Marriage at Cana, and the Last Supper.[193] In a late twelfth-century German manuscript, strongly influenced by Byzantine models, one fork lies on the table in a Last Supper scene.[194] Two large specimens, each paired with a knife, are to be clearly seen in another Last Supper on the magnificent twelfth-century *Pala d'Oro* of the high altar of St. Mark's Cathedral in Venice, made to order in Constantinople.[195]

Although so elusive in Western art, the fork begins to be listed from time to time in the inventories and wills of the late Middle Ages. Sometimes the entries link its use with the eating of fruit or sweetmeats: "I . . . beqwethe . . . my silvir forke for grene gyngour."[196] In the early fourteenth century, the Pope at Avignon speared his meat with a variant of the fork, a little golden skewer, while at the beginning of the fifteenth century, the Duke de Berry ate his strawberries from skewers of crystal with handles of silver and gold.[197]

The impression that medieval forks on the whole were used for sweet and sticky things is strengthened by a casual comparison, made in the mid-thirteenth century by a Franciscan, William of Rubruck, in his report to Louis IX of France on the eating habits of the Tartars: "With the point of a knife or a fork especially made for this purpose—like those with which we are accustomed to eat pears or apples cooked in wine—they offer to each of those standing round one or two mouthfuls."[198] The passage adds one more thread of evidence to the theory that the table fork came to Byzantium first from the East, not from Rome.

Even in the grandest French and English inventories forks are hard to find, although in fourteenth-century Italy Francesco Di Marco Datini, the merchant, had twelve, carefully locked away in his own room.[199] Any table fork that did find a place in the records was a proud possession, made of precious materials. Probably it was brought out rarely, to dazzle guests, and regarded as an investment, something to be sold or melted down for that ready money needed so often for one crisis or another. Certainly an entry in the inventory of Valentina d'Orléans in 1409 suggests

**38. Cook with Kitchen Fork.**
*Maciejowski Manuscript,* illuminated in Paris, ca. 1250 (New York, Pierpont Morgan Library, MS. 638, fol. 20r).

that her single fork was kept more for its value than for use: "A gold fork with her arms on it, with one prong broken."[200] Late in the sixteenth century, Queen Elizabeth of England, on one of those ceremonial, acquisitive visits which so alarmed her hosts,

39. Boy with Fire Fork.
*The Luttrell Psalter,* East Anglian, ca. 1340 (London, British Museum, MS. Add. 42130, fol. 206v). Courtesy of the British Library Board.

thought it worth her while to pocket "a salt, a spoon, and a fork, of fair agate."[201]

Forks conquered Europe very slowly, so slowly indeed that many sixteenth- and seventeenth-century references show that they were still unfamiliar, if not totally unknown, in France and England. Nevertheless, to deepen the mystery of their strange, shadowy existence, they make a bold appearance twice in an eleventh-century manuscript with its roots deep in the past. This, made in the monastery of Montecassino in Italy in 1022/23, is a copy of a ninth-century encyclopedia, *De Universo,* compiled by Rabanus Maurus at Fulda in Germany. Rabanus' work itself looks back over the years, being a glossed version of a seventh-century encyclopedia written in Spain, the *Etymologiae* of Isidore of Seville.

The Montecassino manuscript is richly illustrated, having more than three hundred and sixty pictures filled with late antique elements, clumsily rendered but still recognizable. It is thought that just as the text is ultimately derived from Isidore's, so too this cycle of pictures may have its source in a seventh-century illustrated manuscript of the *Etymologiae.* Tantalizingly, no such manuscript is known to have survived for comparison. Even so, the existence of an early model seems the most likely explanation for the homogeneity of style and the hundreds of late classical details which can be detected in the Montecassino manuscript.[202] The fact that in the seventh century Spain was under the influence of Byzantium lends a little support to the theory, but it is weakened by the undeniable truth that no Byzantine representation of a fork from such an early period has been discovered so far.

The problem is baffling, and it is a relief to turn to the pictures themselves, which are hearteningly clear. In fig. 40 the diner is not using his fork to toy with any fragment of green ginger or stewed pear, but to steady a substantial joint. In a far later, fifteenth-century illustrated German copy of Rabanus' encyclopedia, the fork has vanished from the scene.[203] Nothing could demonstrate more convincingly the fork's feeble hold on life in the Middle Ages. Here and there it was known, here and there admired, and yet it never became an accepted part of the table setting. It emerged for a moment now and then into the spotlight, only to slip away again into the wings to await its next entrance.

40. Table Forks.
Rabanus Maurus, *De Universo*, Montecassino, 1022–23 (Montecassino, Biblioteca dell'Abbazia, codex 132, bk. XXII, chap. I, *De mensis et escis*).

# 7

# Manners Maketh Man

The diner's behavior was affected in a thousand details by the way his table was laid and his meal served. A more subtle influence came from the vision of ideal conduct that hovered hopefully, if sometimes indistinctly, over every well-bred dinner party. In practice, there must have been many a villain with impeccable table manners, but in theory it was stoutly maintained that outward behavior revealed the inner man. This being so, good manners were important not simply because they contributed to the harmony of an occasion, but because they expressed the spiritual grace of the person who displayed them. In an early fifteenth-century treatise on the parish priest and his duties, the good priest and the bad show their true colors at mealtimes. The good one eats slowly and sparingly, never asks for second helpings, and thinks "more of the feast of the mind than that of the stomach." The bad priest rudely shovels in his food, gulps it down, grabs for more, and does not let go of his knife for a split second.[1]

Considered from this point of view, table manners were not trifles but matters of true significance. When Sir Ector delivers the elegy for Lancelot in Malory's *Le Morte Darthur,* he lists the dead man's beautiful manners among his noble achievements: "thou was the mekest man and the jentyllest [most refined] that ever ete in halle emonge ladyes."[2]

The proper tone for a meal was set by the prayer with which it began and ended, giving thanks to God for blessings and bounty. Good manners were the reflection of this mood of grateful love. A man was expected to be sensitive to the feelings of his fellow diners, and if necessary prepared to subdue or conceal his own in order to fit in and make others comfortable. Even self-denial might be less than laudable if flaunted in the face of weaker brethren. England's first Franciscans, in the thirteenth century, deliberately chose for themselves a life of harsh privation. Nevertheless, they mastered the art of tempering rigor with tact. Visitors were offered beer and then, instead of putting them to shame with ostentatious abstention, the friars sat with their guests and "pretended to drink out of charity."[3]

Few diners were expected to emulate such heroic courtesies, but in a hundred tiny ways they were encouraged to think first of their companions. Gossip about bad news, business failures, or medical details was discouraged, loud criticism of the cooking frowned on. Officious attempts to point out flies on the food were firmly forbidden.[4]

Gratitude to God for the plenty one was privileged to enjoy had to be expressed by generosity to others. The ideal of sharing was much admired and colored all behavior at table. When eating with a companion, instead of sharply eyeing his plate to see what special tidbit he had got hold of, a diner was expected to offer delicacies from his own.[5] It was an even more gracious courtesy to share with social inferiors. Bishop Grosseteste, in the mid-thirteenth century, gave this advice to the Countess of Lincoln on the proper way to behave when she sat at dinner with her household: "Command that your dish be so refilled and heaped up . . . that you may courteously give from your dish to all the high table."[6]

To share with the truly poor and needy was not merely an act of kindness but a sign of grace, revealing a love of Jesus and the desire to follow in his footsteps. The table of a prosperous man was expected to be loaded with food, both as visible proof of good fortune and insurance that there were always plenty of leftovers for distribution after the meal. Self-denial was admired when limited to self, scorned when used as a pious pretext for domestic economy. In the twelfth century, St. Thomas Becket's table arrangements struck just the right balance: "Amidst all this [splendor] he was singularly frugal, and his luxurious table provided rich store for almsgiving."[7]

Regrettably, while it was gratifying to share with superiors, and delightful to do so with friends, the idea of sharing with the destitute had not quite the same compelling attraction. Love of God was not always a sufficiently pointed goad to action; sometimes fear of hell was used as the spur to generosity. The most familiar awful warning was the story of Dives, the rich man damned forever because he grudged even a crumb to the beggar Lazarus. Some halls were decorated with scenes of Dives at his table, Lazarus in the dust, but it remains unclear whether such valiant attempts to drive the lesson home ever distracted diners from their rhythmic munching.

Even well-intentioned sinners found it hard to live up to their high principles. Henry, Duke of Lancaster, wrote a devotional treatise, *Le Livre de Seyntz Medicines* (1354), with a rather touching analysis of his own spiritual condition. He certainly knew how he ought to behave, but had to make a rueful admission: although he loved to eat well himself, it cost him a pang to think of sharing the delicacies from one of his splendid dinners with the really hungry.[8]

Most people found it much more congenial to be nice to their pets than considerate to the poor. Fortunately, kindness to animals was regarded as yet another infallible indication of a man's good nature. Happy, well-fed creatures provided encouraging evidence of an affable, open-handed master. Cotgrave, in his *Dictionarie* (1611), sets down under *"Manger"* the proverb "Donner à manger au chien et au chat," with this translation: "to maintain hospitality, keep a plentifull house." The fifteenth-century French illustration to another proverb, "The house reveals its owner," shows a praiseworthy proprietor standing in his pleasant, orderly room, a contented falcon on his wrist and an affectionate dog by his side.[9]

The petting of dogs during dinner was not encouraged, but there was some gap between theory and practice. Certainly their presence was taken for granted. In fig. 41, a greyhound is up on his hind legs, front paws on the tablecloth, surveying the possibilities, while in fig. 28, two small, curly-haired lap dogs are right on the table, rummaging busily in the golden plates under the indulgent eye of the Duke de Berry himself. The Duke would have felt quite at ease with the lord in Caxton's story who "had a lytyll dogge which he loved wel and gaf hym mete and ete upon his table."[10]

Hospitality, to be worthy of the name, had to be shown not only to a guest but to his horse. Froissart, describing his visit to the great Gaston, Count de Foix, in 1388, mentions with approval a tiny, significant detail: "When he saw me, he welcomed me warmly and made me a member of his household, where I stayed for over twelve weeks, with my horses fed and well looked after in every way."[11] In the fourteenth-century romance *Sir Gawain and the Green Knight,* the hero has the same agreeable experience. He finds that his horse has been expertly cared for during a stay at a strange castle, and takes this as one more proof of his host's meticulous courtesy.[12]

41. Hopeful Friend.
*Les Grandes Heures de Rohan,* French, 1419–27 (Paris, Bibliothèque Nationale, MS. lat. 9471, fol. 2v). Photo. Bibl. nat. Paris.

It would be hard to decide which was more pampered, a man's horse or his dog. Froissart himself wrote a poem in which he lets his own animals debate the issue. Each is convinced the other is the spoiled darling, but it is soon clear to the fair-minded reader that there is scarcely a pin to choose between them. The horse is anxiously cosseted at every stage, both at home and on a journey, while the dog gets a bite of bread and butter to sustain him before dinner, and platefuls of rich stew. In misfortune, his master would share the last mouthful with him.[13]

This ideal of sweet and generous affability, however, was held in check by the principle of hierarchy. "A place for everyone, and everyone in his place" was a maxim very dear to the medieval heart. Each person occupied his own precisely defined position on the social ladder; he and everyone around him knew exactly where that was and the degree of honor due to it. To move or be moved up and down the scale were actions deliberately taken and carefully noted. Questions of precedence were debated with relish, seating plans anxiously made, torn up, and made again. To slide a man into just the right slot, the right position on the right table was a rewarding but demanding art. Nightmare visions of ruined tempers and offended guests haunted ambitious hosts and newly appointed marshals on the night before a major feast.

The importance given to seating arrangements is well illustrated by a medieval commentary on the story of the thief crucified with Jesus. At the last moment, on the cross, he turned to Jesus for help, and was comforted with the words, "Today thou shalt be with me in paradise" (Luke 23:43). This easy promise of welcome worried many, for how could a criminal mingle on familiar terms with the saints? It had to be carefully explained that an invitation to heaven was like an invitation to a dinner party: everyone entered the hall through the same door, but once inside was seated in strict order of precedence. The saints were honored at high table; those who had tried to be good found their places at the side tables. Sinners like the thief, who had squeaked in by the skin of their teeth, sat on the floor and felt very relieved to be there at all.[14]

A man's place at table varied with his fortune; all his life he was a player in a tense game of snakes and ladders. In the fifteenth century, Margery Kempe, a difficult companion, so irritated her fellow pilgrims by lachrymose devotions that they "made her sit at the table's end, below all the others."[15] Even there she made their blood boil, because the host for the occasion, mesmerized by her non-stop piety, still insisted on serving her before everyone else, thus outrageously standing the natural order on its head.

On the other hand, John of Salisbury, an English scholar, recalls with relish his own social promotion at the hands of Pope Adrian IV. John was only a clerk in the household of the Archbishop of Canterbury when he was sent on business to the Papal Court in 1156. Nevertheless, the Pope singled him out for most gratifying attentions: "It was his delight to have me eat with him at his very own table, where, against my protestations, he willed and ordered that we use a common cup and plate."[16]

Humility might be laudable, but there was a time for all things. To allow oneself to be maneuvered into a place beneath one's dignity merely sharpened contempt. No commentary is needed on this terse sentence: "He sate beneth his wyfe."[17] It was another matter to humble oneself deliberately and willingly before another. Such behavior was regarded as a special sacrifice at the altar of politeness, though rarely received quite in the spirit intended. After his victory at Poitiers in 1356, the Black Prince of England entertained his prisoner, King John II of France, and insisted on serving at the King's table. King John must have longed to reverse the roles, especially as the prince persisted in rubbing salt into the wound: "He constantly kneeled before him [the King], saying: 'Beloved Sire, do not make such a poor meal, even though God has not been willing to heed your prayers today.' "[18]

If the King felt any twinge of ingratitude, he kept it to himself. Others were less forbearing. In 1170, Henry II of England crowned his son, in the hope of securing a peaceful succession to the throne after his own death. On the day of coronation, King Henry rounded off the celebration by waiting on his own child at dinner. This was heady wine for the new king, who became more arrogant by the minute. When the Archbishop of York pointed out that no other prince in the world had such a waiter, the insufferable young man replied: "Why doost thou marvell at that? My father in doing it, thinketh it not more than becommeth him: he being borne of princelie bloud onlie on the mother's side, serveth me that am a king borne having both a king to my father and a queene to my mother."[19]

The example which inspired these feats of courtesy was the behavior of Jesus at the Last Supper when he knelt to wash the feet of his disciples. Such a reversal of the natural relationship between leader and followers stirred much turmoil in the medieval mind, torn between admiration and disapproval. Something of this struggle may be suspected behind the formation of the legend of St. Martial, who was said to have helped Jesus by bringing in the water and the towels, and thus in fact taking care of all the menial work involved. He may be found sometimes, hovering usefully in the background of Last Supper illustrations.[20]

The struggle comes out into the open in a little exchange between Joinville and his master, St. Louis, King of France: "King Louis asked me if I washed the feet of the poor on Maundy Thursday. 'Your Majesty,' I exclaimed, 'what a terrible idea! I will never wash the feet of such low fellows.' 'Really,' said he, 'that is a very wrong thing to say; for you should never scorn to do what our Lord himself did as an example for us.' "[21] In the *Hours of Jeanne d'Évreux* there is a picture of St. Louis washing the feet of some beggars, while Joinville stands behind him, arms tightly folded, the very image of outrage at the licensed eccentricities of holiness.[22]

This nervous obsession with hierarchy and order was a natural response to conditions. The medieval period was a violent and passionate one, crying out for a straitjacket of rules and regulations. Life was only too often crude and coarse, and this in turn prompted an equally natural preoccupation with elegance, refinement, and dexterity. The desire of anyone with a social pretension to his name was to rise above the roughness of everyday life, to improve on nature, to set as wide a gulf as possible between himself and the peasant. His best efforts, of course, were reserved for public appearances; what he did in the privacy of his own home might be a very different matter.

It was important, particularly for a woman, to show a certain lack of interest in food when invited out to dinner. Peasant appetites, like peasant manners, were not for public view. St. Bernardino of Siena, in the fourteenth century, told of a very greedy woman who prided herself on her refinement. One of the servants brought her a basket of cherries, and silently watched her gobbling them up. As soon as her husband appeared, the pace slackened. The wife picked up one cherry at a time and delicately nibbled it, while asking the servant condescendingly, "How do people eat cherries out there in the country?" There was a disconcerting reply: "They eat them just as you did yours in your room this morning, in great handfuls."[23]

If the temptation to eat heartily could not be resisted, and it rarely was, then at least there must be no sign of overindulgence.

No satisfied belching, no patting of the well-rounded stomach, no bursting at the seams was permitted. To make room for the meal, a discreet loosening of the belt before dinner began was the recommended procedure.[24] Sometimes circumstances demanded the supreme sacrifice. The writer of *La Clef d'Amour*, a twelfth-century French adaptation of Ovid's *Art of Love*, strongly urged any woman dining with her lover to choose the mustard sauce and wave away the garlic.[25] Della Casa in his *Galateo* (1551/55) felt that spitting in company might be avoided with a little self-control: "You should . . . take care, as far as you can, not to spit at mealtimes. I have often heard that the people of some countries are so demure that they never spit at all, and we might well refrain from doing so for a short time."[26]

The medieval admiration for craftsmanship and technical mastery in all the arts is reflected in the attitude toward table-service, and in particular toward the carver's task. Expert eyes followed every move of the knife, and displays of clumsiness were not appreciated: "Thou art as meet to be a great man's carver as a cow to bear a saddle."[27] Virtuoso performances were much relished, and first-class artists knew just how to milk the applause. Even on the hunting-field, the ceremonial breaking-up of a deer before a great lord was done by carvers so skilled that they ostentatiously refused to turn up their sleeves, supremely confident that not a drop of blood would be spattered on their clothes.[28]

Only the torments of first love might be accepted, grudgingly, as an excuse for a disastrous lapse. In a thirteenth-century romance, the hero, Jehan, is a young Frenchman living with a family in England, as the daughter's language tutor. Needless to say, he falls in love with his pupil while laboring to improve her incorrigibly English accent. The lessons he can handle, but when asked to carve at table before the family he stands in a trance, unable to move a muscle. Called sharply to attention by a hungry heroine he starts, but the knife slips in his hand and badly slashes his fingers. He is hurried away to his bedroom, covered in blood and shame, only to revive when the remorseful Blonde comes to comfort him with a little affection and a lot of cold chicken, cooked to perfection in a special grape juice sauce.[29]

Order, freshness, and neatness in a dining room gave great pleasure; slovenliness, then as now, was the sign of an incompetent housekeeper. St. Bernardino in a sermon thundered against wives who made their husbands a pigsty instead of a home: "In the room in which he eats, the floor is covered with melon rind and bones and salad leaves ... He wipes the trenchers off; the dog licks them, and so washes them. Know you how he lives? Like a brute beast. Women, bow your heads! It is the woman who rules the house."[30]

A twelfth-century biography of St. Thomas Becket gives special praise to the saint for the delightful refinement of his dining hall, in phrases which reveal the practical utility of clean, appetizing arrangements: "He ordered his hall to be strewn every day with fresh straw or hay in winter, and with green rushes or leaves in summer, that the hosts of knights, who could not find room on the benches, might find the floor clean and wholesome, lest they should soil their precious coats and fine shirts."[31]

Medieval realities may have fallen far short of perfection; hundreds of stories about horrid conditions could be effortlessly gathered, not to mention such significant hints as the prudent advice murmured in a fifteenth-century French courtesy book: always look at the seat to make sure it is acceptably clean before settling down to dinner.[32] Nevertheless, the ideal shone out hopefully in a murky world. Indeed, the medieval attitude contrasts very favorably with that of the Romans, who were not only in the habit of throwing bones, shells, and assorted débris on the floor during a meal, but were quite prepared to admire works of art based on the theme. Several examples have been found of mosaics designed with this subject, bluntly classified by contemporaries as "the unswept pavement."[33]

The happy dream of propriety and elegance warmed by loving generosity was easier to bring to life in a small company than a large one, at an unpretentious rather than a splendid occasion. Grand events strained every nerve, and in the process badly frayed them. The greater the affair, the greater were the problems of organization, the more numerous the pitfalls into which to stumble, the more prickly the feelings which had to be smoothed and gratified. The Scylla and Charybdis of a formal banquet were excessive muddle and excessive, glum formality.

Froissart describes the ceremonial dinner party given to celebrate the entrance of Queen Isabella of France into Paris in 1389. The crush of people was so great that the high table had to be protected not only by a wooden barrier but by serjeants-at-arms, royal ushers, and mace-bearers. Five hundred ladies were seated at side tables, ravenous in the midst of plenty because attendants could not fight their way through the crowds to serve them. Into this confusion was trundled the entertainment: a tower on wheels, representing Troy; an assault tower, also on wheels, manned by Greeks, and a model ship packed with a hundred soldiers. A refreshing battle had been planned but, not surprisingly, things got out of hand:

> The entertainment could not last long because of the great crush of people round it. Some were made ill by the heat, or fainted in the crowd. A table near the door of the parliament chamber was overturned by force. The ladies who were sitting at it had to get up hurriedly, without ceremony. The great heat and the stink of the crowd almost caused the Queen to faint, and a window which was behind her had to be broken to let in the air. . . . The King saw what was happening and ordered the performance to stop. This was done and the tables were quickly cleared and taken down, to give the ladies more room. The wine and spices were served hurriedly and, as soon as the King and Queen had gone to their apartments, everyone else left also.[34]

While some banquets degenerated into football scrums, others had the life frozen out of them by the excesses of etiquette. The English are notorious for taking their pleasures sadly, and foreign observers are sometimes stunned by the solemnity of state occasions. At the very end of the fifteenth century, a Venetian was invited to a City of London banquet at which two Sheriffs were appointed, and wrote down his impressions: "At this feast . . . I noticed how punctiliously they sat in their order, and the extraordinary silence of everyone."[35] A few years earlier, a Bohemian, Leo of Rozmital, was traveling in England, and one day was allowed to watch Edward IV's queen at dinner. Once again: "Everyone was silent and not a word was spoken."[36] No wonder that a fifteenth-century schoolboy found private snugness preferable to public splendor: "I sytt oftyn tymes emongest them at melys tyme the whych be of more dignite and worshipe then I, wher I may not speke except they appose [question] me, but I hade lever [rather] fare hardely and sytt emongest my companyons wher I may be mery and speke what I wyll."[37]

The technical difficulties of serving a large company swiftly and well helped to shorten tempers. In the first place there was the problem of cooking for many people, a matter not always solved to everyone's satisfaction. The *Great Chronicle* describes the first mayoral banquet held in the London Guildhall and dismisses the food in one terse phrase: "Ful Rawe."[38] A late thirteenth-century

Latin poem, *The Lament of the Roast Swan,* has the insistent and
ominous refrain: "Misery, misery! Now I am black and badly
burnt."[39] William the Conqueror was so enraged when presented
with a half-roasted crane that he tried to knock down the steward
who brought it.[40] If the King had to be content with a raw bird
that day, what did the rest of the company have to swallow? The
situation must have been only too familiar, as it is chosen both at
Notre Dame in Paris and at Amiens Cathedral to illustrate the vice
of ingratitude: a servant on his knees is shown presenting a dish
to his mistress and rewarded for his pains with a kick in the
stomach.[41]

To add to the cook's worries and the diner's discontent, dishes
might be not merely underdone when they left the kitchen, but
cold when they reached the table. Because of fire hazards, the
kitchen was usually at a little distance from the hall, and sometimes in a separate building. Although there might be a covered
passage between the two, food could not always be rushed along
it. Set up in this corridor would be the surveying-board, on which
final touches were added to those dishes intended for high table.
Elegant arrangements take time and encourage creeping chill
(fig. 42).

Even when a certain creation was not delayed in the corridor it
might be cold by the time it was actually tasted. One of the
carver's many responsibilities was to complete the cook's work at
the table. Not only did he carve a joint into acceptable slices, but
he combined these with the proper sauce, which had been sent up
with the meat. John Russell's instructions on how to deal with a
crab may stand for all. After a preliminary, heartfelt remark,
echoed through the centuries ever since, "Crabbe is a slutt to
kerve," he describes how to take the flesh from the claws, remove
any sinews, and then mix it with a sharp vinegar sauce and re-
arrange it in the shell. It is no wonder that the last piece of advice
reads:

> Send the crabbe to the kychyn there for to hete,
> agayn hit facche to thy soverayne sittynge at mete.
> [Send the crab back to the kitchen to be reheated,
> then bring it back to your lord sitting at dinner.][42]

42. (*opposite*) Serving Hatch.
*Guiron,* Flemish, ca. 1480–1500 (Oxford, Bodleian Library, MS. Douce
383, fol. 1).

Jcy commence le quart volume de Guion le courtois / Et dist comment
vne damoiselle vint a la court du roy artus / et de son message.

u temps que
le roy artus ten
gnoit en sa plus
grant prosperite
honneur et haul
tesse et quil estoit ame de ses subgies
et voisins Craint et doubte de ses

ennemis Et que par sa grant
largesse et bonte de cheualerie
tout le monde pres et loms par
loit de sa bonte qui estoit telle que
a son pouoir exaulchoit lordre
de cheualerie et pour ce et tous
cheualiers estoit ame et serui

Even when hot, the portion might be meager. Whereas the ideal feast was lavish, brimming with good things and plenty for all comers, in hard reality budgets had to be balanced. One way of maintaining solvency was to distinguish in both quality and quantity between dishes served to high table and dishes for the also-ran. The problem was an old one. Roman dinner parties too could be sternly stratified, and not many hosts, Roman or medieval, were prepared to emulate Pliny the Younger's self-sacrifice. In one of his letters, Pliny mentions his custom of serving exactly the same wine to all his guests. "Even the freedmen?" an incredulous friend enquires; "that must cost you a lot." Pliny then blandly explains how he keeps his bills within reason: "On the contrary—because my freedmen do not drink the sort of wine I do, but I drink theirs."[43] Medieval hosts who failed to follow in these footsteps were inclined to favor cookery books which suggested helpfully: "tak chekine chopped for comons, for a lord tak hole chekins."[44]

The serving of wine well illustrates the nice calculations which went to the making of a dinner party. It was the custom to mix wine with water, on grounds both of health and morals. Indeed the cardinal virtue of temperance is often shown from the eleventh century on with a wine cup in one hand and a water bottle in the other, the very personification of sensible moderation.[45] Moderation, however, was always approved of with more conviction for the lower orders than for one's peers. In the thirteenth century Joinville describes his own household arrangements: "I used to buy a good hundred barrels of wine, and always had the best drunk first. I had wine mixed with water issued to my servants, and gave the same to my squires, but with a lesser proportion of water. At my own table a large flask of wine and a bottle containing water were placed before each of the knights, so that he might mix his drink as he wished."[46] It was usual for wine to be issued to guests, that is, served on request from supplies kept firmly off the table itself. Only special diners enjoyed the privilege of wine standing on the table in full view and within arm's reach. No wonder that a poor wandering scholar of the twelfth century wrote: "Wine from a tavern tastes more sweet to me than that which the bishop's butler mixes with water."[47]

When the kitchen was a little distance from the hall and the household was a large one, there were innumerable opportunities for the spiriting away of dishes for private feasts in private rooms.

If this happened one can be reasonably certain that it was not high table which went short.

With all this medieval portion control it is hardly surprising that at least one courtesy book offers advice on what to do when seated at a board which, far from groaning, is barely whimpering:

> And whan the borde is thynne as of servyse
> Nought replenesshed with grete diversite
> Of mete and drinke, good chere may then suffise
> With honest talkyng.
> [When the table is rather bare,
> and not kept filled with great variety of meat and drink,
> good cheer and pleasant talk must be enough.][48]

It is hard to chat cheerfully when one is both hungry and ruffled by a servant's rudeness. Guests were not the only ones who were sharply sensitive to distinctions of rank; servants if anything knew even better who was on the way up or down, and were not prepared to waste their sweetness on the desert air. Not much attention was devoted to the unimportant, and a servant was offered the rather chilling advice to concentrate on the main chance and act accordingly:

> in especyal, use ye attendaunce
> Wherein ye shal your self best avaunce.[49]

The tribulations of the second-class guest did not end here. Rank and importance determined how comfortable a man would be at a winter dinner party. As may be seen in fig. 28, the Duke de Berry at his New Year feast sits with his back to a roaring fire, protected by a screen from too much heat. In *Sir Gawain and the Green Knight,* the hero, an honored visitor, is offered a fur-lined cloak to wear indoors when he arrives on Christmas Eve at Bercilak's castle.[50] A fifteenth-century schoolboy was not so cosseted: "The moste part of this wynter my handes were so swellynge with colde that I coulde nother holde my penn for to wrytt nother my knyff for to cutt my mete at the table."[51]

The fourteenth-century poet Deschamps strongly urged his fellow courtiers to stay away from the king's court between November and February: "As for the courtiers' lodgings, God knows how cold they are and how grudgingly the fuel is doled out; in hall, everyone shivers, servants and squires are not permitted to wear cloaks. If you don't want to dance this sort of dance, in this cold weather it is best to stay away."[52] Deschamps implied that it was sensible to stay at home, and indeed home had certain distinct advantages. As a guest, the diner's comfort was determined by his host's standards of generosity and the servants' interpretation of them. At home, a man could sit at his own table, eat his own food, piping hot from the kitchen, bully, or at least coax, his own servant, draw up as close as he liked to the fire, undo his belt, and never share his cup with a fellow-guest. In Lydgate's retelling of an old fable, a mouse shows his guest, a frog, around the mill he calls his home and explains the tranquil pleasures of independence:

> "See," quoth the mouse, "thys ys a mery lyfe.
> Here ys my lordshyp and dominacion.
> I lyve here esyly out of noyse and stryfe.
> Thys cloos all hoole ys in my subieccion.
> [This whole room is my territory.]
> As I have appetyte, I dyne late or sone;
> For Gyb, the catte, hathe here nothyng to done."⁵³

Strong feelings about the comfort of home are revealed by Matthew Paris in an entry in his *Chronicle* for the year 1248. Henry III that October had instituted a new fair at Westminster, and, to make sure there would be lots of business, he forbade other fairs to take place at the same time. The merchants were less than enthusiastic: "They had no shelter except canvas tents . . . they were cold and wet . . . their feet were soiled by the mud, and their goods rotted by the showers of rain; and when they sat down to take their meals there, those who were accustomed to sit down to their meals in the midst of their family by the fireside, knew not how to endure this state of want and discomfort."⁵⁴

The slow, steady growth of pleasure in creature comforts is one reason for the move away from the great hall to the small dining chamber in the later medieval period. Traditionally, the whole household ate together, under the sharp, benevolent eye of its lord. It was an official family, a unity, and the shared meal expressed and strengthened the bonds between master and men. In the mid-thirteenth century, Bishop Grosseteste advised the Countess of Lincoln to stick to the good old ways: "So far as possible for sickness or fatigue, constrain yourself to eat in the hall before your people, for this shall bring great benefit and honour to you."⁵⁵ A century later, the poet Langland was grumbling that the head of the house liked to slip away to his chimney-corner in a private room, "to eten bi hym-selve." No good could come of the change:

> Elying is the halle . . .
> There the lorde ne the lady. liketh noughte to sytte
> [There is something wrong with the hall
> where the lord and lady do not care to sit.][56]

Langland saw nothing but selfishness in the changing attitudes, a sharp tearing of the social fabric. The lord was concerned only with his own comfort, indifferent to his people's welfare, careless of his obligations to the poor and the weary traveler knocking at the gate.

Despite all a poet or a moralist could say, snug privacy had tempting charms. The fact that it did not gain a really firm grip on the imagination of the age may be attributed not to any reviving consciousness of duties to be borne but to one distinct drawback. Solitary dining could be rather dull. In a period when not many people read at all, and fewer still read much, the company of others guaranteed amusement, or at least distraction. The kinds of entertainment offered by a feast will be considered in the next chapter.

# 8

# Entertainment: Surprise and Sotelty

The quiet meal at home has many charms, and several advantages over the grand dinner party, but in one respect it cannot begin to compete with its rival: in entertainment. A medieval feast worthy of the name proceeded at a leisurely pace, with plenty of time between courses to be filled by an enterprising host with incidental delights and surprises. To feed the guests was only a part of the program. The aim was to excite and satisfy every sense: taste, touch, sight, smell, and hearing.

The one amusement sure to be shared by the simplest meal for two and the most elaborate banquet was conversation. In this matter, each kind of occasion had its own pleasures and pitfalls. Sitting at unbuttoned ease among his friends, a man could chat in comfort about any subject that floated into his head. As the old man in More's *Dialogue of Comfort* (1534) explains disarmingly: "To talk much . . . is to me little grief. . . . It is . . . all the lust of an old fool's life to sit well and warm with a cup and a roasted crab, and drivel and drink and talk."[1] No one, save his listeners, could grudge him this innocent satisfaction; for them, the stories and opinions may have worn thin with time.

Relentless repetition takes the savor from the best of jokes. Pictures of unleavened bread and bitter herbs, two essential ingredients of the Jewish Passover feast, the seder, are usually present in the Haggadah, the book of readings for the occasion. One fourteenth-century Spanish manuscript shows the herb, with the words "*Maror zeh*" (this bitter herb) written above. Below, a man points across the dining table to his own bitter herb, his wife.[2] After ten or twenty years of marriage, ten or twenty seders, only true love could bring the shadow of a smile to her lips in dutiful response.

The tedious commonplace and the threadbare joke were penalties imposed from time to time for eating comfortably at home. Dining in a great household could also be a dull affair, when guests were on their best behavior and painfully conscious of rank and protocol. But to be seated at the center of affairs had certain advantages. By its nature, any great man's hall was a whispering gallery of news and views. There was a constant bustle of visitors, and round them swirled eddies of rumor and opinion about the people, events, and ideas of the moment. This was one reason why Froissart the chronicler derived so much professional satisfaction from his stay at the court of Count Gaston de Foix in the autumn of 1388. His host's domain, just north of the Pyrenees, was most conveniently placed for gossip on the borders of French territory in Languedoc, English territory in Gascony, and the Kingdom of Navarre in Spain:

> Reports from every country and kingdom were to be heard, for, because of the reputation of the master of the house, they were brought there in great abundance. At Orthez I was informed of most of the feats of arms which had taken place in Spain, Portugal, Aragon, Navarre, England, Scotland and within the borders of Languedoc, for while staying there I met knights and squires from all those nations who had come to visit the Count. And so I gathered information either from them or from the Count himself, who was always willing to talk to me of such matters.[3]

Not every great house was quite so well situated as Gaston de Foix's for the stimulating exchange of views, but every man of consequence could be expected to provide some other kind of amusement, at least for the year's major celebrations. He might maintain a troupe of entertainers, or make use of someone else's for the occasion, or, indeed, have the best of both worlds by allowing his own men to perform at another hall while he enjoyed fresh faces and new acts at his own. By the beginning of the fourteenth century such small, mobile bands of players had become a familiar part of the festive scene. Froissart noted that, at suppertime, Gaston de Foix "would remain at table for about two hours, and he . . . enjoyed having travelling entertainers to perform between the courses. After he had watched them, he sent them round the tables of the knights and squires."[4]

Churchmen liked to be amused at the dinner table as much as everyone else. The Account Rolls of Selby Abbey in Yorkshire list payments to players who appeared there at the great feasts of the year from 1431 to 1532. An entry for the first year is typical: "And to the players before the Lord Abbot at the feast of the Nativity of the Lord, 12d."[5] The accounts for 1479/80 suggest that the abbot made sure his guests would not grow bored with the same stale old routines. Welcomed to the abbey in that year were the following troupes: the players of Sir John Conyers, Sir James Tyrell, Lord Scrope, the Duke of Gloucester, and the Earl of Northumberland, together with one of the King's company and three men who seem to have belonged to nobody in particular.[6]

Only the occasional entry hints at the kind of routines the entertainers offered: "In reward given to the players . . . that is Tumblers this year [ca. 1500], 2s."[7] Other sources show that tumblers, or acrobats, were indeed very popular, together with jugglers, animal trainers, conjurors, and comedians. Manuscript borders swarm with such performers. Knives are juggled, planks held on chins, goblets set on sticks and balanced on foreheads. Little dogs jump through hoops and men dance while playing a triangle and gripping a candlestick with two candles between the teeth.[8] One boy balances a sword on its point in the palm of his hand and another makes a wheel roll up and down his arm.

Today we tend to conjure up a sinuous, erotic dance when we picture Salome performing before Herod at dinner and persuading him to reward her with John the Baptist's head. The medieval imagination was filled with quite a different image: "Herodias' doughter was a tumbestere, and tumblede byfore him and other grete lordes of that contre."[9] Salome was an acrobat, expertly somersaulting her way into Herod's heart. On a roof boss in Norwich Cathedral she has bounced with such brio before the King and his guests that her dress has split right down the back.[10] In a fourteenth-century wall painting at Idsworth church in Hampshire, before a table laid for dinner Salome arches her body backward until her head almost touches the ground, and still manages to juggle with three swords, one in each hand and one in mid-air.[11] Such inexhaustible energy is coupled with modest decorum. In the *Holkham Bible Picture Book* Salome, far from showing any inclination to shed veil after veil, achieves a handstand which leaves her skirt still demurely in place around her ankles.

Comedy was supplied by the fool, licensed, within limits, to make fun of master and visitors alike. It was a job for the seasoned diplomat, and not every fool had the tact to sense the line between permissible wit and outrageous rudeness. We have a glimpse of one in action in More's *Utopia* (1516). A long and serious discussion at the dinner table about the condition of England is interrupted more and more frequently by "a certain jesting parasite," who stands behind the guests and leans over their shoulders to add his contribution to the argument. His comments about one man become so personal that a furious quarrel flares up, and the host has to cut in swiftly to smooth ruffled feathers: "The cardinal seing that none end wold be made, sent away the jester by a prevy beck [secret sign], and turned the communication to an other matter."[12]

Of the ingredients considered necessary for a satisfactory supper by Bartholomeus Anglicus, a thirteenth-century English Franciscan, music is listed as number eight: "myrthe of songe and of Instrumentes of musike. Noble men use not to make suppers without harpe or symphony."[13] As in the case of the vaudeville entertainers, musicians were part of a great man's household. They were his men, and their quality was an indication of his taste. Like other performers they played sometimes at home, sometimes away. At supper, Gaston de Foix "liked his clerks to sing songs, rondeaux and virelays for him."[14] A century earlier, Louix IX of France showed his unfailing courtesy to visiting musicians: "When minstrels in some nobleman's service arrived with their viols to entertain him after dinner, the King would always wait till they had finished singing before he would let grace be said."[15]

Music had three principal parts to play at a feast: to punctuate, by announcing the ceremonial high points of the meal; to delight the diners; and to charm away the pangs of indigestion. The bright flourish of trumpets gave the signal for hands to be washed, marked the entrance of each course, and brought the dinner to a formal close. While guests munched, drank, and chattered their way through the meal, the players had the thankless task of providing background music for the hubbub. At the end, and in the intervals between the courses, they had more chance to shine as they entertained a captive and contented audience.

At such times, when people were attentive and prepared to listen, musicians might move easily through the hall, stopping here and there to sing and play at close range, so that the subtleties of words and arrangements would not be lost. For bold effects it was better for them to be concentrated in some commanding position from which the instruments could ring out above the din. By the later medieval period it was usual to have a gallery built over the doors which led out to the service passageway and so to the kitchens. Up there the musicians could look down the hall to the high table at the other end and play directly to the host and the only guests who really mattered.

From such a vantage point trumpets and horns sang out to mark the passage of the feast. For gaiety there were tabors and drums, bells and bagpipes. For softer moods, flutes and recorders were blended with whole families of bowed and plucked instruments, from fiddles and rebecs to viols, lutes, harps, and guitars. Any one of these might be used to accompany a song, either on its own or in some intriguing combination with another. Contrast in tone was prized, and the piquancy of wind and string instruments playing together was much appreciated.

Among the many different kinds of song enjoyed the carol held pride of place in the audience's affections. From account rolls and contemporary records it is clear that trained carol singers turned up regularly on the bill of entertainment designed for an important feast. In his journal, William More, the last Prior of Worcester, wrote down the expenses for his abbey's annual Christmas feast, given to a mixed company of clergy and city officials. Year after year he noted payments to minstrels, entertainers, and carolers: "1518: Item to syngers of carralls 14d./8d./8d. ... 1520: Item rewards for caralls on Christmas day dynar 14d./at supper 8d. ... 1527: Item for syngyng of carrolls on cristmas day and to mynstrells 2s. 6d. 16d."[16] During Henry VII's Twelfth Night feast in 1487, "at the Table in the Medell of the Hall sat the Deane and those of the Kings Chapell, which incontynently [straightaway] after the Kings furst Course sange a Carall."[17]

By its nature, however, the carol did not depend for success on any rigorously high standard of trained ensemble singing, but adapted itself easily to the cheerful inadequacies of amateur performance. In form it consisted of a stanza and a burden. The words of each stanza changed as the song proceeded, but the burden, or refrain, remained the same, repeated after every stanza. Traditionally, carolers joined hands and formed themselves into a line or a circle. While each stanza was sung they marked time on the spot and then began to dance as they took up the words of the burden. As the description of the Twelfth Night celebration suggests, the carol was not always danced, but its essential form had been shaped by these age-old links between rest and motion, verse and refrain. Although the whole group joined in the chorus, the verse was sung by a soloist, and it was this leader alone who had to know all the words of a particular carol;

two lines, repeated again and again, were the only contribution expected from the others.

The carol is a song with a long history, stretching back for thousands of years. It is found in many countries and in many settings. Sometimes it is sung in the open air, sometimes indoors. Sometimes it is a work song for harvest or threshing, sometimes it is festive, for people at play. The Church first feared it as a pagan survival and then thought again, shrugged, and transformed it into a celebration of Christian doctrine. By the later medieval period it had become associated particularly with Christmas and all the concentrated merriment packed into the twelve days between 25 December and Epiphany. Its characteristic setting was the hall, and there it flourished in that atmosphere of relaxed happiness which is induced by good dinners and good company.

It became such an accepted part of the season's festivities that, in a fourteenth-century romance, King Arthur's guests for Christmas knew just what would be on the program even before they had arrived at his castle. They "kayred [rode] to the court caroles to make." Further on in the story, at a second Christmas house party, the visitors stayed up late one night to dance carols, and on another sang their carols round the fire in the hall both during supper and long afterward.[18]

No great courage is needed to sing and dance like this in a group of friends, but sometimes more was demanded. In several carols there are strong hints that guests were expected to put their best foot forward and entertain the company with their own party piece. Forfeits awaited those who could not or would not oblige:

> Make we mery, bothe more and lasse,
> For now ys the tyme of Crystymas.

> Lett no man cum into this hall,
> Grome, page, nor yet marshall,
> But that sum sport he bryng withall,
> For now ys the tyme of Crystmas.

> Yff that he say he can not syng,
> Sum oder sport then lett hym bryng,
> That yt may please at thys festyng,
> For now ys the tyme of Crystmas.

> Yff he say he can nowght do,
> Then for my love aske hym no mo,
> But to the stokkes then lett hym go,
> For now ys the tyme of Crystmas.[19]

Froissart offers a glimpse of just such an occasion in his chronicle for 1363. King John II of France, unlucky victim of an interminable war, arrived in England that January as a prisoner. Perhaps conscious that the next turn of Fortune's wheel might well reverse their roles, Edward III received him with great honor and arranged a splendid party to cheer him up: "He arrived on a Sunday in the afternoon, and between then and supper there was time for much dancing and merriment. The young Lord de Coucy in particular took great pains to dance and sing well when his turn came. He was much applauded by both French and English, for whenever he did a thing he did it well."[20]

Music, song, and dance lent their charms to a dinner and heightened its excitement. Other ingredients added their own touches of drama and beauty. For even the humblest and the hungriest spectator, squashed disregarded in a drafty corner, there was always something to delight the eye and excite the imagination as courses were brought in, dishes presented, carved, accepted, waved aside. Ceremony transformed the simple, daily acts of eating and drinking into high theater. Everyone shared an ingrained sense of occasion, and the great and powerful could be relied on to satisfy it. When about to eat his supper alone, without guests, Gaston de Foix still made his formal entrance into the hall each night as "twelve lighted torches were carried before him by twelve serving-men, and these twelve torches were held up in front of his table, giving a bright light in the hall, which was full of knights and squires."[21]

Whether glimmering by torchlight or shining in the mid-day sun, displays of the best tableware enriched the splendor of the scene, while the liveliness of design and the lavish use of motto and rebus added to the fun and interest. For special occasions flowers and leaves were brought in to decorate the tables and the lucky guests. In his list of details to be attended to for a May wedding, the Goodman of Paris notes that "branches, greenery, violets, chaplets" must be bought in good time "at the Porte-de-Paris." To supplement these there would be needed the services of "a woman chaplet maker who shall deliver garlands on the wedding eve and on the wedding day."[22] Just such a chaplet is being used to put a guest in the right mood in a thirteenth-century stained-glass window at Bourges Cathedral. The Prodigal Son, an innocent abroad with his pockets full of money, has been coaxed to sit down to dinner with two prostitutes. By the end of the evening they will have taken every penny from him, but at this stage in the rake's progress he is still enjoying his night on the town. A roast chicken has been brought in and the women are charming their victim out of his senses: one caresses him while the other is about to crown him king of the feast with a garland of flowers.[23]

If all this were not enough to amuse the most jaded diner there was always the possibility of jolting him out of his indifference with a well-planned surprise. The medieval public would have dearly loved the detachable jam stain and the plastic spider that do duty today at countless family dinner tables throughout the Western world when children reach a certain age. Lacking these, they made do with whatever came to mind and hand. Even the Goodman of Paris, that model of sober common sense, had his own recipe for making a glass of white wine turn red before the astonished drinker: *"To Make White Wine Red at Table*: Take in summer the red flowers that grow in the corn . . . and let them dry until they can be made into powder, and cast it privily into the glass with the wine and the wine will become red."[24]

A more ambitious, or more desperate host might consider the use of a jumping chicken to liven up a tedious party. In one of the great medieval bestsellers, the late thirteenth-century *Book of Secrets of Albertus Magnus,* there are helpful instructions under the heading "If thou wilt that a Chicken or other thing leap in the dish." Mercury, or quicksilver, is to be put inside the cooked bird, "for seeing Quicksilver is hot, it moveth itself, and maketh it [the chicken] to leap or dance."[25] The mechanical principles involved were not revealed.

Rather than ruin a perfectly good chicken, the economical might prefer to baffle guests with a re-usable puzzle jug. A handsome and elaborate example was dug up in Exeter in 1899 (fig. 43). It was made in the sophisticated potteries of Saintonge in southwest France in the late thirteenth century, and must have been imported for a very prosperous customer. Liquid poured into its mouth passes down the hollow handle, across the base, and out again through the spout. The main body of the jug is made to look like a three-storied building, its walls pierced with windows. Bishops or abbots can be glimpsed through these openings, standing just inside on the first and third floors, while from the middle one women lean out of windows to listen to fiddlers playing below. The jug is so fretted with holes that its ability to retain the contents is a baffling mystery until the inner structure is explained.

43. Exeter Puzzle Jug.
Polychrome ware from Saintonge, southwest France, late thirteenth century (Exeter City Museum, Devonshire).

Just as mystifying to the uninitiated was the Tantalus cup. In this, by means of concealed hollows and tubes, the level of wine sinks as the drinker tilts the cup, and he is left either frustrated and dry or frustrated and soaking wet as the liquid pours out from the base all over his lap. Horace Walpole in the eighteenth century loftily dismissed such "tricks of waterworks to wet the unwary" as both tedious and offensive, but in the medieval period they were considered to be enchantingly ingenious, and sharp eyes were always on the lookout for new examples. Villard de Honnecourt, the thirteenth-century architect who worked for the Cistercian order and traveled even as far as Hungary on its behalf, kept a notebook filled with sketches of architectural details, ornamental motifs, and oddities which had caught his attention as he moved from place to place. On one page he found space to draw his own design for a particularly infuriating cup in which, while the drinker's lips never manage to touch the wine, a bird perched at the brim seems able to sip to its heart's content. These are his instructions for making the masterpiece:

> Here is a syphon which may be made in a cup in such a way that there is a little tower in its middle, and in the middle of that a tube reaching down to the bottom of the cup. The tube must be as long as the cup is deep. And in the tower there must be three cross-channels against the bottom of the cup so that the wine in the cup may go into the tube. Above the tower, there should be a bird with its beak held so low that it may drink when the cup is full. The wine will then flow through the tube and the foot of the cup, which is double. The bird should obviously be hollow too.[26]

The theatrical effects which could be achieved by such means were well understood by designers and much appreciated by their public. Examples may be found in the most unlikely places. One of the more poignant meetings in the literature of travel took place in the mid-thirteenth century in the depths of Mongolia. In 1253, William of Rubruck, a Franciscan, had been sent on a diplomatic mission to the Great Khan by Louis IX of France. After months of painful journeying he arrived at the court of Mangu Khan in Caracorum, and there he stumbled upon a fellow European, a Christian taken prisoner by the Mongols long ago in Belgrade: "There was a certain master goldsmith called William, a Parisian by birth, whose surname is Buchier, and his father's name Laurent Buchier, and he thinks he still has a brother on the Grand Pont called Roger Buchier."[27]

William of Rubruck discovered that this unlucky man had pleased his master, and perhaps comforted himself, by creating for Mangu Khan a magnificent drink dispenser. There in the wilderness stood a triumph of the western goldsmith's art, a great silver tree with four branches, round each of which was twined a golden serpent. A silver basin lay beneath each branch, ready to receive not the familiar wines of France but the mare's milk, the rice wine, and the honey drinks which the Mongols loved. On top of the tree stood a silver angel, and only when he raised a trumpet to his lips and blew did the liquids begin to pour through the branches and into the basins below.

William, an ideally inquisitive reporter for such an expedition, soon found out what set the machine to work:

> Underneath the tree he [the goldsmith] made a crypt in which a man can be secreted, and a pipe goes up to the angel through the heart of the tree. At first he had made bellows but they did not give enough wind. Outside . . . there is a chamber in which the drinks are stored, and servants stand there ready to pour them out when they hear the angel sounding the trumpet. . . . And so when the drinks are getting low the chief butler calls out to the angel to sound his trumpet. Then, hearing this, the man who is hidden in the crypt blows the pipe going up to the angel with all his strength, and the angel, placing the trumpet to his mouth, sounds it very loudly. When the servants . . . hear this, each . . . pours out his drink into its proper pipe, and the pipes pour them out from above and below into the basins prepared for this, and then the cupbearers draw the drinks and carry them round the palace to the men and women.[28]

It was a splendid design, gallantly carried out, and it is sad to think that its creator probably never found his way home again to the Grand Pont of Paris.

William of Rubruck would have been a credit to his host at any dinner party because of the marvelous anecdotes he could tell about his extraordinary mission and all the strange things he had seen on the way. Medieval diners loved to hear such stories. The most admired and celebrated of all entertainers were the *disours* and *gestours,* the tellers of tales who, often to the accompaniment of music, dramatically recounted the best stories in their repertoire. It was their custom to divide a particularly elaborate narrative into installments, spread over several occasions, with each dinner ending, of course, on a cliff-hanger of suspense. As they traveled from hall to hall and country to country, they carried with them those stories of Arthur and Roland, of bold knights and eastern magicians, which filled the imagination of the age.

At times their place would be taken by a reader. Several poems by Chaucer and Gower were written to be read aloud for the amusement of an audience. When Froissart arrived at Gaston de Foix's court he just happened to have with him his own book, *Meliador,* which he had plumped out by the judicious addition of all the songs composed by Wenceslas of Bohemia, Duke of Luxembourg and Brabant: "Those things, thanks to the skill with which I had inserted them in the book, pleased the Count greatly, and every night after supper I used to read some of them to him. While I was reading no one presumed to speak a word, for he insisted that I should be heard distinctly, and not least by himself."[29]

Even in monasteries such recitals were associated with eating. In the forty-second chapter of the sixth-century Benedictine Rule, the foundation of western monasticism, it is ordained that immediately after supper one monk is to read aloud to the others a passage from Cassian's works or some other edifying book. Often the reading took place during the meal itself. A charming mid-fifteenth-century Parisian miniature shows the mystic Henry Suso seated at supper in a Dominican refectory, jotting down notes on the words he is hearing. The reader declares that wisdom is worth more than any worldly riches, while above his head hovers the figure of Wisdom herself, surrounded by the jewels and money bags to be rejected, and sending down rays of encouragement and inspiration to Henry. His fellow diners, not blessed with a mystic's special vision, munch on stolidly around him.[30]

Medieval diners were not content merely to listen; whenever possible they liked to sit cocooned in story as they ate. The wealthy would hang their halls with tapestries, the merely prosperous with painted cloths. The chief function of such draperies, of course, was to keep a room warm, or a bench soft (fig. 44). In December 1392, Henry, Earl of Derby, later Henry IV, on his way to a January arrival in Jerusalem paused for a few days at Venice. There he waited while a featherbed was bought and a set of tapestries made for his cabin. The dank mist and rain of Venice must have been a warning to Henry of wintry rigors in the Holy Land.[31]

Henry's hangings were probably quite plain and utilitarian. To purchasers with more time on their hands such large surfaces

et fut auſſi come une ſemblance merueil
leuſe & auaproict celui ſon vist ny pent
il auoir nul meillier ne auſſi bon. Et p
reste ſaiſon que ie vous ay dit mort eſte
le ſires du morholt dirlande vint & a
denx proies qui mil meille de lui ny eſte
deuant celui temps fort que t aymeit
ſe tuit ore ly contes apartlei de teſte cho
ſe. et ſeconvne a nue matere.

T dit ly contes que
atelui iour q̄ leſ
preudeſ delam
auſon le roy Artus
euxt recen t. en
lenr compaignie et
Hz leur auoret ottroye ſonne de la tabl
ſonde ſe auentnue leu voulont uider ſt
vient tont mainten alatabl ſonde et
comancent a reſgarder ca ⁊ le pour ſau
ilz peuſſent en auoir deſ ſieges trou
uer bien nouuell. La on Hz aloient ſe
gardunt part leſ ſieges dune part et
dautre Hz ſegardent auſſi roi pur a
uentnue lou ſiege qui y Dire auoit
eſte au morholt dirlande et pronu
erent le nom deſ. eſtript ſe ſuent
trop duleur leur le nll . . . .

begged for decoration and offered splendid opportunities for the display of personal emblems and the re-telling of favorite stories. The Duke de Berry owned many sets of tapestries, and as he moved from one of his houses to another some of them traveled with him, so that wherever he stayed he could be surrounded by scenes and characters that he enjoyed. In fig. 28 the Duke dines with his back to a chimney piece wrapped in a tapestry covered with the bears and swans which were his own special devices, while against the wall hangs a large tapestry filled with fighting men.

Along the top of this hanging there can be seen a line or two of commentary on the scene below. This combination of text and picture is quite usual in tapestry. Descriptions of the action run above or below the scene, angels hold up scrolls of verse, characters are firmly labeled, their names running down a thigh, along a scabbard, round a hat band. Tapestries were not intended to be viewed simply as an agreeable pattern of shapes and colors, dimly perceived in the shadows of a hall; they were to be read.

When Thomas More as a boy designed a painted cloth to hang in his father's house in London, he not only worked out in detail the nine scenes to be represented there but composed the explanatory verses to be written over each one.[32] For a far grander building and occasion, that tedious but fashionable poet, Alexander Barclay, was specially summoned in April 1520 from his monastery in Ely to help with the decoration of a temporary banquet hall, set up for the splendid Field of the Cloth of Gold meeting between Henry VIII and Francis I of France at Guisnes, near Calais. His job was to design a decorative scheme for the hall and compose suitable and relevant inscriptions and mottoes to accompany the pictures.[33]

These examples from private and public life indicate an assumption by the designers that their viewers will take a lively interest in the subject matter of a scene and the details of its story line. A few hints here and there suggest that at least sometimes when a set of tapestries was first displayed an actual narrator may have stood beside the hangings, reciting the story and pointing out the highlights of the crowded scenes. Some verses by John

44. (*opposite*) Preparing for a Party.
*Tristan*, French, fifteenth century (Chantilly, Musée Condé, MS. Fr. 404, fol. 233). Photo. Bibl. nat. Paris.

Lydgate, *The Legend of St. George*, have been preserved in a copy made by John Shirley, a prosperous London publisher and bookseller in the mid-fifteenth century. In a note on this poem Shirley explains that it is "the devyse of a steyned halle of the lyf of Saint George ... made with the balades at the request of th' armorieres [armor-makers] of London for th' onour of theyre brotherhoode and theyre feest of St. George." Lydgate's poem begins with these lines:

> O yee folk that heer present be,
> Wheeche of this story shal have inspeccion,
> Of Saint George yee may beholde and see
> His martirdome and his passyon.[34]

The words seem addressed to an audience assembled in their guild hall to view the new hangings they have just paid for, and ready to study them for flaws and inconsistencies with eyes sharpened by determination to find value for money or know the reason why.

Music and song, dancing and story, spectacle and surprise, these were the magic ingredients that changed dinner into feast, simple meal into special memory. Each element, of course, was as old as time, and any one by itself had the power to lift the spirits and charm the senses. From a happy blend of all together there developed in the later medieval period three fresh and elaborate diversions: the disguising, the mumming, and the interlude.

Nothing about these was startlingly new; the originality lay in their use of familiar pleasures to enliven a very old synopsis. As the most casual reader of romance knows well, a feast is the occasion when mysterious strangers appear, plots thicken, and adventures begin. Into a hall crowded with contented diners steps an uninvited visitor, and at once events take a turn for better or for worse. In story after story indeed, King Arthur, a connoisseur if ever there was one of the first-class adventure, refuses to sit down to eat his dinner at all until such an entrance has been made and he has been satisfyingly surprised. It is a hoary old device, but one that never completely fails to please, or cause ears to prick, eyes to brighten, and heads to turn with the question, "What will happen next?" This motif, the unexpected arrival at the feast and the consequences that flow from it, shapes each of the three entertainments to be considered here.

Two strands of meaning may be detected in the word *disguise* in Middle English. There is the one familiar today, in which a disguise is a costume or mask which alters its wearer's normal appearance and makes him unrecognizable, and there is another, in which a disguise is simply an extraordinary, fantastic costume, something outlandish but not necessarily concealing. The characteristic flavor of a *disguising* was produced by a blend of both.

The disguising was weak on plot but very strong on costume. A group of people, as strangely and gorgeously dressed as ingenuity and funds would permit, entered the hall at some suitable moment and performed a dance or sang a song before sweeping out in a stately exit. It was an expensive entertainment because the costumes were all-important; its natural setting was the great court feast. To judge from later Tudor and Stuart examples, as well as from the medieval evidence, those who took part in the disguising were not necessarily professional players, but often members of the court, and this naturally added to the fun. Even a king, if so inclined, might lead the revels. For the Christmas festivities of 1393 two costumes of white satin were made for Richard II, a dancing doublet and a short jacket. The jacket was embroidered, at a cost of six pounds, with leeches, water, and rocks, and embellished with fifteen whelks and fifteen mussels of silver gilt and fifteen cockles of white silver. The embroiderers charged slightly less, five pounds, for the doublet, which they covered with gold orange trees from which hung one hundred oranges in silver gilt.[35] It is possible that these were ordered for Christmas disguises, and quite in character for Richard II to want to take a part. If so, he may have been a forerunner of that long line of English monarchs who loved to star in such amusements, from Henry VIII to Charles I.

Some idea of the kinds of costume devised for these events may be gathered from the Wardrobe accounts of Edward III for the Christmas seasons of 1347 and 1348, which contain the earliest detailed descriptions of disguise costumes at an English court. From these it appears that the performers were divided into groups, each distinguished by a special costume. In 1347, fourteen people wore angels' heads with silver haloes; fourteen wore bearded men's faces, and fourteen more had women's faces. Three other groups were transformed into birds and beasts with the aid of fourteen peacock heads and wings, fourteen swan heads and wings, and fourteen dragon heads. The two remaining groups each received a headdress which left the wearer's face visible but must have been difficult to carry off with style. One consisted of legs waving in the air and the other of a mountain with rabbits sitting on top. To wear with these masks and head-dresses there were tunics, most of which are simply described as "of diverse colours," but some must have been intended to be matched with the corresponding mask: "fourteen tunics painted like peacocks' tails" obviously went with "fourteen peacocks' heads and wings," while perhaps "fourteen white tunics" were for the swans to wear. For Christmas 1348 there are fourteen red and fourteen green tunics and an assortment of extraordinary head-pieces: twelve men's heads with bats' wings, twelve heads each surmounted by an elephant's head, twelve more crowned with a lion's head, twelve wildmen's heads, and seventeen girls' heads.[36]

The impression gathered from these accounts that at least sometimes the players performed in groups is strengthened by an illustration in the *Romance of Alexander* which shows five dancers, all in matched costumes. They are not masked, but wear very long-tailed hoods. Another picture in the same manuscript shows five performers hand in hand. This time each has a different beast head: ass, monkey, goat, ox, and vulture.

A certain air of mystery always surrounded the disguisers, and it was deliberately fostered. The fantastic costumes and masks were enough by themselves to set the performers apart from the spectators, but two conventions created other, invisible barriers between the groups. The disguisers might sing a song, but they never spoke directly to the guests, and when their dance began they danced by themselves, never choosing partners from their audience. Such silence and aloofness were the special characteristics of the mummers also.

Although the root meaning of the words *mumming* and *momerie* remains uncertain, it is clear from a mass of evidence that those who took part in such an entertainment did not speak. Mumming was a very old folk custom, its origins lost in the mists of time, in which a company of people, disguised by masks, animal head-dresses, or simply blackened faces, made its way from house to house. Wherever the mummers entered they played a game of dice with their hosts, or offered presents, or performed a dance, all in complete silence except for some accompanying music. It was a custom associated with winter festivals, and it must have been distinctly unnerving to hear the knock on the door and see a stream of grotesquely masked, totally unknown men pour in out of the wild darkness, over the threshold and into the hall.[37]

At some time in the later Middle Ages this folk custom was tamed, groomed, and transformed into an agreeable social amusement. Mumming by total strangers was frowned on, and many ordinances were passed against it because of the obvious danger that it could be used by the unscrupulous as a cover for robbery and violence. Mumming by known friends or respectable officials, however, was encouraged, and it became a rather delightful way to make a call or pay a compliment. The first mumming of this kind recorded in England took place during January of 1377, but its organization was so smooth and assured that it seems likely that already by this time such an entertainment was no novelty.

To delight the young Prince Richard, one hundred and thirty substantial citizens of London rode through the city streets and out to Kennington, where the prince was spending Christmas with his mother. Minstrels accompanied them, and the way was specially lighted with torches. The mummers made a procession divided into groups: forty-eight were dressed as esquires, and forty-eight as knights. After these came two riders, impersonating an emperor and a pope, followed by twenty-four cardinals. At the tail end rode a sinister rearguard, "with black visors, not amiable, as if they had been Legates from some forrain Princes."

Once they had made their entrance into the hall at Kennington they saluted the prince and indicated in dumbshow that they wanted to play dice with him. Tactfully, loaded dice had been brought, to make quite sure that Richard would win "a boule of gold, a cup of gold, and a ring of gold," all presents brought by the mummers. After the prince had collected these winnings, his mother and other members of the court had their turn and won gold rings. The strange, exciting visit ended with a dance. Like disguisers, mummers never mingled with their audience, and so "ye prince and ye lordes dansed on ye one syde, and ye mummers on ye other a great while and then they drank and took their leave and so departed toward London."[38]

In the following century the disguising and the mumming became considerably more sophisticated. The essential ingredients, the grand entrance, the elaborate costumes and masks, the silence, were all retained, but the visit was set in the framework of a little story. No longer were swans and angels, popes and ambassadors jumbled together at random. Each character to make an appearance had a part to play in a coherent drama. A handful of such entertainments has been preserved, each devised by the poet John Lydgate and performed in the decade between 1420 and 1430. The word "mumming" appears in their titles, but the texts that have come down to us contain verses intended by Lydgate to be spoken as a commentary on the silent action.[39]

These mummings were prepared for festive occasions, usually in the Christmas season, and designed as graceful compliments to the most important member of the audience. When the Lord Mayor of London was the guest of the Goldsmiths' Company in February 1429, "upon Candelmasse day at nyght, after souper," Lydgate was commissioned to devise a suitable entertainment. He managed to hammer out a story line which would please the guest of honor and show off his patrons' professional skills to the best advantage. A Presenter, impersonating Fortune, stepped forward to introduce and explain the dumb-show. In silence, King David and the twelve tribes of Israel entered the hall, bearing on their shoulders the Ark of the Covenant, which was solemnly offered to the mayor. It is likely that this ark was a choice example of the goldsmith's art and a highly acceptable gift. All pleasure must be tempered with a little pain, and before the mayor could take his present home he had to endure a short lecture on the subject of justice and mercy, written on a scroll which was discovered inside the Ark, handed over to the Presenter and read aloud by him to the assembled company. As was only proper at a cheerful party, the mayor was urged to consider "how that Mercy shal Rygour modefye." Whether his hosts were uneasily aware of one or two skeletons in the company cupboards remains unclear.

In any case, the goldsmiths must have felt bound to put their best foot forward on this evening as, less than a month before, at a feast on 5 January, the Mercers' Company had entertained the same guest of honor. Once again Lydgate had devised an appropriate mumming, this time with spectacular stage machinery. Three boats on wheels were drawn into the hall and from them disembarked oriental merchants, strangely and richly dressed, carrying presents for the mayor. These are not described, but it is possible that they were rolls of silk, a splendid advertisement for the mercers and the luxury trade which made them rivals to be reckoned with even by the powerful goldsmiths. As usual, Lydgate provides a Presenter, whose function is to clarify the action, although it cannot truthfully be claimed today that he succeeds, as the surviving text of his remarks is notably obscure.

At Christmas time in 1424, Lydgate arranged a mumming to entertain the three-year-old Henry VI and his mother. It is to be hoped that the little boy enjoyed the presents at the end, because he must have found the spoken commentary overwhelming. Lydgate's Presenter points out a group of three characters and explains that they are the gods Bacchus, Ceres, and Juno. Wishing to honor the King of England, they have decided to send him gifts: "Wyne, whete and oyle by marchandes that here be." In dumb-show, the gods dispatch merchants to kneel at the King's feet and offer him these three gifts, symbols of peace and plenty for his realm.

On a fourth occasion, a May Day dinner enjoyed by the aldermen and sheriffs of London, probably in 1429, Lydgate, not unnaturally, chose a celebration of spring as the appropriate theme. A Presenter describes and comments on the season, and introduces two personifications, of Spring and May herself. The text does not make quite clear what these figures did, but it seems likely that they offered flowers and branches of fresh green leaves to every guest.

In Lydgate's mummings, the Presenter is all-important, explaining both the action and its significance, and labeling the characters for the audience: "Loo, first komethe in Dame Fortune." The mummers themselves occasionally break their silence with a song, while in the last entertainment preserved, the *Mumming at Hertford* acted before the King in 1430, there are actually three speakers. The theme is a comic debate between henpecked husbands and their wives. The Presenter explains the argument, one spokesman gives the wives' defense and another, the King's Advocate, diplomatically defers judgment on the question of women's right to rule their husbands until the next Christmas.

It can be guessed from this that there was a temptation to push the mumming closer and closer to real drama. The mumming in fact survived for a long time, and the desire for spoken dramatic entertainment at a feast was satisfied instead by the *interlude*, in which all the characters spoke for themselves.

An *interlude*, as the name implies, was a play short enough to be sandwiched between other festivities. References to this kind of amusement in England crop up here and there in the records throughout the fourteenth century; indeed, the earliest surviving fragment of an interlude, eighty-four lines of dialogue explicitly entitled *Hic incipit Interludium de Clerico et Puella*, is found in a manuscript dated ca. 1300, and there is the possibility that this may be based on an earlier model, now lost as a play but still existing in *fabliau* form.[40] Apart from this there is nothing until a cluster of complete interludes appears at the end of the fifteenth century. Although so much has vanished, the assured sense of stagecraft in these late examples strengthens the belief that they sprang from healthy roots and long tradition.

From the chance, contemporary references to these long-lost, long-forgotten plays that have been gleaned so far, it is clear that originally an interlude might be performed anywhere, outside or indoors, from a church gate to a dining hall.[41] By the last quarter of the fifteenth century, the period from which several of these entertainments have survived, they seem to have been specially associated with feasting, and either played at the end of the meal or divided into episodes and performed between the courses. On the title page of *Fulgens and Lucres*,[42] written by Henry Medwall probably in 1497, it is stated that this interlude has been "devyded in two partyes to be played at ii. tymes."

In the play itself, *A* and *B,* the two characters who comment on the action and coax it along, keep up a stream of patter about the diners who make up the audience. The play begins as *A* enters and remarks that the guests have already eaten something but have not yet finished; the first part ends with the comment that the audience is getting hungry again and must not be kept from the rest of the meal. Just before this point, *A* remarks that the climax of the play is to take place "Sone in the evynyng aboute Suppere." All these stage notes suggest that while the first part was inserted between courses at dinner, the second was to be played some hours later, at suppertime. This gap in time between the scenes explains why the second part opens with *A* puffing in to remind his listeners of the story so far before they are allowed to settle back for the rest of the play.

Unlike the mumming and the disguise, which depended for much of their effect on an atmosphere of romantic fantasy and mystery produced by silence and ceremony, flamboyant costume and tantalizing mask, the interlude tried to spin a web of intimacy between the audience and the players. Not only did the characters speak, they tossed remarks from time to time to the spectators at large, or singled out one man in the crowd as a special target.

The playing space was the hall itself, on any part of the floor not already occupied by people and tables. Because costumes and props were kept to a minimum it was possible for an actor, when the action required it, to slip unnoticed into the room and mingle with the guests until the moment came for him to lift up his voice, step out from the crowd, and make the play begin. Sometimes actors would be planted in the audience as spectators, to comment on the action and needle the other characters. In *Fulgens and*

*Lucres, A* and *B* both pretend to be innocent bystanders. When *A* has a sudden suspicion and accuses *B* of being an actor, *B* is properly indignant.

This easy, close relationship between actors and audience is illustrated by an anecdote about Sir Thomas More noted down by his son-in-law. From 1490 to 1492 More was a page in the household of Cardinal Morton in London, and there "though he was young of years, yet would he at Christmas-tide suddenly sometimes step in among the players, and never studying for the matter, make a part of his own there presently among them which made the lookers-on more sport than all the players beside."[43] The story was still remembered in the 1590s, when a place was found for it in the play *Sir Thomas More*. A little band of interlude players is to act before More and his guests when the Lord Mayor comes to supper. Unfortunately, at the critical moment one of them, called Luggins, has slipped out to rent a false beard for a young boy in the cast. The actors panic, but More gallantly steps into the breach and saves the scene with some masterly ad-libbing until Luggins bursts in with the beard.[44]

For subject matter, the interlude writers cast their net wide, ready to use any theme from domestic farce to morality, biblical story to classical legend. Many of these short plays were written by humanists and intended for performance before a sophisticated audience, and the interludes often take the form of an animated debate about an abstract idea: the nature of true nobility, or the essence of good government.

Unlike the mummers and disguisers, who were usually people of some social consequence, entertaining their peers or paying stately compliments to their superiors, the interlude players were university and law students, or professional entertainers, brothers to the jugglers and acrobats, forerunners of the Burbages and Alleyns of the Elizabethan-Jacobean stage. Naturally enough, money might be spent like water on the costumes to be worn by a king, a lord mayor, or a court beauty. Interlude actors found much firmer fingers on the purse-strings. In consequence the emphasis of an interlude is far more on the dialogue and action than the stage machinery, and the plays are written with a careful eye to the number of actors to be employed. On the title page of *Like Will to Like* (1568), for example, sixteen characters are listed, with the encouraging note, "Five may easely play this enterlude." Helpfully, the characters are arranged in groups, so that a producer will know at a glance how to deploy the men at his command, confident that no actor will be playing two characters on stage at the same time. So The Prologue, Tom Tospot, Hankin Hangman, and Tom Collier are all bracketed together in a package deal for one actor.

Interludes were regarded quite casually and cheerfully as make-weight entertainments, designed to fill awkward gaps in festive programs. The title page of *The Nature of the Four Elements* (ca. 1517) by John Rastell suggests how adaptable the players were expected to be. The author has calculated that the whole inter-lude will last "the space of an hour and a halfe." If that amount of time is not available, no matter: "Ye may leve out muche of the sad mater . . . and than it wyll not be paste thre quarters of an hour of length." If on the other hand the actors find they are expected to amuse the audience for more than ninety minutes there is no need for panic. They can always "brynge in a dysgy-synge."[45] With such endearing flexibility, an interlude could be squeezed or stretched into any available space in the proceedings, and prove an invaluable prop and stay to harried hosts.

To the three kinds of dramatic entertainment considered here there may be linked a fourth, the *entremet,* which contributed its own touch of theatrical magic to a feast. Just as the word "inter-lude" means something "played between," so *entremet* derives from *intromitto,* "to let into, introduce." In the late Roman world the *intermissum* was an extra course or luxurious delicacy, added on grand occasions to a dinner. The term *entremet* is French, and although known in England it was not used there so frequently as *sotelty,* or subtlety.

The English word fails to convey any sense of addition to a meal, but it does suggest the special character of the dish it de-scribes. Through its associations with skill and craftsmanship, *sotelty* came to be applied to any ingenious contrivance, and so to the examples of a cook's virtuosity that were brought in with a flourish to grace a table.

Not all sotelties were spectacular, but none could be produced by raw beginners in the kitchen. The Goodman of Paris devotes one whole section of recipes to "*Entremets,* Fried Dishes and Glazed Dishes."[46] This contains instructions on how to make such dishes as pancakes, fish and meat jellies, tarts, glazed and stuffed chickens. Of these, perhaps only the glazed chicken is very deco-rative, but all call for a certain refinement of technique, and all could be classed as special delicacies for a party.

When the Goodman turns his attention to specimen menus,

however, the entremets he mentions are the very ones that the modern reader hazily associates with the ceremonial of a feast: "The boar's head for the entremet"; "Entremet borne on high: swan, peacocks, bitterns, herons and other things."[47] Such noble beasts and birds, agreeably linked in the medieval mind with high luxury and the pleasures of the chase, were brought in whole and made to look not merely lifelike but heraldic, with gilded beaks and tusks and bodies striped and slashed with brilliant color.

An echo of the ceremony with which such sotelties were presented to the guests may be caught in the many "Boar's Head" carols which have survived from the fifteenth and sixteenth centuries. Wild boar was often the star attraction of a Christmas feast, and the head was brought in to the sound of its own special songs, ranging from the merely cheerful to brisk reminders of the season's doctrinal significance:

> The boris hed in hondes I brynge,
> With garlondes gay and byrdes syngynge;
> I pray you all, helpe me to synge,
> Qui estis in convivio.[48]

> The borys hede that we bryng here
> Betokeneth a Prince withowte pere
> Ys born this day to bye us dere;
> Nowell, nowelle! . . .
>
> This borys hede we bryng with song
> In worchyp of hym that thus sprang
> Of a virgine to redresse all wrong;
> Nowell, nowelle![49]

Something of the way in which these dramatic moments were enjoyed is suggested by a picture on the fourteenth-century brass of a wealthy merchant in the Church of St. Margaret, at King's Lynn in Norfolk. Robert Braunche lies in state between his wives, and beneath his feet is engraved an animated feast scene, in which tiny figures turn their heads expectantly to watch two peacocks carried to the table as trumpets sound and fiddlers play. It is not known for certain what occasion is commemorated here, but it is plain that Robert Braunche cherished very happy memories of one particular dinner party (fig. 45).

Peacocks, swans, and boars' heads were all cooked and ready to be eaten, though peacocks were notoriously tough, but sotelty-

makers were not expected to restrict themselves to edible materials. Their job was to make guests gasp with delight and hosts
beam with satisfaction by creating spectacular table decorations,
and to achieve this end they were prepared to use any means that
lay to hand. Chaucer's Parson, who naturally disapproved of such
frivolity, made a few remarks on the subject which suggest that
sotelty dishes might be surrounded by cut-out paper decorations,
or brought flaming into the hall: "Pride of the table appeereth . . .
ful ofte . . . in . . . swich manere bake-metes and dissh-metes,
brennynge of wilde fir and peynted and castelled with papir
[decorated with paper battlements and towers]."[50]

For the banquet Wolsey gave in honor of the French ambassadors at Hampton Court in the 1520s, "the cooks wrought both
night and day in divers subtleties and many crafty devices, where
lacked neither gold, silver, ne any other costly thing meet for their
purpose."[51] At a feast during the celebrations for the wedding of
Prince Afonso of Portugal in 1490, the guests were enchanted to
find their tables dotted with sumptuous tents and fortresses:

> And it was a beautiful thing to see the way the tables were
> arranged, for on each one there were three large covered plat-
> ters of food, and on top of the two at either end of the table
> were tents of white and purple damask, which were the colors

45. The Peacock Feast.
*Braunche Brass* (detail), St. Margaret's Church, King's Lynn, Norfolk,
1364 (London, National Monuments Record, B. B67/8217).

of the Princess; the tents were embroidered and very gallant, with many little golden streamers. . . . And the centre dish was a fortress . . . made of delicate wood and cloth of golden taffeta, which was a very beautiful thing and very costly. And on entering the hall, one saw that the tables were so beautiful and so warlike, that there was much to rejoice in seeing, as it was a new thing, the like of which had not been seen before.[52]

Sotelties were so admired that they were often kept as trophies, or given away to favored friends. Some found the most unlikely homes. At the Portuguese royal wedding, no sooner had the guests been dazzled by the decorations than the tables were stripped for action so that everyone could settle down to the serious business of the occasion and begin to eat: "The youths of the chamber who had charge of the tables removed the tents, which they kept for themselves, but the castles, because they were of such a size that they could not fit beneath the tables, were given to persons who requested them for monasteries and churches, in which they were hung for a long time, and looked very beautiful."[53]

At Wolsey's banquet, the cardinal used a sotelty as a diplomatic gift to one of the French visitors: "There was a chessboard, subtly made of spiced plate [sweetmeats] with men to the same . . . my

lord gave the same to a gentleman of France, commanding that a case should be made for the same in all haste to preserve it from perishing in the conveyance thereof into his country."⁵⁴

A sotelty might represent anything, from a mountain to a mermaid, the only limits being those set by the imagination and skill of its maker. For Wolsey's important party his cooks created one masterpiece after another: "There were castles with images in the same; Paul's Church and steeple . . . as well counterfeited as the painter should have painted it upon a cloth or wall. There were beasts, birds, fowls of divers kinds, and personages, most lively made and counterfeit in dishes; some fighting (as it were) with swords, some with guns and crossbows, some vaulting and leaping, some dancing with ladies."⁵⁵

Though dazzling as a virtuoso display, this stream of creations lacked a certain coherence. For some elegant dinner parties an attempt was made to devise decorations specially appropriate for the occasion, or to choose a theme to be illustrated by all the sotelties presented. At one late fifteenth-century wedding feast, the sotelty crystallized the hopes of both families: "a wif lying in childe-bed."⁵⁶ During another fifteenth-century dinner the Christmas story was retold in three sotelties, representing Gabriel's visit to Mary, the angel's appearance to the shepherds, and the homage of the Three Kings to the baby Jesus.⁵⁷ For another, each sotelty personified one of the seasons, with Spring, for example, appearing as

> A galaunt yonge man, a wanton wight,
> pypynge & syngynge, lovynge & lyght,
> Standynge on a clowd. . . .⁵⁸

We know neither the size of such table ornaments nor the amount of attention they received from cheerful, chattering diners. There was more than a touch of the schoolmaster in the medieval makeup and, like the tapestry makers, the designers of these sotelties clearly intended that their creations should be studied with some care, for they were sent to table festooned with helpful labels and explanatory mottoes. At the dinner party where the sotelties represented the four seasons, Summer was personified by a hot, angry young man surrounded by flames and plainly labeled: "his name was thereon, & cleped Estas [he was called Summer]."⁵⁹ It is possible that, on particularly important occasions, these mottoes and labels were read aloud for the benefit of those seated too far away to fathom the grand design

for themselves. Half the fun of the "wif lying in childe-bed" sotelty would have been lost if teasing guests and blushing, brand-
new bride and groom had been allowed to overlook its mock-sinis-
ter "scriptour": "I am comying toward your bryde. If ye dirste
onys loke to me ward, I wene ye nedys muste [if you dare glance
in my direction once I think you must (conceive a child)]."

Whether or not everyone present appreciated the full
significance of a sotelty, official accounts of a feast took care to
describe the decorations and note down the messages that came
with them. Occasionally there was a lapse. The Herald who wrote
an account of the Queen's coronation banquet in 1487 left an
incomplete record because of a breakdown in communications: he
could not record the verses which had accompanied a sotelty because they had not been sent over to his office in time.[60]

Statesmen were not slow to realize that a sotelty with a message
could be devised to embody political hopes and score diplomatic
points. At the coronation banquet for Henry V in 1413, six cyg-
nets were arranged on the table in pairs around one great swan.
The swan represented the King, and each cygnet carried in its
beak one half of a message suitably uplifting for the start of a new
reign. One bird, for example, bore the words "Eyez pete," and its
partner completed the sentence with "des comunalte" (have pity
. . . on the realm). After this, twenty-four swans made their appearance, all presenting identical scrolls, this time written in English: "noble honour and glory."[61]

Sentiments like these could scarcely be faulted by the most cap-
tious critic, but the sotelties devised for a coronation sixteen years
later were somewhat more controversial. After a series of military
victories, Henry V had laid claim to the crown of France. He died
before he could force France into complete submission, and so the
chance was lost forever, but the guardians of his baby son were
determined to press the matter. In November 1429, at the age of
eight, the little boy, who had succeeded to the throne in 1422, was
considered old enough to be crowned Henry VI. At his banquet,
despite the trifling fact that Charles VII had been made King of
France at Rheims four months earlier, every sotelty was an elaborate allusion to the union of the two countries under one, English,
king. A typical example showed Mary with Jesus on her lap, holding out a crown to Henry, while on one side St. Denis of France
and on the other St. George of England looked on with approval.
Accompanying this tableau were verses, composed by the ever-
useful Lydgate, which made its significance crystal-clear. Mary

and the two rival saints were asked to bless the young king, who was

Bore [born] by discent and by title of right
Justly to reigne in England and in France.[62]

Inevitably, as sotelties became more elaborate they grew larger, so large indeed that it was sometimes impossible to set them any longer on the table. Instead they had to be wheeled onto the floor of the hall, where life-size actors took the place of small-scale models. In France, the term *entremet* covered both the table ornament and its grander cousin, but in England sotelty referred only to the first, and the term *pageant* was used to cover the second. By a stroke of good fortune, the details of one pageant entertainment are known to us, and a contemporary illustration of the event has been preserved (frontispiece). On Twelfth Night, 6 January 1378, Charles V of France gave a feast in honor of his Christmas guests, the Emperor Charles IV of Bohemia and his son, Wenceslas of Luxembourg. To amuse and impress them a sumptuous pageant was produced, representing the crusaders' conquest of Jerusalem.

Into the hall, unseen stagehands wheeled two large stage props, a tower and a boat. On the tower's battlements stood Saracens with darkened faces, ready to repel boarders, while the boat contained assorted Christian knights and Peter the Hermit, the preacher who led the First Crusade. A scaling-ladder was set against the tower and up this swarmed the legendary crusaders of the past. First on the ladder was Godfrey of Bouillon, who actually managed to capture Jerusalem in 1099, while close at his heels came the magnificent, though unsatisfactory, Richard Coeur-de-Lion who, a century later, suddenly abandoned his campaign and went home without achieving the great goal.

The pageant offered a splendid opportunity for a rousing mock-battle, presented for the most part in dumbshow, although the Saracens are said to have called to each other in Arabic. This must have been pleasure enough for most of those present that day, but it is possible that the entertainment, like the much simpler English sotelties just described, may have been devised to sugar a political pill. It is thought to have been planned by one of the French king's counselors, Philippe de Mézières, who schemed fruitlessly for years to persuade the rulers of Europe to go on yet another crusade.[63]

Something of the fascination these entertainments held for

their audience is caught by a reference in Chaucer's *Franklin's Tale*. Chaucer moved in English court circles, and traveled on several diplomatic missions to France, Flanders, and Italy between 1367 and 1378. It is conceivable that he was lucky enough to be a guest on some occasion when a pageant was presented. In his poem he describes just such productions as examples of a magician's power:

> For ofte at feestes have I wel herd seye
> That tregetours [magicians, conjurors], withinne an halle large,
> Have maad come in a water and a barge [ship],
> And in the halle rowen [move] up and doun.[64]

Chaucer was enchanted by the magic of these theatrical illusions. The comments of others suggest that the glamor of a great feast in all its aspects cast a spell over the medieval imagination. George Cavendish, gentleman usher to Cardinal Wolsey, concludes his description of a dinner given by Henry VIII in the 1520s to a French delegation, with these words: "So ended this triumphant banquet, the which in the next morning seemed to all the beholders but as a fantastical dream."[65] For a few, precious moments, men and women had been transformed by the richness of their dress, the heightened beauty of their movements as they danced, and their voices as they sang. As Cavendish says of the women dancers, "they seemed to all men more angelic than earthly, made of flesh and bone."[66]

Christine de Pisan, a poet at the French court, must have been moved in the same way by the beauty of these occasions, for in one poem she casts a vision in the form of an after-dinner entertainment. In *Le Dit de la Rose*, written in 1401, she describes an intimate supper party enjoyed by Louis, Duke of Orléans, and his friends one January evening in his town house in Paris. As they sit comfortably together at the table, talking of books, music, and love, there is a startling interruption. Although the doors are closed and the windows shut, suddenly there appears in the room a company of young girls, looking so beautiful and singing so sweetly that they seem to come from Paradise. They are crowned with flowers, and carry with them gold cups, brimming with red and white roses. Their leader speaks and tells her stunned audience that she is Lady Loyalty, sent by the God of Love to enroll everyone who will promise to serve his mistress with devoted loyalty in a new order, the Order of the Rose. The cups are set down on the table, flowers are distributed, songs are sung. The women vanish as suddenly as they appeared, leaving a laughing, bewildered party of friends, dazed and smothered in roses.[67]

Although the mysterious women speak and sing, the form chosen by Christine de Pisan for their visit is close to that of the mummings devised by Lydgate. It seems likely that she responded to the charm of such entertainments, and saw their possibilities for her poem.

Lydgate himself, in the *Kalendare* he wrote in the 1440s, used the feast and its pleasures as an image of heavenly happiness. His poem is a rhymed calendar of saints' days as they occur throughout the year, and he casts this somewhat intractable material in the form of a carol. As a name is called, each saint steps into the dance, or picks up an instrument and begins to play for the others, until the whole company is circling round the court of Heaven. The dance stops only when December is reached and the Christmas season begins; then everyone sinks down in his place at table to enjoy the most splendid celebration of the year.[68]

The great feast warmed the heart and nourished the imagination long after the last crumbs had been swept away, the last expenses noted down and added up. Its power to move men is suggested by some words of George Cavendish. Writing his life of Wolsey, thirty bitter, turbulent years after the events he described, Cavendish thought back to the banquet given by Henry VIII to the French visitors. As the memories flooded into his mind, the splendor of that occasion masked for a moment the hard and frightening realities of Henry's court: "But to describe the dishes, the subtleties, the many strange devices . . . I do both lack wit in my gross old head and cunning in my bowels to declare the wonderful and curious imaginations in the same invented and devised."[69]

# Notes

The following abbreviations have been used in the notes:

EETS. OS.  Early English Text Society, Original Series (Oxford, 1864–).

EETS. ES.  Early English Text Society, Extra Series (Oxford, 1867–).

*M.E. Dictionary*  *The Middle English Dictionary*, ed. H. Kurath and S.M. Kuhn (Ann Arbor: University of Michigan Press, 1952–).

*O.E. Dictionary*  *The Oxford English Dictionary.*

## Chapter 1

1. *Journal*, Monday, 13 December 1813, in *Byron, Selections from Poetry, Letters and Journals*, ed. P. Quennell (London: Nonesuch Press, 1949), p. 651.
2. *The Roman Cookery Book*, trans. B. Flower and E. Rosenbaum (London: Harrap, 1974), p. 9.
3. R. Hirsch, *Printing, Selling and Reading, 1450–1550* (Wiesbaden: Otto Harrassowitz, 1967), pp. 7, 131.
4. Froissart, *L'Espinette Amoureuse*, ll. 41, 180–84, in *Oeuvres: Poésies*, ed. A. Scheler (Brussels: Devaux, 1870), 1:88, 92.
5. Colin Muset, *Chanson*, in *The Penguin Book of French Verse*, trans. B. Woledge (Harmondsworth: Penguin, 1961), pp. 164–65.
6. E.M. Thompson, *The Carthusian Order in England* (London: S.P.C.K., 1930), p. 285.
7. *Meditations on the Life of Christ*, trans. I. Ragusa and R.B. Green (Princeton: Princeton University Press, 1961), p. 125.
8. John Myrc, *Manuale Sacerdotis*, Bodleian Library, Oxford, MS. 549, fol. 171v.
9. John Myrc, *Festial*, ed. T. Erbe, EETS. ES. 96 (1905), p. 254.
10. C.F. Fiske, *Homely Realism in Medieval German Literature*, in *Vassar Medieval Studies* (New Haven: Yale University Press, 1923), pp. 125–26.
11. Myrc, *Festial*, p. 131.
12. *Providence*, in *The Poems of George Herbert*, ed. H. Gardner (Oxford: The University Press, 1961), p. 107.

13. A. Katzenellenbogen, *Allegories of the Virtues and Vices in Medieval Art* (London: Warburg Institute, 1939), p. 56; fig. 53.
14. Illustrated in the *Rohan Hours* (fifteenth century), Bibliothèque Nationale, Paris, MS. Lat. 9471, fol. 222. Reproduced in *The Rohan Master*, introduction by M. Meiss and M. Thomas (New York: Braziller, 1973), pl. 103.
15. A. Caiger-Smith, *English Medieval Mural Paintings* (Oxford: Clarendon Press, 1963), p. 83.
16. I. Origo, *The World of San Bernardino* (New York: Harcourt, Brace and World, 1962), p. 110.
17. *The Cambridge Medieval History*, vol. 4, pt. 2, *The Byzantine Empire*, ed. J.M. Hussey (Cambridge: The University Press, 1967), p. 91.
18. H. Kraus, *The Living Theatre of Medieval Art* (Bloomington: Indiana University Press, 1967), pp. 77f.
19. Raphael Holinshed, *Chronicles of England, Scotland and Ireland* (London: J. Johnson, 1807), 4:77 (under year 1555).
20. S. Runciman, *The Medieval Manichee* (Cambridge: The University Press, 1947), p. 158.
21. Thompson, *Carthusian*, p. 105.
22. Origo, *San Bernardino*, pp. 14–15.
23. Henri Grégoire, *Les Sauterelles de Saint Jean-Baptiste*, in *Byzantion*, (Paris, 1930), 5:109–21.
24. O. Chadwick, *Western Asceticism* (London: S.C.M. Press, 1958), pp. 33–36; A.H. Hind, *An Introduction to a History of Woodcuts* (New York: Dover, 1963), 2:726, 800.
25. H. Waddell, *The Desert Fathers* (London: Constable, 1946), pp. 113–14.
26. Ibid., p. 95.
27. Chadwick, *Asceticism*, p. 126.
28. Waddell, *Desert*, p. 136.
29. D.J. Chitty, *The Desert a City* (Oxford: Blackwell, 1966), p. 129.
30. Jocelin of Brakelond, *The Chronicle*, trans. H.E. Butler (Oxford: The University Press, 1949), pp. 39–40.
31. A.R. Myers, *The Household of Edward IV* (Manchester: The University Press, 1959), p. 83.
32. William FitzStephen, *The Life and Death of Thomas Becket*, trans. G. Greenaway (London: Folio Society, 1961), p. 56.
33. *Italian Relation of England*, trans. C.A. Sneyd (Westminster: Camden Society, vol. 37, 1847), p. 21.
34. R.W. Southern, *Western Society and the Church in the Middle Ages*, in Pelican History of the Church, vol. 2 (Harmondsworth: Penguin, 1970), p. 112.
35. Einhard, *The Life of Charlemagne*, trans. L. Thorpe (London: Folio Society, 1970), p. 63.
36. *Sir Cleges*, ll. 98–105, in *Middle English Metrical Romances*, ed. W.H. French and C.B. Hale (New York: Prentice-Hall, 1930).
37. Matthew Paris, *English History*, trans. J.A. Giles (London: Bohn, 1852–54), 2:340.
38. Randle Cotgrave, *A Dictionarie of the French and English Tongues* (London, 1611), s.v. "Pois."

39. *Italian Relation*, p. 25.
40. Dante, *The Divine Comedy*, trans. D.L. Sayers and B. Reynolds (Harmondsworth: Penguin, 1962), vol. 3, *Paradise*, canto 17, ll. 59–60.
41. Paris, *English History*, p. 412.
42. J.J. Norwich, *The Kingdom in the Sun* (London: Longmans, Green, 1970), p. 252.
43. *Book of Vices and Virtues*, ed. W. Nelson Francis, EETS. OS. 217 (1942), pp. 50–51.
44. *Jacob's Well*, pt. 1, ed. A. Brandeis, EETS. OS. 115 (1900), p. 144, chap. 21, "On Gluttony."
45. *Book of Vices and Virtues*, p. 53.
46. Ibid., p. 53; *Jacob's Well*, p. 144.
47. John Bickerdyke, *The Curiosities of Ale and Beer* (London, 1889), pp. 135, 139.
48. *The Game and Play of the Chess* (1475), in *Selections from William Caxton*, ed. N.F. Blake (Oxford: Clarendon Medieval and Tudor Series, 1973), p. 90.

## Chapter 2

1. *Religious Lyrics of the Fifteenth Century*, ed. Carleton Brown (Oxford: Clarendon Press, 1939), no. 83.
2. John Myrc, *Festial*, ed. T. Erbe, EETS. ES. 96 (1905), p. 286.
3. *Book of Vices and Virtues*, ed. W. Nelson Francis, EETS. OS. 217 (1942), pp. 48–49.
4. Robert Grosseteste, *Rule for the Countess of Lincoln*, in *Walter of Henley's Husbandry*, ed. E. Lamond (London: Royal Historical Society, 1890), p. 141.
5. *The Tale of Beryn*, ed. F.J. Furnivall and W.G. Stone, EETS. ES. 105 (1909), ll. 363–67, 428–33.
6. Robert Mannyng of Brunne, *Handlyng Synne*, ed. F.J. Furnivall, EETS. OS. 123 (1903), ll. 7281–82.
7. *Fifteenth Century Diatorie*, in *The Babees Book*, ed. F.J. Furnivall, EETS. OS. 32 (1868), p. 56, l. 27.
8. *La Male Regle*, in Hoccleve's *Minor Poems*, vol. 1, ed. F.J. Furnivall, EETS. ES. 61 (1892), ll. 317–18.
9. *Jacob's Well*, pt. 1, ed. A. Brandeis, EETS. OS. 115 (1900), p. 104.
10. *Peter Idley's Instructions to his Son*, ed. C. d'Evelyn (Oxford: The University Press, 1935), pt. 2, l. 916.
11. Robert Mannyng, *Handlyng Synne*, ll. 7303–4.
12. *An Alphabet of Tales*, ed. M.M. Banks, EETS. OS. 126–27 (1904–5), no. 108.
13. *Sir Gawain and the Green Knight*, ed. J.R.R. Tolkien and E.V. Gordon (Oxford: Clarendon Press, 1925), l. 1135.
14. Andrew Boorde, *Dyetary of Helth*, ed. F.J. Furnivall, EETS. ES. 10 (1870), p. 248.
15. *Jacob's Well*, p. 142.
16. *Book of Vices and Virtues*, p. 51.

17. Thomas Tusser, *500 Points of Good Husbandrie*, ed. E.V. Lucas (London: James Tregaskis and Son, 1931), *Huswiferie: Morning Workes*, p. 163.
18. Erasmus, *Praise of Folly*, trans. B. Radice (London: The Folio Society, 1974), p. 93.
19. A.R. Myers, *The Household of Edward IV* (Manchester: The University Press, 1959), pp. 203, 216.
20. Froissart, *Chronicles*, trans. G. Brereton (Harmondsworth: Penguin, 1968), pp. 469–70.
21. E. Power, "Thomas Betson," in *Medieval People* (Garden City, N.Y.: Doubleday Anchor, 1954), pp. 134–35.
22. Quoted in R. Warner, *Antiquitates Culinariae* (London: R. Blamire, 1791), p. 134.
23. Ibid.
24. *The Rule of St. Benedict*, in O. Chadwick, *Western Asceticism* (London: S.C.M. Press, The Library of Classics, vol. 12, 1958), p. 318.
25. Quoted in G.G. Coulton, *Social Life in Britain from the Conquest to the Reformation* (Cambridge: The University Press, 1956), pp. 374–75.
26. Froissart, *Chronicles*, p. 263. See also *Chronicles*, ed. W.P. Ker (London: D. Nutt, 1901–3), 4:136.
27. John Lydgate, *The Siege of Thebes*, ed. A. Erdmann, EETS. ES. 108 (1911), ll. 151–55.
28. William Caxton, *English and French Dialogues*, ed. H. Bradley, EETS. ES. 79 (1900), p. 26, ll. 27–32.
29. Myers, *Edward IV*, p. 90.
30. Tusser, *Husbandrie*, p. 164.
31. L.F. Salzman, *Building in England down to 1540* (Oxford: Clarendon Press, 1952), p. 56.
32. *A Fifteenth Century Schoolbook*, ed. W. Nelson (Oxford: Clarendon Press, 1956), pp. 1–2, no. 1.
33. Ibid., p. 2.
34. William Horman, *Vulgaria* (1519), ed. M.R. James (Oxford: Roxburghe Club, 1926), p. 239.
35. I. Origo, *The Merchant of Prato* (New York: Knopf, 1957), p. 316.
36. *The Tale of Beryn*, l. 709.
37. Boorde, *Dyetary*, p. 286.
38. *The Brewers' First Book* (1423), ll. 378–79, 491, in R.W. Chambers and M. Daunt, *A Book of London English* (Oxford: Clarendon Press, 1931).
39. For Sloth as an idle peasant, see for example British Museum, London, MS. Add. 28162, fol. 8v (late thirteenth century).
40. G.L. Remnant, *A Catalogue of Misericords in Great Britain* (Oxford: Clarendon Press, 1969), p. 196; British Museum, London, MS. Add. 24098, fol. 25b (Flemish, early sixteenth century).
41. Hoccleve, *La Male Regle*, ll. 145–52, 185–92.
42. *Book of Vices and Virtues*, p. 48.
43. *Tale of the Frogge and the Mowse*, ll. 400, 405, in *Lydgate's Minor Poems*, vol. 2, ed. H.N. MacCracken, EETS. OS. 192 (1933–34), p. 580.
44. *The Flower and the Leaf*, ll. 411–13, in *Chaucerian and Other Pieces*, ed. W.W. Skeat (Oxford: The University Press, 1897), p. 374.

45. *The Cely Papers,* ed. H.E. Malden (London: Camden Society, 3d ser. vol. 1, 1900), p. xlv.
46. *The Tale of Beryn,* ll. 285–86.
47. *Book of Vices and Virtues,* p. 47.
48. *A Hundred Merry Tales* (London: printed by John Rastell, 1526), no. 78. Quoted in Boorde, *Dyetary,* p. 330, n.

## Chapter 3

1. Alexander Barclay, *Eclogues,* ed. B. White, EETS. OS. 175 (1928), p. 9, *First Eclogue,* l. 292.
2. *Household Accounts of Richard de Swinfield,* ed. J. Webb (London: Camden Society, o.s. [2 vols.], vol. 62, 1855), p. cx.
3. Herbert Thurston, *Lent and Holy Week* (London: Longmans, Green, 1904), p. 41.
4. St. Augustine, *De Civitate Dei,* trans. V.J. Bourke (New York: Image Books, 1958), chap. 21, 4.
5. St. Augustine, *Confessions,* trans. R.S. Pine-Coffin (Harmondsworth: Penguin, 1961), bk. 10, chap. 31, p. 235.
6. *Jacob's Well,* pt. 1, ed. A. Brandeis, EETS. OS. 115 (1900), p. 143.
7. *The Prioress's Tale,* ll. 514–15, in *Works of Geoffrey Chaucer,* ed. F.N. Robinson (Oxford: The University Press, 1957), p. 162.
8. John Myrc, *Festial,* ed. T. Erbe, EETS. ES. 96 (1905), p. 253.
9. Ibid., p. 254.
10. *Speculum Sacerdotale,* ed. E.H. Weatherly, EETS. OS. 200 (1935), p. 4.
11. Myrc, *Festial,* p. 82.
12. Thurston, *Lent and Holy Week,* p. 47.
13. Ibid., p. 41.
14. Gen. 3:17.
15. 1 Tim. 4:4.
16. St. Augustine, *Confessions,* 10:31, p. 237.
17. *Lenten Stuffe,* in *Works of Thomas Nashe,* ed. R.B. McKerrow (Oxford: Basil Blackwell, 1958), 3:203.
18. Barclay, *Fifth Eclogue,* ll. 87–103; Froissart, *L'Espinette Amoureuse,* ll. 185–94, in *Oeuvres: Poésies,* ed. A. Scheler (Brussels: Devaux, 1870), vol. 1.
19. J.J. Norwich, *The Kingdom in the Sun* (London: Longmans, Green, 1970), p. 157.
20. Froissart, *Chronicles,* trans. G. Brereton (Harmondsworth: Penguin, 1968), p. 165.
21. T. Tusser, *500 Points of Good Husbandrie,* ed. E.V. Lucas (London: James Tregaskis and Son, 1931), p. 29.
22. Ibid., p. 82.
23. W. Horman, *Vulgaria* (London, 1519), ed. M.R. James (Oxford: Roxburghe Club, 1926), p. 240.
24. *Swinfield Accounts,* vol. 59, p. 13.
25. E.M. Carus-Wilson, *Medieval Merchant Venturers* (London: Methuen, 1967), pp. 132–33.

26. Tusser, *Husbandrie*, p. 125.
27. *Godstow Nunnery, The English Register*, ed. A. Clark, EETS. OS. 142 (1911), p. xxxi.
28. Tusser, *Husbandrie*, p. 50.
29. *Godstow Nunnery*, p. xxxi.
30. Jocelin of Brakelond, *The Chronicle*, trans. H.E. Butler (Oxford: The University Press, 1949), p. 76.
31. Nashe, *Lenten Stuffe*, p. 179.
32. Ibid., p. 185.
33. R.H. Tawney and E. Power, *Tudor Economic Documents* (London: Longmans, Green, 1924), 2:104ff.
34. Tusser, *Husbandrie*, p. 24.
35. Izaak Walton, *The Compleat Angler* (Harmondsworth: Penguin, 1939), *The First Day*, chap. 1, p. 29.
36. Froissart, *Chronicles*, ed. W.P. Ker (London: D. Nutt, 1901–3), 3:301.
37. Joinville, *Life of St. Louis*, trans. M.R.B. Shaw (Harmondsworth: Penguin, 1963), p. 245.
38. From Poggio Bracciolini (1380–1459), *Facetiae*, quoted in *Fons Perennis*, ed. S. Morris (London: Harrap, 1962), no. 53.
39. John Taylor, *Jack a Lent* (1617), in *Early Prose and Poetical Works* (London: Hamilton, Adams, 1888), pp. 187–88.
40. Rabelais, *Gargantua*, trans. J. Le Clercq (New York: Modern Library, 1944), bk. 4, chap. 29, pp. 584–85.
41. E.L. Guilford, *Select Extracts Illustrating Sports and Pastimes in the Middle Ages* (London, 1920), p. 52.
42. H. Rashdall, *The Universities of Europe in the Middle Ages* (Oxford: Clarendon Press, 1936), 1:334–35.
43. Matt. 6:16–21.
44. Beryl Smalley, *English Friars and Antiquity in the Early Fourteenth Century* (Oxford: Blackwell, 1960), p. 144.
45. Henry Howard, Earl of Surrey, *Poems*, ed. E. Jones (Oxford: Clarendon Press, 1964), p. 30, *London, hast thow accused me*.
46. Einhard, *Life of Charlemagne*, trans. L. Thorpe (London: Folio Society, 1970), p. 64.
47. *A Fifteenth Century Schoolbook*, ed. W. Nelson (Oxford: Clarendon Press, 1956), no. 30, p. 8.
48. Taylor, *Jack a Lent*, pp. 194–95.
49. Tusser, *Husbandrie*, p. 92, *March's Husbandry*, stanza 3.
50. William Dunbar, *Poems*, ed. J. Kinsley (Oxford: Clarendon, Medieval and Tudor Series, 1958), no. 33, p. 77.
51. Helen Waddell, *The Wandering Scholars* (London: Constable, 1927), p. 150.
52. William Hone, *The Everyday Book* (London: William Hone, 1827), 2:439.
53. Early sixteenth-century carol in Douce MS. frag. 54, *Anglia* 12 (1889):588.
54. 1 Tim. 5:23.
55. Sermon by Robert Rypon, quoted in G.R. Owst, *Literature and Pulpit in Medieval England* (Oxford: Basil Blackwell, 1961), p. 435.

56. Petronius, *The Satyricon,* trans. W. Arrowsmith (Ann Arbor: University of Michigan Press, 1959), p. 36.
57. John Russell, *The Boke of Norture,* in *The Babees Book,* ed. F.J. Furnivall, EETS. OS. 32 (1868), p. 154, ll. 554–57.
58. Nashe, *Lenten Stuffe,* p. 200.
59. Thurston, *Lent and Holy Week,* p. 46.
60. I. Origo, *The Merchant of Prato* (New York: Knopf, 1957), p. 282.
61. St. Jerome, *Epistle 34, Ad Nepotianum,* quoted in Thurston, *Lent and Holy Week,* p. 35.
62. Carus-Wilson, *Medieval Merchant,* p. 50.
63. *A Fifteenth Century Schoolbook,* no. 31, p. 8.
64. J.J. Norwich and R. Sitwell, *Mount Athos* (New York: Harper and Row, 1966), p. 64.
65. David Knowles, *The Monastic Order in England* (Cambridge: The University Press, 1941), p. 459.
66. *Sir Gawain and the Green Knight,* ed. J.R.R. Tolkien and E.V. Gordon (Oxford: Clarendon Press, 1925), ll. 890–900.
67. H.T. Riley, *Memorials of London and London Life* (London: Longmans, Green, 1868), p. 644.
68. Taylor, *Jack a Lent,* p. 187.
69. *A Noble Boke off Cookry,* ed. Mrs. A. Napier (London: Elliot Stock, 1882), p. 47.
70. *Two Fifteenth Century Cookery Books,* ed. T. Austin, EETS. OS. 91 (1888), p. 74.
71. Ibid., pp. 96, 33.
72. *Noble Boke off Cookry,* p. 47.
73. *Two Fifteenth Century Cookery Books,* p. 96.
74. *A Noble Boke off Cookry,* p. 37.
75. Giraldus Cambrensis, *Autobiography,* trans. H.E. Butler (London: Jonathan Cape, 1937), p. 71.
76. Margaret W. Labarge, *A Baronial Household of the Thirteenth Century* (New York: Barnes and Noble, 1966), p. 169.
77. Knowles, *Monastic Order,* p. 462.
78. John R.H. Moorman, *Church Life in England in the Thirteenth Century* (Cambridge: The University Press, 1946), pp. 335–36; see also Knowles, *Monastic Order,* p. 462.
79. Dante, *The Divine Comedy, Paradise,* trans. D. Sayers and B. Reynolds (Harmondsworth: Penguin, 1962), canto 21, ll. 130–32.
80. *An Open Letter to the Christian Nobility of the German Nation* (1520), in *Martin Luther's Three Treatises* (Philadelphia: Fortress Press, 1960), p. 75.
81. Russell, *Norture,* p. 153, l. 547.
82. Thurston, *Lent and Holy Week* pp. 50–54; T.H. White, *The Book of Beasts* (London: Jonathan Cape, 1954), pp. 267–68.
83. Frederick II of Hohenstaufen, *The Art of Falconry,* trans. C.A. Wood and F. Marjorie Fyfe (Stanford: The Stanford University Press, 1943), pp. 51–52.
84. *Gerard's Herball,* ed. M. Woodward (London: Spring Books, 1964), p. 284.
85. *The Travels of Leo of Rozmital, 1465–7,* trans. M. Letts (Cambridge: Hakluyt Society, ser. 2, vol. 108, 1957), p. 58.

86. Robert Henryson, *Poems,* ed. C. Elliott (Oxford: Clarendon Press, 1963), p. 23, *The Taill how this foirsaid Tod maid his Confessioun to Freir Wolf Waitskaith,* l. 751.
87. Owen Chadwick, *Western Asceticism* (London: S.C.M. Press, The Library of Christian Classics, vol. 12, 1958), *The Sayings of the Fathers,* pp. 129–30.
88. Thurston, *Lent and Holy Week,* p. 183.
89. *Swinfield Accounts,* vol. 59, p. 68.
90. Evelyn Cecil, *A History of Gardening in England* (New York: E.P. Dutton, 1910), p. 18.
91. C.L. Kingsford, *Prejudice and Promise in Fifteenth Century England* (Oxford: Clarendon Press, 1925), p. 29.
92. Goldsmiths' Company Wardens' Accounts and Court Minutes, vol. B., 1492–99, p. 335.
93. C.H. Talbot, *Medicine in Medieval England* (London: Oldbourne, 1967), p. 174.
94. Carus-Wilson, *Medieval Merchant,* p. 95.
95. Froissart, *Chronicles,* 4:149.
96. Rashdall, *Universities of Europe,* 3:35; see also C.H. Haskins, *Studies in Medieval Culture* (New York: Ungar, 1958), p. 69.
97. Owen Chadwick, *John Cassian* (Cambridge: The University Press, 1968), p. 160.
98. Moorman, *Church Life,* p. 338.
99. Knowles, *Monastic Order,* pp. 463–64.
100. Jocelin of Brakelond, *The Chronicle,* p. 110.
101. Gottfried von Strassburg, *Tristan,* trans. A.T. Hatto (Harmondsworth: Penguin, 1960), p. 53.
102. Quoted in *O.E. Dictionary* s.v. "refection."
103. Moorman, *Church Life,* pp. 177–78; *Swinfield Accounts,* vol. 62, pp. clxvi, clxvii.
104. Henryson, *Poems, Taill of the Uponlandis Mous,* p. 8, l. 248.
105. *Godstow Nunnery,* vol. 130, sec. 871, p. 648.
106. Hone, *Everyday Book,* 1:429.
107. Venetia Newall, "Easter Eggs," *Journal of American Folklore* 80 (1967):19.
108. Joinville, *St. Louis,* p. 257.
109. Henryson, *Poems, Taill of the Uponlandis Mous,* p. 9, l. 289.
110. *Speculum Sacerdotale,* p. 62.
111. Ben Jonson, *Masque of Christmas* (1616), in *Masques and Entertainments,* ed. H. Morley (London: Routledge, 1890), pp. 202–3.
112. Myrc, *Festial,* p. 63.
113. *Jacob's Well,* p. 136.
114. *Walter of Henley's Husbandry,* ed. E. Lamond (London: Royal Historical Society, 1890), p. 9.
115. For details in these two paragraphs, see L.F. Salzman, *Building in England down to 1540* (Oxford: Clarendon Press, 1952), pp. 64–80.
116. Nashe, *Summer's Last Will and Testament,* in *Works,* vol. 3, p. 287, ll. 1725–29.
117. Tusser, *Husbandrie,* p. 61.

118. The will of Stephen Thomas of Lee, Essex, 1417–18, in *The Fifty Earliest English Wills*, ed. F.J. Furnivall, EETS. OS. 78 (1882), p. 40.
119. Jocelin of Brakelond, *The Chronicle*, pp. 92–93.
120. *Promptorium Parvulorum*, ed. A.L. Mayhew, EETS. ES. 102 (1908), 362/2.
121. My thanks are due to Mr. Michael Winton, Local History Librarian of the Borough of King's Lynn, for details on the Braunche brass.

## Chapter 4

1. G.L. Remnant, *A Catalogue of Misericords in Great Britain* (Oxford: Clarendon Press, 1969), pp. 6, 48; J.C.D. Smith, *Church Wood-carvings, a West Country Study* (Newton Abbot: Davis and Charles, 1969), p. 100.
2. Remnant, *Catalogue*, p. 107.
3. *Caxton's Aesop*, ed. R.T. Lenaghan (Cambridge: Harvard University Press, 1967), p. 81.
4. Remnant, *Catalogue*, p. 47.
5. H. Kraus, *The Living Theatre of Medieval Art* (Bloomington: Indiana University Press, 1967), p. 115 and pl. 83; A. Katzenellenbogen, *Allegories of the Virtues and Vices in Medieval Art* (London: Warburg Institute, 1939), pl. 73B.
6. British Museum, London, MS. Royal 10E. IV, fols. 137–48.
7. *A Selection of English Carols*, ed. R. Greene (Oxford: Clarendon, Medieval and Tudor Series, 1962), p. 144, no. 82.
8. *Hali Meidenhad*, ed. O. Cockayne, EETS. OS. 18 (1866), p. 37.
9. William Langland, *Piers the Plowman*, ed. W.W. Skeat (Oxford: The University Press, 1886), B. Passus 5, ll. 155–65.
10. J. Strutt, *The Sports and Pastimes of the People of England* (1801), ed. J.C. Cox (London: Methuen, 1903), p. 22; *The Manciple's Prologue*, ll. 15–49, in *Works of Geoffrey Chaucer*, ed. F.N. Robinson (Oxford: The University Press, 1957), p. 224.
11. M. Keen, *The Outlaws of Medieval Legend* (London: Routledge and Kegan Paul, 1961), p. 19.
12. Matthew Paris, *English History*, trans. J.A. Giles (London: Bohn, 1852–54), 1:126.
13. A. Franklin, *La Vie Privée au Temps des Premiers Capétiens* (Paris: Emile-Paul, 1911), 2:234.
14. *Aulularia*, ll. 363–71, in *Plaute*, trans. A. Ernout (Paris: Société d'édition les belles lettres, 1959), vol. 1; Jean Renart, *Galeran de Bretagne*, in *The Penguin Book of French Verse to the Fifteenth Century*, trans. B. Woledge (Harmondsworth: Penguin, 1961), p. 130.
15. Henry, Earl of Derby, *Expeditions to Prussia and the Holy Land, 1390–1 and 1392–3, being the Accounts kept by his Treasurer during two years*, ed. L. Toulmin Smith (Westminster: Camden Society, n. s., vol. 52, 1894–95), p. 101.
16. Quoted in *M.E. Dictionary* s.v. "Cook."

17. Remnant, *Catalogue*, pp. 85, 48.
18. Albertus Magnus, *The Book of Minerals*, trans. D. Wyckoff (Oxford: Clarendon Press, 1967), pp. 128–29.
19. E. Panofsky, *I Primi Lumi: Italian Trecento Painting and its Impact on the Rest of Europe*, in *Renaissance and Renascences in Western Art* (New York: Harper Torchbook, 1969), p. 143 and fig. 105.
20. Petronius, *The Satyricon*, trans. W. Arrowsmith (Ann Arbor: University of Michigan Press, 1959), pp. 3–4.
21. *The Ancrene Riwle*, trans. M.B. Salu (London: Burns and Oates, 1955), p. 168.
22. Richard de Bury, *Philobiblon*, trans. E.C. Thomas (London: The King's Classics, 1903), p. 108.
23. P.M. Kendall, *Richard III* (London: George Allen and Unwin, 1955), p. 108.
24. *Three Fifteenth Century Chronicles, with Historical Memoranda by John Stowe*, ed. J. Gairdner (Westminster: Camden Society, n. s., vol. 28, 1880), p. 111.
25. O. Chadwick, *Western Asceticism* (London: S.C.M. Press, 1958), p. 315.
26. *The Life of Ailred of Rievaulx by Walter Daniel*, ed. F.M. Powicke (London: Nelson, 1950), pp. lviii–lix, 4.
27. R.W. Southern, *Western Society and the Church in the Middle Ages*, in Pelican History of the Church, vol. 2 (Harmondsworth: Penguin, 1970), p. 352.
28. J.H. Round, *The King's Sergeants and Officers of State* (London: Tabard Press, 1970), pp. 254–55; E.G. Kimball, *Serjeanty Tenure in Medieval England* (New Haven: Yale University Press, 1936), p. 43.
29. Round, *King's Sergeants*, pp. 243–49.
30. Plautus, *Pseudolus*, trans. P. Nixon (London: Loeb Classical Library, 1932), p. 236.
31. I. Origo, *The Merchant of Prato* (New York: Knopf, 1957), p. 210.
32. John Russell, *The Boke of Norture*, in *The Babees Book*, ed. F.J. Furnivall, EETS. OS. 32 (1868), p. 149.
33. *The Goodman of Paris*, trans. E. Power (New York: Harcourt, Brace, 1928), p. 263.
34. Livy, *Ab Urbe Condita*, bk. 39, 6.8–7.3, trans. E.T. Sage (London: Loeb Classical Library, 1936), 11:235, 237.
35. Quoted in D. Hartley, *Food in England* (London: Macdonald, 1964), p. 498.
36. *Sir Gawain and the Green Knight*, ed. J.R.R. Tolkien and E.V. Gordon (Oxford: Clarendon Press, 1925), l. 694.
37. H. Waddell, *The Desert Fathers* (London: Constable, 1936), p. 137.
38. *Selections from Layamon's Brut*, ed. G.L. Brook (Oxford: Clarendon, Medieval and Tudor Series, 1963), p. 65, l. 2240.
39. P.M. Kendall, *The Yorkist Age* (New York: Doubleday, Anchor Books, 1965), p. 320; Round, *King's Sergeants*, p. 250; review by Christopher Driver in *The Guardian*, 21 February 1972.
40. Henry, Earl of Derby, *Accounts*, p. 109; John Harvey, *Medieval Craftsmen* (London: Batsford, 1975), p. 186.

41. *The Lay of Havelok the Dane*, ed. W.W. Skeat (Oxford: Clarendon Press, 1902), ll. 2900–2909.

42. *The Fifty Earliest English Wills*, ed. F.J. Furnivall, EETS. OS. 78 (1882), pp. 133–34.

43. Ibid., pp. 94–95; John Harvey, *Early Nurserymen* (London and Chichester: Phillimore, 1974), p. 35.

44. V. Galbraith, *The St. Albans Chronicle, 1406–20* (Oxford: Clarendon Press, 1937), pp. xxxvi–vii; W.C. Hazlitt, *Old Cookery Books* (London: Elliot Stock, 1902), p. 234; L.F. Salzman, *Edward I* (New York: Praeger, 1968), p. 93.

45. Chaucer, *The Reeve's Tale*, ll. 4136–37, in *Works*, p. 58.

46. *The Tale of Beryn*, ed. F.J. Furnivall, EETS. ES. 105 (1887), ll. 61–62.

47. K.L. Wood-Legh, *A Small Household of the Fifteenth Century* (Manchester: The University Press, 1956), p. xxx.

48. A.R. Myers, *The Household of Edward IV* (Manchester: The University Press, 1959), p. 190.

49. M.W. Labarge, *A Baronial Household of the Thirteenth Century* (New York: Barnes and Noble, 1966), p. 95.

50. A. Fremantle, *The Age of Faith* (New York: Time-Life Books, 1965), p. 173.

51. Origo, *Merchant*, p. 326.

52. *Goodman*, p. 308.

53. Ibid., p. 275.

54. Ibid., p. 246.

55. M.S. Giuseppi, "The Wardrobe and Household Accounts of Bogo de Clare, 1284–6," *Archaeologia* 70 (1920): 9–10.

56. Origo, *Merchant*, pp. 326–27.

57. For another example of this object see *Queen Isabella's Psalter*, English, early fourteenth century, fol. 36r, reproduced on pl. 92 of *The Tickhill Psalter*, ed. D.D. Egbert (New York and Princeton: New York Public Library and Princeton University, 1940).

58. See T. Wright, *A Volume of Vocabularies* (London, 1882), p. 240, and the *M.E. Dictionary* s.v. "Bred."

59. Tindale, commentary on Exod. 16:31 (1530), quoted in *O.E. Dictionary* s.v. "Wafer."

60. *The Cloud of Unknowing*, ed. P. Hodgson, EETS. OS. 218 (1944), p. 105.

61. C.H. Haskins, *Studies in Medieval Culture* (New York: Ungar, 1958), p. 66; Wright, *Vocabularies*, p. 126.

62. *Goodman*, p. 240.

63. Ibid., p. 240.

64. H.T. Riley, *Memorials of London and London Life* (London: Longmans, Green, 1868), p. 438.

65. G. Henderson, *Chartres* (Harmondsworth: Penguin, 1968), p. 76 and pl. 76.

66. *Proverbes en Rimes*, ed. G. Frank and D. Miner (Baltimore: The Johns Hopkins Press, 1937), no. 121.

67. Quoted in M. St. Clare Byrne, ed., *The Elizabethan Home discovered in Two Dialogues* (London: F. Etchells and H. Macdonald, 1925), p. 35.

68. C. Pendrill, *London Life in the Fourteenth Century* (London: Unwin, n.d.), p. 195.
69. *A Fifteenth Century Schoolbook*, ed. W. Nelson (Oxford: Clarendon Press, 1956), p. 54, no. 230.
70. Riley, *Memorials*, p. 438.
71. Quoted in Haskins, *Studies*, p. 67.
72. Riley, *Memorials*, p. 163.
73. Ibid., p. 498.
74. Chaucer, *General Prologue*, ll. 379–80, in *Works*, p. 20.
75. H.F.M. Prescott, *Once to Sinai* (London: Eyre and Spottiswoode, 1957), p. 20.
76. A.R. Myers, ed., *English Historical Documents* (Oxford: The University Press, 1969), 4:1212–13.
77. Riley, *Memorials*, p. 426.
78. *Goodman*, pp. 246–47.
79. R.W. Chambers and M. Daunt, ed., *A Book of London English, 1384–1425* (Oxford: Clarendon Press, 1931), p. 180.
80. Ibid.
81. Paris, *English History*, 2:470.
82. George Cavendish, *The Life and Death of Cardinal Wolsey* (1557), in *Two Early Tudor Lives*, ed. R.S. Sylvester and D.P. Harding (New Haven: Yale University Press, 1962), p. 71.
83. *A Book of London English*, pp. 179–80.
84. Origo, *Merchant*, p. 203.
85. *Goodman*, pp. 309–10.
86. William Horman, *Vulgaria* (1519), ed. M.R. James (Oxford: Roxburghe Club, 1926), p. 227.
87. C.H. Talbot, *Medicine in Medieval England* (London: Oldbourne, 1967), p. 175.
88. *A Pictorial Vocabulary of the Fifteenth Century*, in Wright, *Vocabularies*, p. 256.
89. S.L. Thrupp, *The Merchant Class of Medieval London* (Ann Arbor: University of Michigan Press, 1962), p. 522.
90. Myers, *Edward IV*, p. 173.
91. *Havelok*, ll. 879–908.
92. W. Heyd, *Histoire du Commerce du Levant au Moyen Age* (Leipzig: Harrassowitz, 1923), 2:561.
93. Henry, Earl of Derby, *Accounts*, p. 22.
94. *Goodman*, pp. 272–73.
95. *Proverbes en Rimes*, no. 117.
96. K.M. Briggs, *The Fairies in Tradition and Literature* (London: Routledge and Kegan Paul, 1967), pp. 31, 38. Information about the para was kindly communicated by Miss Marketta Tamminen of the National Museum of Finland. A para at work may be seen on pl. 40 of I. Racz, *Art Treasures of Medieval Finland* (New York: Praeger, 1967).
97. Sir Thomas More, *Utopia*, ed. J. Churton Collins (Oxford: Clarendon Press, 1904), bk. 2, chap. 5, p. 70.
98. Thomas Love Peacock and Mary Ellen Meredith, "Gastronomy and Civilization," *Fraser's Magazine* 44 (December 1851): 366.

99. Walter de Bibbesworth, *Traité*, in Wright, *Vocabularies*, pp. 170–71.
100. *Havelok*, ll. 912–15.
101. Chaucer, *Canon's Yeoman's Tale*, ll. 922–31, in *Works*, p. 217.
102. Horman, *Vulgaria*, p. 224.
103. John of Garland, *Dictionary*, in Wright, *Vocabularies*, p. 123.
104. Langland, *Piers Plowman*, B Passus 17, ll. 244–46.
105. de Bibbesworth, *Traité*; Bartholomaeus Anglicus, *Medieval Lore*, ed. R. Steele (London: Chatto and Windus, 1924), pp. 107, 110; Horman, *Vulgaria*, p. 224.
106. *Goodman*, p. 307.
107. Chaucer, *Canon's Yeoman's Tale*, l. 753, in *Works*, p. 215.
108. Ibid., *Prologue*, ll. 666–67, *Tale*, ll. 727–28, in *Works*, pp. 214, 215.
109. J.G. Hurst, "The Kitchen Area of Northolt Manor," *Medieval Archaeology* 5 (1961): 265.
110. *The Booke of thenseygnementes and techynge that the Knyght of the Towre made to his Doughters*, trans. William Caxton, ed. G.B. Rawlings (London: George Newnes, 1902), the chapter "Of them whiche ought to Come toward theyre Carnall Frendes, in what somever Estate they be."
111. Myers, *Edward IV*, p. 167; *The Household Accounts of Richard de Swinfield*, ed. J. Webb (Westminster: Camden Society, o.s., vols. 59 and 62, 1854–55), 62:cix–x, and n.
112. Origo, *Merchant*, p. 247.
113. Horman, *Vulgaria*, p. 227.
114. D.F. Renn, "The Keep of Wareham Castle," *Medieval Archaeology* 4 (1960): 66 and fig. 20,B8; *The Bayeux Tapestry*, ed. Sir Frank Stenton (London: Phaidon, 1957), pl. 48.
115. *Dulcitius*, sc. 4–5, in *The Plays of Roswitha*, trans. C. St. John (New York: Cooper Square Publishers, 1966), pp. 38–40.
116. John of Garland, *Dictionary*, in Wright, *Vocabularies*, p. 132.
117. Quoted in J.C. Dickinson, *Monastic Life in Medieval England* (New York: Barnes and Noble, 1962), p. 101.
118. Hurst, *The Kitchen Area of Northolt Manor*, p. 278, fig. 73.
119. *A Noble Boke off Cookry*, ed. Mrs. A. Napier (London: Elliot Stock, 1882), pp. 40, 45; *Two Fifteenth Century Cookery Books*, ed. T. Austin, EETS. OS. 91 (1888), pp. 45, 9.
120. Horman, *Vulgaria*, p. 227.
121. Quoted in U.T. Holmes, *Daily Living in the Twelfth Century* (Madison: University of Wisconsin Press, 1962), p. 93.
122. *Swinfield Accounts*, 59:131.
123. Musée Condé, Chantilly, MS. 680, no folio number. Reproduced in L. Fischel, *Bilderfolgen im Frühen Buchdruck* (Constance: Jan Thorbecke Verlag, 1963), p. 77, pl. 45.
124. Smith, *Church Wood-carvings*, p. 88; *Lambeth Homilies* (1225), quoted in *M.E. Dictionary* s.v. "Bred."
125. A safe with pierced sides is to be seen in the calendar picture for January in the British Museum MS. Add. 29433 (Paris), late fourteenth- to early fifteenth-century, fol. 1, reproduced in M. Meiss, *French Painting in the Time of Jean de Berry* (London: Phaidon, 1967), vol. 2, fig. 718.

126. *Swinfield Accounts*, 62:liii.
127. Myers, *Edward IV*, p. 248, n. 225.
128. *Two Fifteenth Century Cookery Books*, p. 77.
129. *Goodman*, p. 250.
130. *Peter Idley's Instructions to his Son*, ed. C. d'Evelyn (Oxford: The University Press, 1935), vol. 2, l. 2282.
131. *Ancrene Riwle*, p. 152.
132. *Goodman*, p. 223.
133. Russell, *Boke of Norture*, p. 128, l. 172.
134. *Culhwch and Olwen*, in *The Mabinogion*, trans. G. and T. Jones (London: Everyman, 1949), p. 98.
135. *Fleta*, bk. 2, chap. 75, *Of the Cook*, trans. H.G. Richardson and G.O. Sayles (London: Selden Society, vol. 72, 1955), 2:248.
136. See N. Denholm-Young, "Who Wrote 'Fleta'?," in *Collected Papers on Medieval Subjects* (Oxford: Blackwell, 1946).
137. Wood-Legh, *Household*, p. 12.
138. Margaret Paston to John Paston, 24 December 1484 (?), quoted in Myers, *Historical Documents*, pp. 1207–8.
139. Hilda Johnstone, *Edward of Carnarvon* (Manchester: The University Press, 1946), p. 28.
140. *Swinfield Accounts*, 59:171.
141. M. Wood, *The English Medieval House* (London: Phoenix House, 1965), pp. 247–55.
142. L.F. Salzman, *Building in England down to 1540* (Oxford: Clarendon Press, 1952), pp. 23, 20.
143. Dickinson, *Monastic Life*, p. 41; Salzman, *Building*, pp. 279–80.
144. Salzman, *Building*, p. 147.
145. Wood, *English House*, p. 254; Salzman, *Building*, p. 185.
146. Wood, *English House*, pp. 277–80.
147. Salzman, *Building*, pp. 235–36.
148. Wood, *English House*, pp. 297–98.
149. G.C. Dunning, "A Pottery Louver from Great Easton, Essex," *Medieval Archaeology* 10 (1966): 74–80, and pl. 2.
150. Salzman, *Building*, pp. 97–98.
151. Ibid., p. 99.
152. Wood, *English House*, pp. 251, 248, 254.
153. C.L. Kingsford, "A London Merchant's House and its Owners, 1360–1614," *Archaeologia* 74 (1924): 150; Dickinson, *Monastic Life*, pp. 36–37.
154. W.A. Pantin, "Medieval English Town-House Plans," *Medieval Archaeology* 6–7 (1962–63): 209. See also Pantin, *Medieval Archaeology* 1 (1957):118–46, and 3 (1959):216–58.
155. *Swinfield Accounts*, 62:cxx; Wood, *English House*, p. 248.
156. Wood, *English House*, p. 254; Dickinson, *Monastic Life*, p. 34.
157. Salzman, *Building*, p. 340.

## Chapter 5

1. Froissart, *Chronicles*, trans. G. Brereton (Harmondsworth: Penguin, 1968), pp. 46–47.
2. *The Goodman of Paris*, trans. E. Power (New York: Harcourt, Brace, 1928), p. 280.
3. R. Warner, *Antiquitates Culinariae* (London: R. Blamire, 1791), p. xxxii.
4. A. Gransden, "Realistic Observation in Twelfth Century England," *Speculum* 47, no. 1 (1972): 48.
5. *The Penguin Book of French Verse to the Fifteenth Century*, trans. B. Woledge (Harmondsworth: Penguin, 1961), pp. 216–17, 328.
6. *Goodman*, p. 280.
7. Thomas of Eccleston, *The Coming of the Friars Minor to England*, trans. P. Hermann, ed. M-T. Laureilhe (Chicago: Franciscan Herald Press, 1961), pp. 181–82.
8. Henry, Duke of Lancaster, *Le Livre de Seyntz Medicines*, ed. E.J. Arnould (Oxford: Blackwell, 1948), pp. 149–50, 194.
9. Ibid., pp. 19–20, 48–49, 68, 75.
10. Ibid., p. 20.
11. A.R. Myers, *The Household of Edward IV* (Manchester: The University Press, 1959), p. 172.
12. *A Noble Boke off Cookry*, ed. Mrs. A. Napier (London: Elliot Stock, 1882), pp. 86, 27.
13. Bartholomaeus Anglicus, *Medieval Lore*, ed. R. Steele (London: Chatto and Windus, 1924), p. 105.
14. C.H. Talbot, *Medicine in Medieval England* (London: Oldbourne, 1967), p. 138.
15. Quoted in M.W. Labarge, *A Baronial Household of the Thirteenth Century* (New York: Barnes and Noble, 1966), p. 88.
16. Bartholomaeus, *Medieval Lore*, p. 103.
17. See for example *Pearl*, ll. 41–46, Chaucer, *The Parlement of Foulys*, l. 206, *Romaunt de la Rose* (Chaucer's translation), ll. 1367–72.
18. *The English Correspondence of Saint Boniface*, ed. E. Kylie (New York: Cooper Square Publishers, 1966), letter 22, p. 108.
19. "American Notes and Queries," 3, no. 12 (20 July 1889): 138.
20. *The Squire of Low Degree*, l. 850, in *Middle English Metrical Romances*, ed. W.H. French and C.B. Hale (New York: Prentice-Hall, 1930).
21. *Goodman*, p. 241.
22. Ibid., p. 300.
23. *The Ancrene Riwle*, trans. M.B. Salu (London: Burns and Oates, 1955), p. 34.
24. *Goodman*, p. 264.
25. Ibid., p. 265.
26. Giraldus Cambrensis, *Itinerary through Wales*, ed. W.L. Williams (London: Everyman, 1908), pp. 68–69.
27. *Testament of Cresseid*, ll. 416–21, in *Robert Henryson, Poems*, ed. C. Elliott (Oxford: Clarendon Medieval and Tudor Series, 1963), p. 102.

28. Quoted in *The Victoria County History of Essex* (Westminster: Constable, n.d.), 2:360.
29. Ibid., p. 361.
30. *Two Fifteenth Century Cookery Books*, ed. T. Austin, EETS. OS. 91 (1888), p. 14.
31. *Goodman*, p. 241.
32. Ibid., p. 258.
33. R.S. Lopez and I.W. Raymond, *Medieval Trade in the Mediterranean World* (New York: Columbia University Press, 1955), p. 352.
34. K.L. Wood-Legh, *A Small Household of the Fifteenth Century* (Manchester: The University Press, 1956), p. xxviii.
35. Deschamps, Ballade *En Hainaut*, in *Penguin Verse*, pp. 240–41.
36. *Proverbes en Rimes*, ed. G. Frank and D. Miner (Baltimore: The Johns Hopkins Press, 1937), no. 108.
37. Bede, *Life of Cuthbert*, in *Lives of the Saints*, trans. J.F. Webb (Harmondsworth: Penguin, 1965), p. 118.
38. I. Origo, *The Merchant of Prato* (New York: Knopf, 1957), p. 22.
39. Sidonius Apollinaris, *To Catulinus that he cannot write him an Epithalamium because of the enemy hosts*, trans. H. Waddell in *Poetry in the Dark Ages*, reprinted in M. Blackett, *The Mark of the Maker* (London: Constable, 1973), p. 236.
40. A.M. Tyssen Amherst, "A Fifteenth Century Treatise on Gardening," *Archaeologia* 54 (1894): 157–72.
41. Ibid., ll. 183–84.
42. C.L. Kingsford, "On Some London Houses of the Early Tudor Period," *Archaeologia* 71 (1920–21): 47.
43. M.D. Lambert, *Franciscan Poverty* (London: S.P.C.K., 1961), p. 13.
44. Giraldus Cambrensis, *Autobiography*, trans. H.E. Butler (London: Jonathan Cape, 1937), p. 71.
45. Quoted in J.J. Norwich, *The Kingdom in the Sun* (London: Longmans, Green, 1970), p. 295.
46. Sir Frank Crisp, *Medieval Gardens* (New York: Hacker, 1966), 1:35–36, 48.
47. *The Life of Christina of Markyate*, trans. C.H. Talbot (Oxford: Clarendon Press, 1959), p. 191.
48. *The Forme of Cury*, in Warner, *Culinariae*, p. 16.
49. *Cookery Books*, p. 86.
50. Ibid., pp. 72, 92, 39.
51. Ibid., p. 69.
52. Ibid.
53. Ibid., pp. 69–70.
54. *The Cambridge Economic History of Europe*, vol. 1, *The Agrarian Life of the Middle Ages*, ed. M.M. Postan (Cambridge: The University Press, 1966), p. 166.
55. See for example *Goodman*, pp. 198–99.
56. Ibid., p. 296.
57. Ibid., pp. 257, 296.
58. *Cookery Books*, pp. 31, 29, 23.
59. Edmund Spenser, *The Shepheardes Calender* (1579), *April*, ll. 138–39, in *Poetical Works* (Oxford: The University Press, 1912), p. 433.

60. *Mary Magdalen,* pt. 1, ll. 536–37, in *The Digby Plays,* ed. F.J. Furnivall, EETS. ES. 70 (1896).
61. Froissart, *Oeuvres,* ed. K. de Lettenhove (Brussels: Devaux, 1868), 6:24–26. The story is contained in one manuscript, Bibliothèque Nationale, Paris, MS. 2366.
62. *Noble Boke,* p. 31.
63. Ibid., p. 84.
64. *Goodman,* p. 251.
65. A. Strickland, *Lives of the Queens of England* (Philadelphia: Lippincott, 1893), 1: 450–51; *The Household Accounts of Richard de Swinfield,* ed. J. Webb (Westminster: Camden Society, o.s., 1854–55), 59:134; 62:cxxi.
66. *A Fifteenth Century Schoolbook,* ed. W. Nelson (Oxford: Clarendon Press, 1956), p. 16, no. 64.
67. S. Thrupp, *The Merchant Class of Medieval London* (Ann Arbor: University of Michigan Press, 1962), pp. 106–7.
68. Henry of Lancaster, *Le Livre de Seyntz Medicines,* p. 34.
69. *The Testament of Dan John Lydgate,* ll. 638–41, in *Lydgate's Minor Poems,* vol. 1, ed. H.N. MacCracken, EETS. ES. 107 (1910).
70. Walter of Bibbesworth, *Traité,* in Thomas Wright, *A Volume of Vocabularies* (London, 1882), p. 150.
71. *Schoolbook,* p. 74, no. 307.
72. *The Miller's Tale,* l. 3261, in *Works of Geoffrey Chaucer,* ed. F.N. Robinson (Oxford: The University Press, 1957), p. 49.
73. Mrs. Evelyn Cecil, *A History of Gardening in England* (New York: E.P. Dutton, 1910), pp. 35–37.
74. Myers, *Edward IV,* p. 190.
75. Cecil, *Gardening,* pp. 35–37, 46; T.H. Turner, "Observations on the State of Horticulture in England, *Archaeological Journal* 5 (1848): 300–302.
76. Sacheverell Sitwell, *Gothic Europe* (London: Weidenfeld and Nicolson, 1969), p. 46.
77. John Lydgate, *London Lickpenny,* l. 60, in *Historical Poems of the Fourteenth and Fifteenth Centuries,* ed. R.H. Robbins (New York: Columbia University Press, 1959), p. 132.
78. J.T. Williams, "Plant Remains in the Fifteenth Century Cloisters of the College of the Vicars Choral, Hereford," *Medieval Archaeology* 15 (1971):117–18.
79. Thrupp, *Merchant Class,* p. 136.
80. H.F.M. Prescott, *Once to Sinai* (London: Eyre and Spottiswoode, 1957), pp. 40, 165.
81. See for example the instructions of Hildegard of Bingen (1098–1179), in W. Ley, *Dawn of Zoology* (Englewood Cliffs, N.J.: Prentice-Hall, 1968), p. 82.
82. Cecil, *Gardening,* p. 38.
83. *Cookery Books,* p. 28.
84. *Noble Boke,* p. 68.
85. *Goodman,* p. 291.
86. *Cookery Books,* pp. 96–97.
87. Ibid., p. 97.

88. Ibid., pp. 97–98.
89. Ibid., pp. 20, 30.
90. *Noble Boke*, p. 121.
91. *Cookery Books*, pp. 106–7.
92. Ibid., pp. 88, 87.
93. *Noble Boke*, p. 54.
94. Goldsmiths' Company Wardens' Accounts and Court Minutes, vol. B, 1492–99, p. 335.
95. *Cookery Books*, p. 29.
96. Ibid., p. 75.
97. *National Trust Guide to the Vyne* (London: Country Life, 1961), p. 13.
98. Bede, *Ecclesiastical History of the English Nation*, trans. J. Stevens (London: Everyman, 1910), p. 4.
99. E. Hyams, *Dionysus* (New York: Macmillan, 1965), p. 188.
100. E. Hyams, ed., *Vineyards in England* (London: Faber and Faber, 1953), pp. 33–35.
101. E.M. Carus-Wilson, *Medieval Merchant Venturers* (London: Methuen, 1967), pp. 267–68.
102. Ibid., pp. 267, 28.
103. Ibid., pp. 267–68.
104. Ibid., p. 8.
105. Ibid., p. 27.
106. H.T. Riley, ed., *Memorials of London and London Life* (London: Longmans, Green, 1868), p. 318.
107. Thrupp, *Medieval Merchant*, p. 136; Froissart, *Chronicles*, ed. W.P. Ker (London: D. Nutt, 1901), 1:L.
108. *Noble Boke*, p. 68.
109. Ibid., p. 114.
110. *Cookery Books*, p. 109.
111. Ibid., p. 103.
112. V. Pritchard, *English Medieval Graffiti* (Cambridge: The University Press, 1967), p. 62.
113. *Cookery Books*, p. 38.
114. *Noble Boke*, p. 109; *Cookery Books*, p. 84.
115. *Cookery Books*, p. 28.
116. Ibid., p. 52.
117. *Goodman*, pp. 295–96, 299.
118. *Cookery Books*, pp. 109, 110.
119. *Noble Boke*, pp. 42–43; *Cookery Books*, pp. 91–92.
120. *Cookery Books*, pp. 91, 16; *Noble Boke*, pp. 75–76.
121. *Cookery Books*, pp. 85, 34, 20.
122. Ibid., p. 91.
123. *Ingulph's Chronicle of the Abbey of Croyland*, trans. H.T. Riley (London: Bohn, 1854), p. 359.
124. Early sixteenth-century carol in Douce MS. frag. 54, printed in *Anglia* 12 (1889): 588.
125. *The Master of Game*, ed. W.A. and F. Baillie-Grohman (New York: Duffield and Co., 1909), p. 97.
126. *Cookery Books*, p. 52; *Noble Boke*, p. 66.
127. *Cookery Books*, p. 93.

128. Ibid., p. 86.
129. John Gower, *Confessio Amantis*, ed. G.C. Macaulay, EETS. ES. 81 (1900), bk. 4, ll. 2732–33.
130. *Noble Boke*, pp. 87, 119–20.
131. *Cookery Books*, p. 92.
132. Ibid., p. 50.
133. *Goodman*, pp. 283, 260; *Master of Game*, p. 97.
134. *Goodman*, p. 260.
135. *Noble Boke*, p. 57; *Cookery Books*, p. 92.
136. *Goodman*, p. 283.
137. *Italian Relation of England*, trans. C.A. Sneyd (Westminster: Camden Society, vol. 37, 1847), p. 11.
138. *Cookery Books*, p. 43.
139. Ibid., p. 83.
140. Ibid., p. 98.
141. *Goodman*, p. 309.
142. *An English Vocabulary of the Fifteenth Century*, in Wright, *Vocabularies*, p. 198.
143. *Noble Boke*, p. 52.
144. *Cookery Books*, p. 20.
145. Ibid., p. 75.
146. *Goodman*, p. 306.
147. *Schoolbook*, pp. 7–8, n. 26.
148. Rabelais, *Gargantua and Pantagruel*, trans. J. Le Clercq (New York: Modern Library, 1944), Prologue to Book I, p. 4.
149. Peter of Blois, *Epistle 14*, in J.P. Migne, ed., *Patrologia cursus completus, series latina* (Paris: Migne, 1844–91), vol. 207, col. 47.
150. Montaigne, *On Experience*, in *Essays*, trans. J.M. Cohen (Harmondsworth: Penguin, 1958), p. 388.
151. *Paris and Vienne* (1485), in *Selections from William Caxton*, ed. N.F. Blake (Oxford: Clarendon Medieval and Tudor Series, 1973), p. 60.
152. *Cookery Books*, pp. 108–10.
153. Ibid., p. 102.
154. Ibid., p. 40.
155. Ibid., p. 106.
156. Ibid., p. 114.
157. Ibid., p. 39.
158. Ibid., p. 9.
159. Ibid., p. 55.
160. Ibid., p. 99.
161. Ibid., p. 98.
162. Ibid., p. 49.
163. Ibid., pp. 49–50.
164. *Noble Boke*, pp. 95–96.
165. Ibid., p. 116.
166. *Cookery Books*, pp. 40–41.
167. Ibid., p. 39.
168. Ibid., pp. 72–73. See also *Noble Boke*, p. 69.
169. *Cookery Books*, p. 70.
170. Ibid., p. 6.

171. *Noble Boke,* pp. 85–86.
172. W.H. St. John Hope, *Heraldry for Craftsmen and Designers* (London: Pitman, 1913), pp. 211–13, pl. 27A; Elspeth M. Veale, *The English Fur Trade in the Later Middle Ages* (Oxford: Clarendon Press, 1966), pp. 209–14.
173. *Cookery Books,* p. 80.
174. Ibid., pp. 34, 38–39.
175. Ibid., p. 71.
176. *Noble Boke,* p. 98.
177. Ibid., pp. 42, 122–23.
178. *Cookery Books,* pp. 86–87.
179. Ibid., p. 40.
180. Walter of Bibbesworth, *Traité,* in Wright, *Vocabularies,* pp. 155–56.
181. *Noble Boke,* p. 45.
182. Ibid., p. 82.
183. *Cookery Books,* pp. 38, 46.
184. Ibid., pp. 70, 17.
185. D.F. Renn, "The Keep of Wareham Castle," *Medieval Archaeology* 4 (1960): 66 and fig. 20, B8.
186. *The Bayeux Tapestry,* ed. Sir Frank Stenton (London: Phaidon, 1957), pl. 48.
187. British Museum, London, MS. Add. 47682, fol. 42v.
188. *Cookery Books,* p. 39.
189. Einhard, *The Life of Charlemagne,* trans. L. Thorpe (London: The Folio Society, 1970), p. 63.
190. *Cookery Books,* p. 39.
191. Ibid., p. 54.
192. All Saints Church, Maidstone, Kent, misericord described in G.L. Remnant, *A Catalogue of Misericords in Great Britain* (Oxford: Clarendon Press, 1969), p. 72.
193. J.S. Purvis, "The Use of Continental Woodcuts and Prints by the 'Ripon School' of Woodcarvers in the Early Sixteenth Century," *Archaeologia* 85 (1935): 122 and pl. 30, fig. 5.
194. Henry, Earl of Derby, *Expeditions to Prussia and the Holy Land, 1390–1 and 1392–3, being the Accounts kept by his Treasurer during two years,* ed. L. Toulmin Smith (Westminster: Camden Society, n.s. 52, 1894–95), see *Index.*
195. Dante, *The Divine Comedy,* pt. 1, *Hell,* trans. D. Sayers (Harmondsworth: Penguin, 1949), canto 29, circle 8, bowge 10, ll. 73–74, 82–84, p. 254.
196. *Huon of Burdeux,* ed. S.L. Lee, EETS. ES. 41 (1883), chap. 116, pp. 408–9.
197. *Cookery Books,* p. 87.
198. *Goodman,* p. 280.
199. *Noble Boke,* p. 98.
200. *Goodman,* p. 223.
201. Ibid.
202. William Horman, *Vulgaria* (1519), ed. M.R. James (Oxford: Roxburghe Club, 1926), p. 229.
203. *Goodman,* p. 261.

204. Ibid., p. 275.
205. Ibid., p. 274.
206. *The Fifty Earliest English Wills*, ed. F.J. Furnivall, EETS. OS. 78 (1882), pp. 91, 46, 22.
207. *Noble Boke*, pp. 31, 27.
208. *Cookery Books*, p. 56.
209. Ibid., p. 6.
210. *Noble Boke*, p. 44.
211. Ibid., p. 45.
212. Ibid., pp. 93, 92; *Cookery Books*, p. 39; *Goodman*, p. 277.
213. *Goodman*, p. 249; *Cookery Books*, p. 73.
214. *Cookery Books*, p. 7.
215. *Goodman*, pp. 285, 295.
216. L.F. Salzman, *Building in England down to 1540* (Oxford: Clarendon Press, 1952), p. 58.
217. *Master of Game*, p. 179.
218. Rudolf Hirsch, *Printing, Selling and Reading, 1450–1550* (Wiesbaden: Otto Harrassowitz, 1967), p. 46.
219. Pepys MS. 1047, English, late fifteenth century. Printed in *Stere Htt Well* (London: Cornmarket Reprints, 1972), p. 13.
220. *Goodman*, pp. 45–46.
221. Myers, *Edward IV*, p. 113.
222. Russell, *Boke of Norture*, p. 163, l. 673.
223. William Caxton, *The Game and Play of Chess* (1475), in *Selections*, p. 90.
224. Origo, *Merchant*, p. 320.
225. *Goodman*, p. 310.
226. Goldsmiths' Company Wardens' Accounts and Court Minutes, vol. B, 1492–99, p. 335.
227. M. Keen, *The Outlaws of Medieval England* (London: Routledge and Kegan Paul, 1961), p. 57.
228. *Goodman*, p. 238.

## Chapter 6

1. Froissart, *Chronicles*, trans. G. Brereton (Harmondsworth: Penguin, 1968), p. 356.
2. G. Masson, *Frederick II of Hohenstaufen* (London: Secker and Warburg, 1957), p. 198.
3. *The Boke of Kervynge*, p. 268; John Russell, *Boke of Norture*, p. 129, ll. 186–87. In *The Babees Book*, ed. F.J. Furnivall, EETS. OS. 32 (1868).
4. *The General Prologue to the Canterbury Tales*, l. 354, in *Works of Geoffrey Chaucer*, ed. F.N. Robinson (Oxford: The University Press, 1957), p. 20.
5. *Sir Degrevant*, l. 391, in *Middle English Romances*, ed. A.C. Gibbs (London: York Medieval Texts, Edward Arnold, 1966), p. 151.
6. *Jehan et Blonde*, ll. 3013–24, in *Oeuvres Poétiques de Philippe de Remi, Sire de Beaumanoir*, ed. H. Suchier (Paris: Firmin Didot, 1885), 2:95.

7. *The Master of Game,* ed. W.A. and F. Baillie-Grohman (New York: Duffield and Co., 1909), pp. 163–64.
8. *Mandeville's Travels,* ed. P. Hamelius, EETS. OS. 153 (1916), p. 144.
9. H.T. Riley, *Memorials of London and London Life* (London: Longmans, Green, 1868), p. 123.
10. R.E. Zupko, *A Dictionary of English Weights and Measures* (Madison: University of Wisconsin Press, 1968), p. 123.
11. Russell, *Norture,* p. 129, ll. 187–92; *Kervynge,* p. 268.
12. Quoted in *M.E. Dictionary* s.v. "bord cloth."
13. William Horman, *Vulgaria* (1519), ed. M.R. James (Oxford: Roxburghe Club, 1926), p. 227.
14. A.R. Myers, *The Household of Edward IV* (Manchester: The University Press, 1959), pp. 192–93.
15. Quoted in *M.E. Dictionary* s.v. "Diapren," v.
16. *Sir Degrevant,* ll. 393–94.
17. I. Origo, *The Merchant of Prato* (New York: Knopf, 1957), pp. 255–56.
18. *The Goodman of Paris,* trans. E. Power (New York: Harcourt, Brace, 1928), pp. 242, 246.
19. Montaigne, *On Experience,* in *Essays,* trans. J.M. Cohen (Harmondsworth: Penguin, 1958), p. 367.
20. Origo, *Merchant,* pp. 255–56.
21. *The Fifty Earliest English Wills,* ed. F.J. Furnivall, EETS. OS. 78 (1882), p. 56, Roger More Esq., of London and Oakham, Rutlandshire.
22. E.M. Thompson, *The Carthusian Order in England* (London: S.P.C.K., 1930), p. 122.
23. A.H. de Oliveira Marques, *Daily Life in Portugal in the Late Middle Ages* (Madison: University of Wisconsin Press, 1971), p. 31.
24. Ibid., p. 209.
25. Quoted in *M.E. Dictionary* s.v. "bord cloth."
26. R.W. Chambers and M. Daunt, *A Book of London English* (Oxford: Clarendon Press, 1931), pp. 180, 188.
27. Walter of Bibbesworth, *Traité,* in *A Volume of Vocabularies,* ed. T. Wright (London, 1882), pp. 171–72.
28. Ambroise, *L'Estoire de la Guerre Sainte,* ed. G. Paris (Paris: Imprimerie nationale, 1897), p. 30, l. 1092.
29. John of Garland, *Morale scolarium,* quoted in C.H. Haskins, *Studies in Medieval Culture* (New York: Ungar, 1958), p. 78.
30. *Sir Gawain and the Green Knight,* ed. J.R.R. Tolkien and E.V. Gordon (Oxford: Clarendon Press, 1925), l. 885.
31. *Promptorium Parvulorum,* ed. A.L. Mayhew, EETS. ES. 102 (1908), 398/1.
32. *Ffor to Serve a Lord,* in *Babees Book,* p. 367.
33. *Goodman,* p. 244.
34. Quoted in *O.E. Dictionary* s.v. "Sleekstone."
35. *Femina,* ed. W.A. Wright (Cambridge: The University Press, 1909), p. 76. My thanks are due to Professor Sherman M. Kuhn, editor of the *Middle English Dictionary,* for this reference.

36. *Gerard's Herball* ed. M. Woodward (London: Spring Books, 1964), p. 194.
37. de Bibbesworth, *Traité*, pp. 173–74.
38. G. Frank and D. Miner, *Proverbes en Rimes* (Baltimore: The Johns Hopkins Press, 1937), n. cxxx.
39. W. Ashley, *The Bread of Our Forefathers* (Oxford: Clarendon Press, 1928), p. 72.
40. Bede, *The Ecclesiastical History of the English Nation*, trans. J. Stevens (London: Everyman, 1951), pp. 73–74.
41. Origo, *Merchant*, p. 317.
42. Ashley, *Bread*, p. 112.
43. B. Smalley, *English Friars and Antiquity in the Early Fourteenth Century* (Oxford: Blackwell, 1960), p. 82.
44. William Langland, *Piers the Plowman*, ed. W.W. Skeat (Oxford: The University Press, 1886), B passus 6, ll. 139, 304–6.
45. Thompson, *Carthusian*, p. 38.
46. *Jacob's Well*, ed. A. Brandeis, EETS. OS. 115 (1900), p. 192.
47. Russell, *Norture*, pp. 130–31, ll. 197–228, p. 133, l. 263.
48. Randle Cotgrave, *A Dictionarie of the French and English Tongues* (London, 1611), s.v. "Pain de mesnage."
49. Myers, *Edward IV*, p. 214.
50. Langland, *Piers Plowman*, B 13, ll. 48, 51, 60.
51. Horman, *Vulgaria*, p. 232.
52. Russell, *Norture*, p. 120, ll. 53–55.
53. *The Myroure of Oure Ladye*, ed. J.H. Blunt, EETS. ES. 19 (1873), p. xxxii.
54. *The Boke of Curtasye*, ll. 685–87, in *Babees Book*, p. 322.
55. Ashley, *Bread*, pp. 105, 111–12.
56. *Kervynge*, p. 269.
57. Myers, *Edward IV*, p. 171.
58. Ibid., p. 172.
59. *Stans Puer ad Mensam*, ll. 36–37, in *Lydgate's Minor Poems*, pt. 2, ed. H.N. MacCracken, EETS. OS. 192 (1933), p. 741; *Curtasye*, p. 300, ll. 77–79.
60. *Aucassin et Nicolette*, ed. M. Roques in *Les Classiques Français du Moyen Age* (Paris: E. Champion, 1925), 41:12, sec. 11, ll. 14–15.
61. Bonvicino, *Fifty Courtesies of the Table*, trans. W.M. Rossetti in *Queene Elizabethes Achademy*, ed. F.J. Furnivall, EETS. ES. 8 (1869), p. 23, ll. 93–96.
62. *Modus Cenandi*, ll. 97–98, in *Babees Book*, p. 41.
63. *Curtasye*, p. 324, ll. 757–62.
64. *Ffor to Serve a Lord*, p. 370.
65. Russell, *Norture*, p. 120, l. 156.
66. *Goodman*, p. 238.
67. Myers, *Edward IV*, p. 190; *Curtasye*, p. 320, ll. 627–28.
68. *Curtasye*, p. 322, ll. 667–84; *Ffor to Serve a Lord*, p. 369.
69. *Ffor to Serve a Lord*, p. 369.
70. *Babees Book*, p. 7, ll. 183–84.
71. G. Brett, "Trenchers," in *Annual, Art and Archaeology Division* (Toronto: Royal Ontario Museum, 1962), pp. 23–27.

72. Cotgrave, *Dictionarie*, s.v. "Sel."
73. A.R. Bridbury, *England and the Salt Trade in the Later Middle Ages* (Oxford: Clarendon Press, 1955), pp. 50–52.
74. *The Victoria County History of Hertfordshire* (London: Constable, n.d.), 4:430, n. 31.
75. Russell, *Norture*, p. 120, l. 57.
76. *Goodman*, p. 301.
77. Russell, *Norture*, p. 120, ll. 58–59.
78. *Curtasye*, p. 303, ll. 129–31.
79. *Babees Book*, p. 7, ll. 160–61.
80. Brett, "Trenchers," p. 24 and pl. 5.
81. William Caxton, *Book of Curtesye*, ed. F.J. Furnivall, EETS. ES. 3 (1868), p. 23, l. 213.
82. *Ffor to Serve a Lord*, p. 369.
83. *Modus Cenandi*, p. 39, ll. 62–63.
84. *Ffor to Serve a Lord*, pp. 368, 371, 372.
85. E.M. Carus-Wilson, *Medieval Merchant Venturers* (London: Methuen, 1967), p. 78.
86. *The Très Riches Heures of Jean, Duke de Berry*, Intro. J. Longnon (New York: Braziller, 1969), p. 19.
87. Henry, Earl of Derby, *Expeditions to Prussia and the Holy Land, 1390–1 and 1392–3, being the Accounts kept by his Treasurer during two years*, ed. L. Toulmin Smith (London: Camden Society, n.s. 52, 1894–95), p. 288, and index s.v. "Silver and Gold Ware."
88. A. Franklin, *La Vie Privée au Temps des Premiers Capétiens* (Paris: Emile-Paul, 1911), 1:317; J. Evans, *English Art, 1307–1461* (Oxford: The University Press, 1949), p. 85.
89. Evans, *English Art*, p. 85.
90. C. Oman, *Medieval Silver Nefs* (London: Her Majesty's Stationery Office, Victoria and Albert Museum, 1963), p. 20.
91. Bonvicino, *Fifty Courtesies*, p. 27, ll. 141–44.
92. Barberino, *Documenti d'Amore*, trans. W.M. Rossetti, in *Queene Elizabethes Achademy*, p. 41; Lydgate, *Stans Puer*, p. 740, ll. 22–23; *Babees Book*, p. 6, ll. 134–35.
93. *The Testament of Dan John Lydgate*, l. 650, in *Lydgate's Minor Poems*, Part 1, ed. H.N. MacCracken, EETS. ES. 107 (1910), p. 353.
94. Richard de Bury, *Philobiblon*, trans. E.C. Thomas (London: The King's Classics, 1903), pp. 107–8.
95. Horman, *Vulgaria*, p. 231.
96. *The Taill of the Uponlandis Mous and the Burges Mous*, ll. 267–68, in *Robert Henryson Poems*, ed. C. Elliott (Oxford: Clarendon Medieval and Tudor Series, 1963), p. 9.
97. *Curtasye*, p. 303, ll. 133–34.
98. Caxton, *Book of Curtesye*, p. 27, ll. 265–66.
99. Origo, *Merchant*, p. 204.
100. *Modus Cenandi*, p. 35, ll. 23–24.
101. Russell, *Norture*, p. 132, l. 232; Barberino, *Documenti d'Amore*, p. 42; Bonvicino, *Fifty Courtesies*, p. 17, ll. 11–12.

102. Myers, *Edward IV*, p. 194.
103. P. Tudor-Craig, *Catalogue of the Richard III Exhibition at the National Portrait Gallery, London, 1973*, item no. 112 and App. 3.
104. Goodman, p. 299.
105. Froissart, *Chronicles*, pp. 386–87.
106. *Curtasye*, p. 323, ll. 713–14.
107. *Ffor to Serve a Lord*, pp. 372–73; *Curtasye*, p. 326, ll. 809–20; Russell, *Norture*, p. 132, ll. 237–56.
108. M. Wood, *The English Medieval House* (London: Phoenix House, 1965), p. 370.
109. St. Bernard of Clairvaux, *Apology to Abbot William of St. Thierry*, ed. C.D. Warner, in *Library of the World's Best Literature* (New York: J.A. Peale and Hill and Co., 1902), 4:1824.
110. *English Wills*, p. 41, John Rogerysson of London, 1419/20.
111. W.H. St. John Hope, *Heraldry for Craftsmen and Designers* (London: Pitman, 1913), p. 174.
112. Evans, *English Art*, p. 85.
113. E.C. Dodd, "On the Origins of Medieval Dinanderie: the Equestrian Statue in Islam," *Art Bulletin* 51 (September 1969): 220–32.
114. *The Rites of Durham* (Durham: Surtees Society, vol. 107, 1902), p. 81.
115. Albertus Magnus, *Book of Minerals*, trans. D. Wyckoff (Oxford: Clarendon Press, 1967), pp. 195–96.
116. C. Oman, "English Medieval Drinking Horns," *Connoisseur* 113 (March 1944): 22, pl. 3, 4.
117. W.H. St. John Hope, "Mazers," *Archaeologia* 50, pt.1 (1887): 139–42.
118. *English Wills*, p. 133; M.W. Labarge, *A Baronial Household of the Thirteenth Century* (New York: Barnes and Noble, 1966), p. 123.
119. *The Grandes Heures of Jean, Duke of Berry*, intro. M. Thomas (New York: Braziller, 1971), pl. 58, fol. 41.
120. *Medieval Archaeology* 11 (1967):291, pl. 34.
121. T. Husband, "Valencian Lusterware of the Fifteenth Century" (New York: *Metropolitan Museum of Art Bulletin* [Summer 1970]: 11–19).
122. Origo, *Merchant*, p. 89.
123. *The Master of Mary of Burgundy*, intro. J.J.G. Alexander (New York: Braziller, 1970), pl. 79, 80, fol. 145v, 146.
124. Earl of Derby, *Accounts*, p. lxviii and index.
125. Myers, *Edward IV*, pp. 189, 190.
126. Russell, *Norture*, p. 131, l. 231.
127. *Ffor to Serve a Lord*, p. 368.
128. Froissart, *Chronicles*, pp. 356–57.
129. *English Wills*, p. 45.
130. Labarge, *Baronial Household*, pp. 122–23.
131. *English Wills*, p. 56.
132. Labarge, *Baronial Household*, p. 123.
133. S. Thrupp, *The Merchant Class of Medieval London* (Ann Arbor: University of Michigan Press, 1962), p. 147; Evans, *English Art*, p. 89.

134. *English Wills,* p. 110, Richard Dixton Esq., Cirencester, Gloucester-shire, 1438; William Carent of Somerset, 1406, quoted in Oman, "Drinking Horns," p. 22.
135. *English Wills,* p. 101.
136. Myers, *Edward IV,* p. 183.
137. Origo, *Merchant,* p. 169.
138. *Sancti Augustini Vita scripta a Possidio episcopo,* ed. W.T. Weisskotten (Princeton: Princeton University Press, 1919), chap. 22, p. 95.
139. *The Household Accounts of Richard de Swinfield,* ed. J. Webb (West-minster: Camden Society, o.s. 59, 1854), pp. 47–48.
140. H.E. Jean Le Patourel, "Documentary Evidence and the Medieval Pottery Industry," *Medieval Archaeology* 12 (1968): 119.
141. *Swinfield Accounts,* p. 70.
142. M. Keen, *Outlaws of Medieval Legend* (London: Routledge and Kegan Paul, 1961), pp. 18–19.
143. Bonvicino, *Fifty Courtesies,* p. 29, ll. 173–76.
144. *Table Manners for Boys,* trans. O.J.A. Russell (London: Wine and Food Society, 1958), p. 11.
145. Goldsmiths' Company Wardens' Accounts and Court Minutes, vol. B, 1492–99, p. 335.
146. Myers, *Edward IV,* pp. 90, 214.
147. *Sir Gawain and the Green Knight,* ll. 122–29.
148. Barberino, *Documenti d'Amore,* p. 40; Bonvicino, *Fifty Courtesies,* p. 23, ll. 85–88.
149. *A Fifteenth Century Schoolbook,* ed. W. Nelson (Oxford: Clarendon Press, 1956), no. 49, p. 12.
150. The Knyght of La Tour Landry, *The Booke of thenseygnementes and techynge that the Knyght of the Towre made to his Doughters,* trans. William Caxton, ed. G.B. Rawlings (London: George Newnes, 1902), p. 87.
151. Lydgate, *Stans Puer,* p. 742, l. 58.
152. *Babees Book,* p. 6, ll. 136–38.
153. Bonvicino, *Fifty Courtesies,* p. 31, ll. 194–96.
154. M. St. Clair Byrne, *Elizabethan Life in Town and Country* (London: University Paperbacks, 1961), p. 57.
155. *Modus Cenandi,* p. 41, ll. 91–93.
156. Ibid., p. 43, l. 107.
157. Russell, *Norture,* p. 130, ll. 201–7, p. 133, ll. 260, 264.
158. *La Pala d'Oro di San Marco* (Florence: Sadea, 1965), pl. 31.
159. Adam de la Halle, *Oeuvres Complètes,* ed. E. de Coussemaker (Paris: A. Durand, 1872), p. 322.
160. Barberino, *Documenti d'Amore,* p. 40.
161. Cotgrave, *Dictionarie,* s.v. "pain."
162. Caxton, *Book of Curtesye,* p. 27, verse 36; *Curtasye,* p. 302, l. 113.
163. *Table Manners for Boys,* p. 9.
164. Alexander Barclay, *Second Eclogue,* ll. 973–78, in *Eclogues,* ed. B. White, EETS. OS. 175 (1927), pp. 89–90.
165. Lydgate, *Stans Puer,* p. 742, l. 65.
166. *Modus Cenandi,* p. 39, ll. 58–59.
167. Bonvicino, *Fifty Courtesies,* p. 25, ll. 101–2.

168. *Kervynge*, p. 279.
169. Ibid., p. 275.
170. Russell, *Norture*, p. 146, ll. 466–68.
171. *Ffor to Serve a Lord*, p. 371.
172. Chaucer, *Reeve's Tale*, l. 3934, in *Works*, p. 56.
173. Chaucer, *Prologue*, ll. 366–67, ibid., p. 20.
174. C.T.P. Bailey, *Knives and Forks* (London: Medici, 1927), p. 4.
175. *Pseudodoxia Epidemica*, bk. 3, chap. 23, in *The Works of Sir Thomas Browne*, ed. G. Keynes (Chicago: University of Chicago Press, 1964), 2:241.
176. C.H. Talbot, *Medicine in Medieval England* (London: Oldbourne, 1967), p. 175.
177. *The Shepherds' Play*, ll. 584–85, in *The Chester Plays*, ed. H. Deimling, EETS. ES. 62 (1892).
178. Istvan Racz, *Art Treasures of Medieval Finland* (New York: Praeger, 1967), pl. 154.
179. Barclay, p. 5, *First Eclogue*, l. 150.
180. S. Bertrand, *La Tapisserie de Bayeux* (Paris: Zodiaque, 1966), p. 284.
181. *Ffor to Serve a Lord*, p. 371.
182. Johannes Kerer, *Statuta Collegii Sapientiae* (1497), ed. J.H. Beckmann (Lindau and Constance: Jan Thorbecke Verlag, 1957), fol. 29r, *De Custodia Cratheris et Coclearis argenteorum*.
183. *Babees Book*, p. 6, l. 145.
184. Quoted in D. Hartley, *Food in England* (London: Macdonald, 1957), p. 535.
185. *English Wills*, p. 45.
186. Labarge, *Baronial Household*, p. 122.
187. Petronius, *The Satyricon*, trans. W. Arrowsmith (Ann Arbor: University of Michigan Press, 1959), pp. 100–101, 168.
188. *The Master of Game*, Appendix, *Curée*, pp. 208–9.
189. T. Talbot Rice, *Everyday Life in Byzantium* (London: Batsford, 1967), p. 170.
190. W. Smith, *Dictionary of Greek and Roman Antiquities* (London: J. Murray, 1890), s.v. "furca"; Daremberg-Saglio, *Dictionnaire des Antiquités Grecques et Romaines* (Paris: Hachette, 1877–1919), s.v. "fuscinula."
191. D.M. Wilson, *Anglo-Saxon Ornamental Metal Work, 700–1100* (London: British Museum, Catalogue of Antiquities of the Later Saxon Period, 1964), 1:168, and pl. 29.
192. Peter Damian, *Institutio Monialis*, chap. 11, in *Patrologiae cursus completus, series latina*, ed. J.P. Migne (Paris: Migne, 1853), vol. 145, col. 744.
193. M. Hadzidakis, "Une Nouvelle Manière de Dater Les Peintures," *Byzantion* 14 (1939): 110–12; G. de Jerphanion, *La voix des monuments* (Rome: Ligugé, 1938), pp. 243–48.
194. Herrade von Landsberg, *Hortus Deliciarum*, ed. J. Walter (Strasbourg, 1852), pl. 30.
195. O. Demus, *The Church of San Marco in Venice* (Washington, D.C.: Dumbarton Oaks Research Library and Collection, 1960), p. 23; *La Pala d'Oro di San Marco*, pl. 31.
196. Quoted in *M.E. Dictionary* s.v. "forke."

197. Origo, *Merchant*, p. 254, n.; M. Meiss, *French Painting in the Time of Jean de Berry* (London: Phaidon, 1967), p. 45.
198. *The Journey of William of Rubruck*, in C. Dawson, ed., *Mission to Asia* (New York: Harper Torchbooks, 1966), p. 98.
199. Origo, *Merchant*, p. 254.
200. E. McLeod, *Charles of Orleans* (London: Chatto and Windus, 1969), pp. 51–52.
201. R. Strong and J. Trevelyan Oman, *Elizabeth R* (London: Secker and Warburg, 1971), p. 69.
202. For detailed discussion, see E. Panofsky, *Hercules Agricola*, in *Essays Presented to Rudolf Wittkower* (London: Phaidon, 1967), pp. 20–23, and F. Saxl, *Illustrated Medieval Encyclopaedias*, in *Lectures* (London: Warburg Institute, 1957), 1:229–41.
203. Vatican Codex Palatinus Lat. 291, illustrations to bk. 22, chap. 1 and bk. 16, chap. 4 of Rabanus Maurus, *De Universo*.

## Chapter 7

1. John Myrc, *Manuale Sacerdotis*, Bodleian Library, Oxford, MS. 549, fol. 171v–172r.
2. Sir Thomas Malory, *The Tale of the Death of King Arthur*, ed. E. Vinaver (Oxford: Clarendon Press, 1955), p. 94.
3. Thomas of Eccleston, *The Coming of the Friars Minor to England*, in *Thirteenth Century Chronicles*, trans. P. Hermann, ed. M-T. Laureilhe (Chicago: Franciscan Herald Press, 1961), pp. 98–99.
4. Bonvicino, *Fifty Courtesies of the Table*, p. 23, ll. 77–80, p. 31, ll. 165–68, 153–56; Barberino, *Documenti d'Amore*, p. 42, trans. W.M. Rossetti, in *Queene Elizabethes Achademy*, ed. F.J. Furnivall, EETS. ES. 8 (1869).
5. *Table Manners for Boys* (early fifteenth century), trans. O.J.A. Russell (London: Wine and Food Society, 1958), p. 9; *The Babees Book*, ed. F.J. Furnivall, EETS. OS. 32 (1868), p. 7, ll. 169–75.
6. Robert Grosseteste, *Rule for the Countess of Lincoln*, in *Walter of Henley's Husbandry*, ed. E. Lamond (London: Royal Historical Society, 1890), p. 139.
7. William FitzStephen, *The Life and Death of Thomas Becket*, trans. G. Greenaway (London: Folio Society, 1961), p. 42.
8. Henry of Lancaster, *Le Livre de Seyntz Medicines*, ed. E.J. Arnould (Oxford: Blackwell, for the Anglo-Norman Society, 1940), p. 48.
9. *The Waning of the Middle Ages* (University of Kansas Museum of Art, Exhibition Catalogue, 1969), pp. 20–21, pl. 57, no. 16.
10. *Caxton's Aesop*, ed. R.T. Lenaghan (Cambridge: Harvard University Press, 1967), p. 85, "The XVII fable of the asse and of the yong dogge."
11. Froissart, *Chronicles*, trans. G. Brereton (Harmondsworth: Penguin, 1968), p. 263.
12. *Sir Gawain and the Green Knight*, ed. J.R.R. Tolkien and E.V. Gordon (Oxford: Clarendon Press, 1925), ll. 2047–53.

13. Froissart, *Oeuvres: Poésies,* ed. A. Scheler (Brussels: Devaux, 1870–71), vol. 2, *Le Debat dou Cheval et dou Levrier,* ll. 36–40.
14. William Langland, *Piers the Plowman,* ed. W.W. Skeat (Oxford: The University Press, 1886), B. Passus 12, ll. 192–205.
15. *The Book of Margery Kempe,* ed. W. Butler-Bowden (Oxford: The World's Classics, 1954), p. 80.
16. John of Salisbury, *The Metalogicon,* trans. D.D. McGarry (Berkeley and Los Angeles: University of California Press, 1962), bk. 4, chap. 42, p. 274.
17. William Horman, *Vulgaria* (1519), ed. M.R. James (Oxford: Roxburghe Club, 1926), p. 235.
18. Froissart, *Chronicles,* p. 144.
19. Raphael Holinshed, *Chronicles* (London: J. Johnson, 1807), 2:130, under the year 1170.
20. For example, in *Le Sacramentaire de Saint-Etienne de Limoges,* ca. 1100, ed. J. Porcher (Paris: Les Editions Nomis, n.d.), pl. 6 (fol. 46v).
21. Joinville, *The Life of St. Louis,* in *Chronicles of the Crusades,* trans. M.R.B. Shaw (Harmondsworth: Penguin, 1963), p. 169.
22. *The Hours of Jeanne d'Evreux* (early fourteenth century), The Cloisters, Metropolitan Museum of Art, New York, fol. 148v.
23. I. Origo, *The World of San Bernardino* (New York: Harcourt, Brace and World, 1962), pp. 43–44.
24. William Caxton, *Book of Curtesye,* ed. F.J. Furnivall, EETS. ES. 3 (1868), p. 21, ll. 197–201.
25. Gaston Paris, *Le Poésie du Moyen Age* (Paris: Hachette, 1906), 1:200.
26. Della Casa, *Galateo,* trans. R.S. Pine-Coffin (Harmondsworth: Penguin, 1958), p. 98.
27. John Palsgrave, *Lesclarcissement de la Langue Francoyse* (London, 1530), ed. R.C. Alston (Menston, England: The Scolar Press, 1969).
28. *The Master of Game,* ed. W.A. and F. Baillie-Grohman (New York: Duffield and Co., 1909), Appendix, *Curée,* pp. 208–9.
29. *Jehan et Blonde,* ll. 436–39, 475–78, in *Oeuvres Poétiques de Philippe de Remi, Sire de Beaumanoir,* ed. H. Suchier (Paris: Firmin Didot, 1885), vol. 2.
30. I. Origo, *The Merchant of Prato* (New York: Knopf, 1957), p. 179.
31. FitzStephen, *Life of Becket,* p. 42.
32. S. Glixelli, "Les contenances de Table," *Romania* 47 (1921):10.
33. J. Balsdon, *Life and Leisure in Ancient Rome* (New York: McGraw-Hill, 1969), p. 53; W. Deonna and M. Renard, *Croyances et Superstitions de Table dans la Rome Antique* (Brussels: Collection Latomus, vol. 46, 1961), pp. 107–21, pl. 15.
34. Froissart, *Chronicles,* pp. 357–58.
35. *The Italian Relation of England,* trans. C.A. Sneyd (Westminster: Camden Society, vol. 37, 1847), p. 44.
36. *The Travels of Leo of Rozmital, 1465–7,* trans. M. Letts (Cambridge: The University Press, for the Hakluyt Society, 2nd. ser., vol. 108, 1957), pp. 46–47.
37. *A Fifteenth Century Schoolbook,* ed. W. Nelson (Oxford: Clarendon Press, 1956), no. 50, p. 12.

38. S.L. Thrupp, *The Merchant Class of Medieval London* (Ann Arbor: University of Michigan Press, 1962), p. 150.
39. "Olim Pacus colueram," from *Carmina Burana* (late thirteenth century), in *The Penguin Book of Latin Verse*, trans. F. Brittain (Harmondsworth: Penguin, 1962), pp. 267–68.
40. R. Warner, *Antiquitates Culinariae* (London: R. Blamire, 1791), p. xii, n.
41. A. Katzenellenbogen, *Allegories of the Virtues and Vices in Medieval Art* (London: Warburg Institute, 1939), p. 80; H. Kraus, *The Living Theatre of Medieval Art* (Bloomington: Indiana University Press, 1967), p. 102 and pl. 71.
42. John Russell, *Boke of Norture*, ll. 598–99, in *Babees Book*, p. 158.
43. Pliny the Younger, *Letters*, trans. B. Radice (Harmondsworth: Penguin, 1963), bk. 2, letter 6, pp. 63–64.
44. *A Noble Boke off Cookry*, ed. Mrs. A. Napier (London: Elliot Stock, 1882), p. 27.
45. Katzenellenbogen, *Allegories*, p. 55.
46. Joinville, *St. Louis*, p. 291.
47. The Archpoet (ca. 1130–67), *Meum est propositum*, in *Penguin Book of Latin Verse*, p. 209.
48. Caxton, *Book of Curtesye*, p. 27, ll. 253–56.
49. Ibid., p. 13, ll. 118–19.
50. *Sir Gawain and the Green Knight*, ll. 878–81.
51. *A Fifteenth Century Schoolbook*, no. 20, p. 6.
52. Eustache Deschamps, *Ballade*, in *The Penguin Book of French Verse*, vol. 1, trans. B. Woledge (Harmondsworth: Penguin, 1961), p. 245.
53. John Lydgate, *The Tale of the Frogge and the Mouse*, ll. 400–405, in *Minor Poems*, vol. 2, ed. H.N. MacCracken, EETS. OS. 192 (1933–34), p. 580.
54. Matthew Paris, *English History*, trans. J.A. Giles (London: Bohn, 1852–54), vol. 2, p. 273.
55. Grosseteste, *Countess of Lincoln*, p. 141.
56. Langland, *Piers Plowman*, B. Passus 10, ll. 94–95.

## Chapter 8

1. Sir Thomas More, *A Dialogue of Comfort against Tribulation*, ed. L. Miles (Bloomington: Indiana University Press, 1965), pt. 2, Introduction, p. 66.
2. Spanish Haggadah, fourteenth century, British Museum, London, OR. MS. 1404, fol. 18, reproduced in Bezalel Narkiss, *Hebrew Illuminated Manuscripts* (Jerusalem: Macmillan, *Encyclopaedia Judaica*, 1969), pl. 14.
3. Froissart, *Chronicles*, trans. G. Brereton (Harmondsworth: Penguin, 1968), bk. 3, p. 266.
4. Ibid., p. 265.
5. G. Wickham, *Early English Stages, 1300–1600* (London: Routledge and Kegan Paul, 1959), 1:333.

6. Ibid.
7. Ibid., p. 335.
8. See for example Lilian M.C. Randall, *Images in the Margins of Gothic Manuscripts* (Berkeley and Los Angeles: University of California Press, 1966), figs. 347, 410–414, 421, 447–448.
9. Quoted in G.R. Owst, *Literature and Pulpit in Medieval England* (Oxford: Basil Blackwell, 1961), p. 118.
10. M.D. Anderson, *Drama and Imagery in English Medieval Churches* (Cambridge: The University Press, 1963), p. 102.
11. E.W. Tristram, *English Wall Painting of the Fourteenth Century* (London: Routledge and Kegan Paul, 1955), p. 185 and pl. 42.
12. Sir Thomas More, *Utopia*, ed. J. Churton Collins (Oxford: Clarendon Press, 1904), bk. 1, p. 29.
13. Quoted in G.G. Coulton, *Social Life in Britain from the Conquest to the Reformation* (Cambridge: The University Press, 1956), p. 375.
14. Froissart, *Chronicles*, p. 265.
15. Joinville, *Life of St. Louis,* in *Chronicles of the Crusades,* trans. M.R.B. Shaw (Harmondsworth: Penguin, 1963), p. 331.
16. *A Selection of English Carols,* ed. R. Greene (Oxford: Clarendon Medieval and Tudor Series, 1962), pp. 15, 29.
17. Ibid., p. 28.
18. *Sir Gawain and the Green Knight,* ed. J.R.R. Tolkien and E.V. Gordon (Oxford: Clarendon Press, 1925), ll. 43, 1025–26, 1652–55.
19. *A Selection of English Carols,* pp. 58–59, no. 5.
20. Froissart, *Chronicles*, p. 168.
21. Ibid., p. 265.
22. *The Goodman of Paris,* trans. E. Power (New York: Harcourt, Brace, 1928), pp. 241, 244.
23. Henry Kraus, *The Living Theatre of Medieval Art* (Bloomington: Indiana University Press, 1967), p. 11, pl. 3.
24. *Goodman,* p. 300.
25. *The Book of Secrets of Albertus Magnus,* ed. M.R. Best and F.H. Brightman (Oxford: Clarendon Press, 1973), p. 98.
26. *The Sketchbook of Villard de Honnecourt,* ed. T. Bowie (Bloomington: Indiana University Press, 1959), pl. 28.
27. *The Journey of William Rubruck,* in *Mission to Asia,* ed. C. Dawson (New York: Harper Torchbooks, 1966), p. 157.
28. Ibid., p. 176.
29. Froissart, *Chronicles,* p. 264.
30. Reproduced in *La Librairie de Bourgogne,* intro. Léon Gilissen (Brussels: Cultura, 1970), pl. 13.
31. Henry, Earl of Derby, *Expeditions to Prussia and the Holy Land, 1390–1 and 1392–3, being the Accounts kept by his Treasurer during two years,* ed. L. Toulmin Smith (Westminster: Camden Society, n. s. 52, 1894–95), p. 281.
32. Leslie Paul, *Sir Thomas More* (London: Faber and Faber, 1953), p. 26.
33. Geoffrey Webb, *The Office of Devisor,* in *Fritz Saxl Memorial Essays,* ed. D.J. Gordon (London: Nelson, 1957), p. 300.
34. D. Pearsall, *John Lydgate* (London: Routledge and Kegan Paul, 1970), p. 181.

35. W. Paley Baildon, "A Wardrobe Account of Richard II, April 1393–April 1394," *Archaeologia* 62, pt. 2 (1911): 503.
36. Wickham, *English Stages,* p. 188.
37. E. Welsford, *The Court Masque* (Cambridge: The University Press, 1927), pp. 20, 30, 31.
38. Ibid., p. 39; Wickham, *English Stages,* pp. 197–98.
39. For the discussion that follows, see Wickham, *English Stages,* pp. 191–207; Pearsall, *Lydgate,* pp. 183–88; John Lydgate, *Poems,* ed. J. Norton-Smith (Oxford: Clarendon Medieval and Tudor Series, 1966), pp. 122–27.
40. *Early Middle English Texts,* ed. B. Dickins and R.M. Wilson (London: Bowes and Bowes, 1951), p. 132.
41. R.M. Wilson, *The Lost Literature of Medieval England* (London: Methuen, 1970), pp. 213, 214, 232; Welsford, *Masque,* p. 47, n.; *Gawain and the Green Knight,* ll. 471–75.
42. For the discussion of *Fulgens and Lucres,* see R. Southern, *The Staging of Plays before Shakespeare* (London: Faber and Faber, 1973), pp. 95–126.
43. William Roper, *The Life of Sir Thomas More* (ca. 1553), in *Two Early Tudor Lives,* ed. R.S. Sylvester and D.P. Harding (New Haven: Yale University Press, 1962), p. 198.
44. *Tudor Interludes,* ed. Peter Happé (Harmondsworth: Penguin, 1972), pp. 375–76.
45. Southern, *Staging,* p. 206.
46. *Goodman,* pp. 275–85.
47. Ibid., p. 232.
48. *A Selection of English Carols,* p. 91, no. 32.
49. Ibid., pp. 91–92, no. 33.
50. *The Parson's Tale,* in *Works of Geoffrey Chaucer,* ed. F.N. Robinson (Oxford: The University Press, 1957), p. 241.
51. George Cavendish, *The Life and Death of Cardinal Wolsey* (1557), in *Two Early Tudor Lives,* p. 71.
52. Quoted in A.H. de Oliveira Marques, *Daily Life in Portugal in the Late Middle Ages* (Madison: University of Wisconsin Press, 1971), p. 34.
53. Ibid.
54. Cavendish, *Wolsey,* p. 74.
55. Ibid., pp. 73–74.
56. *A Feste for a Bryde,* in *The Babees Book,* ed. F.J. Furnivall, EETS. OS. 32 (1868), pp. 376–77.
57. John Russell, *The Boke of Norture,* in *Babees Book,* pp. 164–66.
58. Ibid., p. 167.
59. Ibid.
60. Wickham, *English Stages,* p. 211.
61. *A Noble Boke off Cookry,* ed. Mrs. A. Napier (London: Elliot Stock, 1882), pp. 4–5.
62. Wickham, *English Stages,* p. 211; Pearsall, *Lydgate,* p. 169.
63. L.H. Loomis, "Secular Dramatics in the Royal Palace, Paris, 1378, 1389, and Chaucer's 'Tregetoures,' " *Speculum* 33 (1958):242–55.
64. Chaucer, *The Franklin's Tale,* in *Works,* p. 139, ll. 1142–45.
65. Cavendish, *Wolsey,* p. 76.

66. Ibid.
67. Christine de Pisan, *Le Dit de la Rose,* in *Oeuvres Poétiques,* ed. M. Roy (Paris: Société des Anciens Textes Français, 1891), 2:32–37, ll. 83–263.
68. *Kalendare,* in *Lydgate's Minor Poems,* pt. 1, ed. H.N. MacCracken, EETS. ES. 107 (1910), pp. 363–76.
69. Cavendish, *Wolsey,* p. 75.

# Suggestions for Further Reading

Davis, Dorothy. *A History of Shopping*. London: Routledge and Kegan Paul, 1966.

Drummond, J.C., and Anne Wilbraham. *The Englishman's Food*. London: Jonathan Cape, 1964.

Harrison, Molly. *The Kitchen in History*. Reading, U.K.: Osprey Publishing, 1972.

Hartley, Dorothy. *Food in England*. London: Macdonald, 1964.

Hazlitt, W.C. *Old Cookery Books*. London: Elliot Stock, 1902.

Mead, William Edward. *The English Medieval Feast*. London: Allen and Unwin, 1931.

"Old English Cookery," *The Quarterly Review* 178 (1894), pp. 82–104.

Serjeantson, M.S. "The Vocabulary of Cookery in the Fifteenth Century," in *Essays and Studies of the English Association*, vol. 23 (1937).

# Index